Tolley's Managing ~~Dismissals~~

G000117153

Practical guidan dismissing fairly

2nd Edition

by

Daniel Barnett, Barrister, Lincoln's Inn

Members of the LexisNexis Group worldwide

United Kingdom	LexisNexis UK, a Division of Reed Elsevier (UK) Ltd, 2 Addiscombe Road, Croydon CR9 5AF
Argentina	LexisNexis Argentina, BUENOS AIRES
Australia	LexisNexis Butterworths, CHATSWOOD, New South Wales
Austria	LexisNexis Verlag ARD Orac GmbH & Co KG, VIENNA
Canada	LexisNexis Butterworths, MARKHAM, Ontario
Chile	LexisNexis Chile Ltda, SANTIAGO DE CHILE
Czech Republic	Nakladatelství Orac sro, PRAGUE
France	Editions du Juris-Classeur SA, PARIS
Germany	LexisNexis Deutschland GmbH, FRANKFURT and MUNSTER
Hong Kong	LexisNexis Butterworths, HONG KONG
Hungary	HVG-Orac, BUDAPEST
India	LexisNexis Butterworths, NEW DELHI
Ireland	LexisNexis, DUBLIN
Italy	Giuffrè Editore, MILAN
Malaysia	Malayan Law Journal Sdn Bhd, KUALA LUMPUR
New Zealand	LexisNexis Butterworths, WELLINGTON
Poland	Wydawnictwo Prawnicze LexisNexis, WARSAW
Singapore	LexisNexis Butterworths, SINGAPORE
South Africa	LexisNexis Butterworths, Durban
Switzerland	Stämpfli Verlag AG, BERNE
USA	LexisNexis, DAYTON, Ohio

First published in 2002

Re-printed in 2003

© Daniel Barnett 2004

The original edition of this work was previously published as *Avoiding Unfair Dismissal Claims* by John Wiley & Sons Ltd

A CIP Catalogue record for this book is available from the British Library.

ISBN 0 7545 2213 X

Typeset by Letterpart Ltd, Reigate, Surrey

Printed and bound in Great Britain by Cromwell Press, Trowbridge, Wiltshire

Visit LexisNexis UK at www.lexisnexis.co.uk

Preface

Since the first edition of this book was published, the number of unfair dismissal claims has continued to rise. According to the 2003/04 annual report of the Employment Tribunal Service, there were over 115,000 tribunal claims lodged last year (a 17% rise on 2002/03). Of these, almost 40,000 claims were for unfair dismissal.

This increase in claims is due to a combination of a rise in the value of awards and an increasing public awareness of rights in the workplace. Additionally, access to legal advice has widened enormously with the developing popularity of conditional fee agreements, and the cultural shift of trade unions from acting as workplace negotiators to professionally managed organisations providing effective advice to, and representation for, their members.

The growth in claims is also due to the increasing body of case law governing the dismissal process. But most fundamentally, it is due to a lack of familiarity by many small and medium-sized enterprises with the correct procedures to go through before dismissing employees. Unfair dismissal claims are won or lost depending on the behaviour of the employer before the dismissal – and very little can be done afterwards to save the situation if the correct procedures have been overlooked.

Claims will still be brought by resentful employees against even the best and fairest employers. Such employers will lose working time in defending the claim, possibly incurring significant legal costs along the way. But if the advice in this book is followed, the prospects of having to pay compensation to that employee are much reduced.

This book aims to assist such organisations, in much the same way as trade unions provide guides for employees on their employment rights, and it explains the procedures that employers should follow when dismissing in a variety of circumstances. It also aims to set out the evidence that must be gathered along the way, so as to increase the prospect of a tribunal validating the employer's actions if they should come to be examined under a forensic microscope a year or so later at a tribunal hearing.

For convenience, the name 'Fred' has been adopted throughout this book for the employee who is claiming unfair dismissal. This is illustrative shorthand that, I think, makes much easier reading than repeated use of 'the employee'.

There are a number of people I wish to thank. Countless clients have contributed ideas – often inadvertently – which have gone into this book. I also owe a debt to a wide variety of other lawyers who have discussed issues in this book with me, including Neil Russell, Harry Sherrard, Nigel Brain, Michael Creamore, Andrew Conway, Marc Jones, Keir Hirst, Jeremy Taylor, Michael Davies, Gillian Howard, Gemma Webb, Richard Woodman, Paul

Housego, Kate Brearley, Julian Yew, Stephen Levinson, Eugenie Verney, Charlotte Hamer, Adam Turner, Lynden Lever, Matt Dean, David Pollard, Justin Nelson, Simon Quantrill, Anne Copley, David Reade, Andrew Macmillan, Alain Cohen, Vernon Hadida, Yvonne Gallagher, Rachel Lester, Kate Sandison, Richard Linskell, John Bowers QC, Jayne Nevins, Judith Watson, Michael Duggan, Stephen Breen, Joanna Wade, Stephen Melzack, David Salt, Richard Stephens, Clare Primett, Piers Martin, Shaman Kapoor and Richard Samuel. Apologies if I've left anyone off! Finally, Henry Scrope of DiscLaw Publishing, which produces the quite wonderful website www.emplaw.co.uk, has proven a valuable sounding board.

I owe particular thanks to my fellow barristers, especially Simon Brown, David Barr, Keith Morton and Paul McGrath, and to the clerking team at 1 Temple Gardens for their contributions and support.

Finally, a big thanks to Miranda Barnett for being a wonderful wife and employment lawyer.

The law is stated as at 1 September 2004, save that it takes full account of the new rules regarding mandatory dismissal and grievance procedures which come into force on 1 October 2004.

Daniel Barnett
Barrister
1 Temple Gardens
www.danielbarnett.co.uk

Contents

Table of Cases

Table of Statutes

Table of Statutory Instruments

Chapter I
The Law of Unfair Dismissal: An Overview

Can the employee get his claim off the ground?   1.1

There are several hurdles which Fred will have to overcome before an employment tribunal can even hear his claim of unfair dismissal. They are as follows:

Is he an employee?   1.2

Fred cannot claim unfair dismissal if he is not actually employed by you. The law recognises a distinction between the employed and the self-employed. If Fred is self-employed (as, for example, a window-cleaner might be) and you terminate his services, he cannot claim unfair dismissal.

The main pointers a tribunal will look at to decide whether he is employed or self employed are:

General pointers

- what the job advertisement said;

- the contract between the parties (or any offer letter) – what does it say?

- the tax status of the worker – PAYE is a strong indicator of employment; paying the worker's invoices without deduction of tax is a strong indicator of self-employment. Note that this is not determinative: *AirFix Footwear Ltd v Cope [1978] ICR 1210*, where a person treated as self-employed by the Revenue was treated as an employee by the employment tribunal, or *Express & Echo Publications v Tanton [1999] ICR 693, CA* where the opposite was the case;

- whether there are other workers doing similar duties for the employer, and whether they are employed or self-employed;

1

- the extent of control exercised by the employer over the worker;

- who arranges a replacement if the worker cannot attend work. If the employer arranges a replacement, this will normally indicate employee status. If the worker can arrange his own replacement, this will normally indicate self-employed status. However, whilst often conclusive (*Express & Echo Publications v Tanton [1999] ICR 693, CA*), it is not necessarily so (*MacFarlane v Glasgow City Council [2001] IRLR 7, EAT; Byrne Brothers (Formwork) Ltd v Baird [2002] IRLR 96*);

- who provides the equipment;

- who pays for any professional insurance.

Specific pointers towards employee status

- the existence of a staff handbook or collective agreement which governs the individual's work;

- provision of a formal induction, or provision of training;

- whether the employer moves the worker around from job to job;

- the worker receives sick pay;

- the employer can overrule the worker, when the worker decides how or when the job is to be done;

- the employer has exercised disciplinary powers over the worker, or if the worker has utilised a grievance procedure;

- the contract contains restrictive covenants.

Specific pointers towards self-employed status

- the worker works from his own premises;

- the worker is responsible for his own expenses, rather than being able to reclaim them from the employer;

- the worker works for other employers / organisations;

- the worker issues invoices before receiving payment;

- the worker stands to make (or lose) money depending on how well he does his job (note: do not confuse this with an employee on commission);

- the worker has invested his own money in being able to perform the job properly (e.g. purchased equipment, paid for his own training).

- the worker has his own business cards (rather than company business cards) or has his own advertisements (eg in Yellow Pages);

- the worker had some influence over his rate of pay (eg he tendered against others for the work).

Although the provision of paid holiday used to be a powerful indicator towards status as an employee, this is no longer the case since the introduction of the *Working Time Regulations 1998* (*SI 1998 No 1833*), which requires employers to allow paid holiday for large numbers of self-employed workers.

It can sometimes be quite difficult to determine Fred's status, although it is crucial in determining his right to claim unfair dismissal.

Agency workers   1.3

Historically, workers who were supplied through an agency, and who were paid by that agency, would not have been regarded as your employee.

However, courts have recently been taking a more pragmatic view, and saying that if an individual has been working for an employer for at least a year, even if his wages are paid through an agency, the reality is that the individual is an employee of the company. Note that most contracts between yourself and the employment agency will, nowadays, specify whether the individual is regarded as your employee, or the agency's employee. However, this is not binding on tribunals, if the individual brings a claim against you, and it may be worthwhile seeking legal advice if you are considering dismissing an agency worker who has been with you for more than 12 months.

Example

> Mrs Dacas was on the books of the Brook Street Bureau employment agency. She worked, through the agency, for Wandsworth Council as a cleaner for four years. After being dismissed, she brought an unfair dismissal claim against both Wandsworth and Brook Street. The Court of Appeal said that the reality of the situation was that she had, over time, become Wandsworth's employee and she was entitled to claim unfair dismissal against the Council (although her claim was not allowed to proceed on other, technical, grounds) – *Dacas v Brook Street Bureau [2004] IRLR 358.*

Readers should be aware that the position on agency workers may soon change, when the draft *EU Agency Workers Directive* is implemented. This gives agency workers similar rights to employees, although at the time of writing the full implications of this impending legislation are not clear.

Has he been employed for at least a year?   1.4

Fred must normally have worked for at least one year before he is allowed to claim unfair dismissal. If he has not worked for one year, he cannot bring a claim. There are a number of exceptions to this rule, which are discussed at **18.15** below.

Is he under the normal retirement age?   1.5

If Fred is over the normal retirement age for his job, he cannot claim unfair dismissal. A word of caution – the normal retirement age is not necessarily the state pension age. This is discussed further at **10.9**. Note that this rule will change in December 2006, although it is not yet clear whether the retirement age limit will be abolished or just changed.

Was he dismissed?   1.6

Unless Fred is actually dismissed, he cannot claim unfair dismissal. An employment tribunal will take a fairly robust attitude as to what constitutes a dismissal. A dismissal can occur without the use of phrases such as 'you are dismissed' – the central question will be whether it was you or Fred who caused the termination of his employment. An employment tribunal will often consider there to have been a dismissal when Fred appears to have resigned (commonly known as 'constructive dismissal').

Generally it will be obvious when Fred has been dismissed, and so this should not be an issue in the case. For example, if he has been dismissed for theft, or for persistent absence or incompetence, then you will admit that he was dismissed. The only real issue for an employment tribunal will be whether the dismissal was fair or unfair.

Sometimes, however, the situation is not quite that straightforward. Complications arise, for example, if Fred has simply stopped turning up to work – has he resigned? What if you tell him 'if you don't resign, you'll be sacked!' and he resigns as a result. Is that a resignation or dismissal? What if you have been reducing his pay or making life difficult for him with a view to forcing his resignation? Or if you told him 'go home and don't come back', meaning 'don't come back today', but Fred interpreted that as being dismissed?

If you think that there might have been a resignation rather than a dismissal (thus preventing Fred from claiming unfair dismissal), you should have a look at the categories set out in **CHAPTER 17** to see if the situation falls within one of the bands of resignation that the law interprets as being a dismissal.

Was the dismissal fair or unfair? 1.7

To show that a dismissal was fair it is, in general, necessary to show that the dismissal was for one of four reasons. It is then also necessary to show that the dismissal was reasonable in all the circumstances.

The reasons are:

(1) Capability or qualifications: If Fred is unable to do his job properly or lacks the appropriate qualifications then this will be a potentially valid ground for dismissing him. Examples include if Fred is unable to work due to ill-health, if his quality of work decreases and it is decided that he is no longer capable of doing the job properly, or if he has misled you over the qualifications he possesses.

(2) Conduct: Conduct at work is one of the most common reasons for dismissal. This can be one incident of serious misconduct (such as theft) or the accumulation of less serious incidents of misconduct (such as aggressive or offensive behaviour, persistent absenteeism or refusal to obey your instructions).

(3) Redundancy: Many people do not realise that redundancy is a form of dismissal and that if the correct procedures are not complied with then it will be an unfair dismissal. Redundancy has a different meaning to a lawyer than to a layman, and unless the situation clearly falls within the lawyer's definition of redundancy then you run the risk of an employment tribunal finding that the dismissal was unfair.

(4) Contravention of a statutory duty: If a law prohibits an employee doing something for which he is employed (e.g. a lorry driver who loses his driving licence) then it will be potentially fair to dismiss him.

It should be noted that the four headings above are not exhaustive. The tribunal has the right, if it considers that there is some other substantial reason for the dismissal that does not fall within the list above, to decide that the dismissal was fair. Each of these categories is considered in full in the following chapters.

Minimum procedures 1.8

Even if a reason for dismissal falls into one of the above categories that is not, of itself, enough to make the dismissal fair. It must be shown that the dismissal was reasonable in all the circumstances, having regard to the size and administrative resources of the employer. Case law has developed some fairly clear criteria as to what must be done, depending on the reason for the dismissal, to comply with the overriding duty to act reasonably.

There are also minimum procedures which an employer must go through (including writing to the employee in advance, inviting him to a meeting, and also offering a right of appeal against your decision to dismiss). If you do not go through these procedures, a dismissal will be automatically unfair – irrespective of how good the underlying reason for dismissal is.

These compulsory minimum procedures have only been required since 1 October 2004, and there are a number of grey areas which may take some time for the courts to resolve.

Chapter 2
How to Dismiss Someone for Incapability

Introduction

There is sometimes a degree of overlap between incapability and misconduct. If Fred is failing to sell a sufficient number of products or is making too many mistakes in the ordinary course of his work this may be due either to incompetence or to laziness/indifference, which would qualify as misconduct. Accordingly the procedures for this sort of incapability/misconduct are very similar.

This chapter will address how to dismiss somebody in the following situations:

* where Fred is simply incompetent – i.e. he is not up to the job;

* where Fred is ill and therefore continuously absent from work (either for a long period or a series of regular short absences);

* where Fred lacks the proper qualifications to do the job.

Dismissing the employee for incompetence

Introduction

It may be difficult to show that Fred is incompetent if he has been doing the same job for a long time but has not been the subject of previous criticisms or warnings. It will be very difficult if he has recently received a good report or a significant pay rise (particularly when compared to his work colleagues).

Incompetence is more commonly a reason for dismissal if Fred has been transferred to a new job and it transpires that he has difficulty fulfilling the job requirements, or if he is employed for a trial period to see whether he is suitable. Note that in the latter situation, Fred will be unlikely to have accrued one year's continuity of service and therefore would lack the right to claim unfair dismissal.

Before dismissing Fred for incompetence you must generally be sure of four things:

- that he *is* incompetent;

- that he has been given the opportunity to improve;

- that he has not improved, and is not likely to do so; and

- that it is not reasonable to offer him an alternative job.

Step 1: You must be sure that he *is* incompetent
2.3

Sometimes this step is fairly easy to satisfy, for example if there has been a clear fall-off in sales due to Fred's work (or lack of it). Sometimes, however, incompetence is simply a matter of impression rather than hard, objective evidence (such as a diminution in production). You should see if there is any more concrete evidence than simple 'impression'. Such evidence might include:

- in a larger organisation, statements from people who are in daily contact with Fred;

- a comparison of Fred's daily output figures (for example, number of contracts negotiated, letters typed or customers served) with those of other employees;

- frequency of complaints received from customers.

At the end of the day you have to be able to show a tribunal that you had a genuine belief (i.e. you were not motivated by dislike of the individual concerned) that it is more likely than not that Fred is incapable of doing the job to a satisfactory standard.

You must be satisfied that it is him that is incompetent
2.4

If you know that one of your employees is not competent, but do not know exactly who, it is generally not justifiable to dismiss all (or both) possible employees. This is because employment tribunals will always view any arbitrary action as extremely serious; it will almost always be arbitrary to dismiss an employee when you cannot be more certain than not that he is the incompetent one.

There is an exception to the above rule. If the nature of the job is such that it is imperative that there can be no risk of future mistakes then it may be justifiable (under the general catch-all 'some other substantial reason') to dismiss more than one person when you cannot be sure whether one or other is the culprit. An example might be where one of two mechanics in a factory makes a fundamental error resulting in a serious risk to other workers, being an error which may re-occur. It may be, in the employer's view, imperative that the incompetent employee be dismissed. If each mechanic blames the other for the error, and the employer (after proper investigation) cannot tell who is telling the truth, he would be justified in dismissing both of them. This is because of the possible dire consequences of continuing to let the incompetent mechanic work outweighing the unfairness involved when dismissing someone who is not personally culpable.

This exception, however, will only be appropriate to rely upon in the rarest of circumstances. Unless it is absolutely crucial that a mistake should not re-occur (and mere financial loss is unlikely to be sufficient) then you must be satisfied that you have correctly identified Fred as being the person responsible for the mistakes when administering disciplinary sanctions.

You must genuinely believe that he is incompetent   2.5

At the end of the day, however, the important thing is that you have to have a genuine belief that Fred is incompetent. If you do not genuinely believe that (or if an employment tribunal decides that you did not believe that) then you will be found to have dismissed Fred unfairly. It is the need to prove to a tribunal that, at the time of dismissal you genuinely believed that Fred was incompetent, which makes it desirable to have the sort of objective evidence referred to above.

Step 2: You must have given him the opportunity to improve   2.6

If you do not think that Fred is capable of doing the job properly you must tell him before you dismiss him, so as to give him the opportunity to improve. He may think that he is doing the job properly, or it may even transpire that he was incorrectly shown how to do his job.

It is never pleasant to tell someone that they are not up to scratch and many employers are reluctant to do so. It is, however, obvious that from Fred's point of view he would prefer to be given a chance to improve than be dismissed without warning or notice.

Explain what he is doing wrong   2.7

You must explain to Fred precisely what it is that he is doing wrong. If his work involves a degree of technical skill then demonstrations of that skill must be both provided and documented.

Give a written warning   2.8

You should put a warning as to his competence in a letter. This is for two reasons:

- Fred will take a written warning more seriously than mere verbal guidance. It has a higher chance of encouraging him to do the job properly and therefore a higher chance of resolving the problem without recourse to dismissal; and,

- in the event that dismissal does become necessary, and Fred claims against you, then you will have clear evidence to put before the tribunal showing that you did warn him as to his competence and that you did give him the opportunity to improve.

Points for a written warning   2.9

The letter should contain the following points:

- full details of the faults being complained of. If there are a very large number of small matters it is sufficient to refer to them in passing (i.e. 'You will recall our conversation yesterday when we discussed the ways in which your work required improvement');

- a warning that you consider the problem to be serious enough to justify dismissal if Fred does not improve;

- a minimum time period during which Fred has the chance to improve before you review his performance (see **2.10** below); and

- an invitation to Fred to discuss the matter further with you.

Give time to improve   2.10

The minimum time period should be sufficient to allow Fred to improve. It is unlikely that a period of less than four weeks will be adequate. A long-standing employee who is being required to perform new tasks can expect to receive a longer period to adjust than a new employee who has no track record of efficiency and who gives no indication of being capable of improvement (although an employee with less than one year's service would not be able to claim unfair dismissal anyway unless he falls into a narrow set of exceptions – see **18.15** below).

During the period for improvement you should monitor Fred's performance carefully. Beware of breathing down his neck – this might be perceived by him (and by an employment tribunal) as a way of putting pressure on him to encourage him to resign. In those circumstances a tribunal would probably view a resignation as a dismissal and, if it did, you would almost certainly be found to have acted unfairly (see **CHAPTER 17**).

Exceptions   2.11

Sometimes it is not necessary to allow a period for improvement. This may be the case when the consequences of Fred's mistakes are so serious, or so potentially serious, that you simply cannot take the risk of another mistake.

Example

A pilot was dismissed after making a faulty landing (for which he was to blame), which caused considerable damage to the airplane. The Court of Appeal held that some jobs, such as flying an airplane or driving a lorry full of hazardous chemicals, require such a high standard of professional skill that even the slightest departure from the norm is enough to justify dismissal – *Alidair v Taylor [1978] IRLR 82.*

Step 3: After giving an opportunity to improve, you must have formed the view that he is not likely to improve   2.12

After the monitoring period has expired you should re-evaluate Fred's performance. If he is now achieving the goals you set the problem will be solved. If he is only a little way short of the goals then you should extend the monitoring period and inform him of what you have decided. It will not be reasonable at this point to dismiss someone who has significantly improved, albeit not to the level that you hoped.

Arrange a meeting   2.13

If Fred has not improved at all, or has failed to improve sufficiently to warrant extending the improvement period, you will need to hold a meeting with him at which the options can be explored. You must write to him before the meeting, stating:

- that in your view his performance has not improved and that you are considering dismissal as a result;

- that you wish to have a meeting with him to discuss (a) whether you are correct in your assessment that he has not improved, and (b) if you are correct, whether there are any reasons why he should not be dismissed;

- that he may bring a workplace colleague or trade union representative to the meeting, together with any colleagues who may be able to attest to his ability and effort.

The letter should also state the date (and place) of the meeting. If it is inconvenient for Fred to attend you must reschedule it to a more convenient time.

Before the meeting takes place, you should give Fred copies of any documents you are relying on (for example, worksheets, complaints from customers or productivity reports) so that he has an opportunity to consider them and prepare an explanation or response.

Consider alternatives   2.14

Before the meeting you must investigate whether there are any alternative positions within the company which could be offered to Fred. This is considered below at **2.16**.

Let him put his case   2.15

At the meeting you must permit Fred to give any explanation that he considers appropriate. See the advice on how to hold a disciplinary/dismissal meeting in **4.40** below.

Step 4: You must be sure that it is not reasonable to offer him another job   2.16

It is necessary for you to consider whether it is possible to re-deploy Fred in a position where he will be able to cope. In a small or medium company the answer will usually be obvious – either there is a position available or there is not.

In a larger company (say, 100+ employees) or a company which is associated with (or linked to) others, you will need to make slightly more extensive enquiries. This can be done by various means, for example:

- sending Fred's details to the personnel department;

- contacting other managers directly with a view to seeing if they have any appropriate vacancies;

- circulating a memo to department heads;

- contacting any associated employers to enquire whether they have any suitable positions.

It is also well worth asking Fred, during the dismissal meeting, whether there are any areas in which he would particularly like to work. It may be that he knows (through the employee grapevine) of vacancies that may soon become available through resignations or otherwise.

Keep a thorough record of all steps you have taken when considering alternative employment – this is the type of evidence which impresses employment tribunals and encourages them to view you with favour.

Considering alternative employment 2.17

If you form the view that there is another job which Fred might be capable of doing, you should ask him, either at the dismissal meeting (or preferably before), whether he wants to do it. Put this enquiry in writing so that you can prove to an employment tribunal that you did make the offer.

If he wishes time to consider his options you must allow him a reasonable amount of time. A week will usually be sufficient unless the new job involves major considerations such as moving house.

It is justifiable to offer Fred a new position which involves a certain reduction in wages. An employee might prefer a lower paid job to no job at all. Therefore a reasonable employer will offer his employee the lower paid job if it is available. Failure to offer suitable alternative employment can render an otherwise fair dismissal unfair.

Dismissal procedure 2.18

If you decide that there is no suitable alternative work that Fred can do and, after having met with him, are unconvinced that there is any legitimate reason for the poor job performance, then you can proceed to dismissal. Ensure that the previous written warning was issued in the last year: if it is more than a year old, a tribunal is likely to regard it as out of date and having expired – in that scenario, you are best off giving another written warning and imposing another monitoring period.

13

Write to Fred, stating:

- what happened at the meeting;

- a summary of any documents he saw and the explanations (if any) he put forward for the lack of improvement since his written warning;

- that he has failed to improve since receiving his written warning;

- if appropriate, that his explanation for the failure to improve is not adequate (explaining why);

- that in the circumstances you have no option but to dismiss him with notice. See **CHAPTER 12** for any payments (such as notice pay) that you must make to him upon dismissal;

- that he has the right to appeal against your decision. If he wishes to appeal, he should put his reasons in writing to you within, say, seven days (note: the manner of requesting an appeal should be appropriate to the nature of Fred's incapacity). See **CHAPTER 11** for appeal procedures.

Dismissing him for absence due to illness or injury

Introduction   2.19

Normally, illness or injury is unconnected with the workplace. An employee might develop an illness because of infection, or suffer an injury in a road traffic accident. In such a situation, tribunals are normally quite willing to hold that a dismissal is fair provided you have followed the procedures below.

Sometimes, the illness or injury is sustained because of something that happened at work. If an employer has caused the employee's illness through negligent working practices (for example, exposure to dangerous substances or providing unsafe working equipment), then tribunals are increasingly saying that the employer should not normally be able to escape the consequences of its negligence and be able to dismiss with impunity.

Example

> Mr Edwards was dismissed from his job as a teacher because of stress-related sick absence. The Employment Appeal Tribunal held that the reason for his absence, namely that he was suffering from work-related stress because of his treatment by the headmaster, should be taken into account when deciding whether his dismissal was fair – *Edwards v The Governors of Hanson School [2001] IRLR 733.*

When this situation arises 2.20

Assuming you are not directly responsible for Fred's illness, then the two situations when dismissal will usually arise are where Fred is frequently absent for short periods and where Fred is absent for one long, continuous period. As you will see the procedure adopted is slightly different depending on which case it is.

Sickness not conduct 2.21

This heading covers absence due to sickness. It should not be confused with absence due to lethargy or indifference (i.e. taking the day off), or even deliberate 'sickies' when holiday has been refused. If Fred is simply taking days off for no particular reason then you should use the 'conduct' section of this book (see **CHAPTER 4**).

Investigating the illness 2.22

Short, frequent absences will usually be due either to a recurring illness (or injury), due to a heightened susceptibility to infection or simply due to hypochondria! The basic question that a tribunal will ask, if Fred claims against you, is 'should you have waited any longer to see what happens, and if so, for how long?' There is a useful website, at www.managingabsence.org.uk, with guidance on how to best reduce sickness absence levels amongst the workforce as a whole.

There are three steps you must take in this situation before you dismiss Fred.

Step 1: Establish the reason for his absence 2.23

This may appear obvious: however, you should discuss with Fred (and preferably obtain in writing) precise details of his ill-health. If he is persistently absent for short periods, you can discuss this at work. If he has been continually absent for a long period, you should write to him and ask him for exact details of his illness and when he thinks he will be ready to return to work.

It is often useful to have a face-to-face meeting to establish the reason for dismissal. If you want to hold such a meeting, you should write to Fred in advance setting out the reason for the meeting. Tribunals normally disapprove of meetings where the employee is taken by surprise and has not had the opportunity to gather his thoughts.

Step 2: Consider whether improvement is likely 2.24

The second step is to consider, with the aid of medical advice, whether Fred's attendance record is likely to improve in the future. To this purpose you should ask Fred to provide you with a brief letter to his GP authorising the GP to provide a short medical report (see **2.26** below if Fred does not give permission).

Even if Fred has been examined by a company doctor, you will need to ask for Fred's permission for the report to be copied to you.

You should write to the GP (or company doctor), enclosing a letter of authority from Fred, asking him to advise you on the following points:

- the nature of the illness;

- if Fred has been absent for one long continuous period, how long he is likely to remain off work;

- if Fred has been persistently absent for short periods, the likelihood of recurrence or of some other illness arising; and

- how any recurrence will affect Fred's ability to work in the future.

Some GPs will require a small payment for such a report – you should check first and offer to pay this if necessary.

Obtain medical advice 2.25

It may be wise, if the GP's response is tentative or unclear, to ask Fred to consent to being examined by a consultant. Although this may cost you around £400–£500, it is clearly preferable to losing an unfair dismissal claim. Consider it an investment – a medium-to-large company (say, 100+ employees) could be seen as acting unreasonably in failing to obtain a consultant's report when the GP's report is unclear.

The reason for obtaining medical advice is that neither you nor Fred are qualified to determine the prospects of his ability to work in the future. Accordingly, in the absence of medical evidence, a tribunal will usually decide you were not in a proper position to judge whether dismissal is an appropriate course.

What if he refuses? 2.26

If Fred refuses to undergo a medical examination at your request, or refuses to authorise his GP to provide a report, then you will have to act on the facts currently within your knowledge. Legally, Fred is not obliged to consent to providing you with medical information unless there is a term in his contract of employment to that effect (and, even then, there is little you can do if Fred withdraws his consent).

If you dismiss Fred as a result of the facts within your knowledge, but without the benefit of medical advice due to his refusal to authorise it, then you cannot be criticised if non-disclosed medical evidence suggests at a later stage that you acted precipitately.

You are not entitled to infer any sinister reason behind Fred's refusal to authorise the release of medical records. He may be reluctant to disclose them for a reason entirely unconnected with his absence from work. If you assume the worst because of Fred's failure to divulge all the details of his personal medical history then you will be acting unfairly in dismissing him. You must only act based on the information that he allows you to have. It is, however, legitimate to assume in the absence of evidence to the contrary, that the current state of affairs (i.e. absence from work) will be ongoing provided that you have tried to investigate the situation, kept Fred informed of your enquiries and invited his comments at all stages.

Step 3: Is dismissal justified?   2.27

The third step is to consider, in view of the medical information as to Fred's ability to work in the future, whether it is reasonable to dismiss him. In doing so you must remember that Fred has a legal right not to be unfairly dismissed, which he can enforce in the tribunals. The decision to dismiss him, which is obviously a draconian remedy from his point of view, must be justifiable in the terms of the cost or lost revenue if you continue to employ him (albeit at a lower level of efficiency).

One trap for the unwary is that if you provide permanent health insurance for Fred, and he only remains entitled to the benefits of the policy as long as he remains employed, the courts will imply a term that you will not dismiss him for a sickness-related reason, if that prevents him receiving the benefits under the policy. Seek specialist legal advice if Fred is in receipt of such benefits.

Example

Mr Aspden, a senior manager, suffered a heart attack, followed by angina and 'flu. He took long-term sick leave. The MD considered that he was malingering and dismissed him. His contract entitled him to sick pay at full salary for the first three months of sickness absence, with 50 per cent salary for the next three months. After 26 weeks' incapacity, an

> insurance-backed income replacement scheme kicked in to provide 75 per cent of last payable salary until death, retirement or the 'date on which the group member ceases to be an eligible employee'. On the evidence the High Court decided that Mr Aspden had not been malingering and was genuinely absent by reason of sickness. The court held there was an implied term that an employer will not terminate a contract of employment during an employee's absence on sick leave while he is receiving permanent health insurance benefit if that results in him losing entitlement to the benefit. Accordingly Mr Aspden was entitled to compensation (the case was adjourned to allow damages to be assessed) – *Aspden v Webbs Poultry and Meat Group (Holdings) Ltd [1996] IRLR 521, QBD.*

Is dismissal necessary?   2.28

In deciding whether dismissal is necessary you should consider the following facts:

- the length of the various absences and the spaces of good health between them;

- your need for the work to be done by that particular employee;

- the impact of Fred's absence on those who work with him;

- any considerations personal to Fred which place an additional obligation on you to retain him (e.g. length of service).

The Disability Discrimination Act   2.29

You must also consider the provisions of the *Disability Discrimination Act 1995.* This Act applies if:

- Fred suffers from a physical or mental impairment which has lasted (or is likely to last) for more than 12 months; and

- his condition has an effect (which is more than merely trivial) on his ability to undertake day-to-day activities.

If the *Disability Discrimination Act* applies, you cannot dismiss Fred unless you can prove to a tribunal that you are objectively justified in doing so. This will involve a tribunal balancing up the detriment to Fred in being dismissed, against the detriment to you in having to keep Fred on the books.

You are also obliged, under the *Disability Discrimination Act*, to make any reasonable adjustments to any physical features of the workplace, or any job-structure arrangements, which may or will remove the effect of Fred's disability. The factors that have to be considered under the Act are:

- making adjustments to premises;

- allocating some of the disabled person's duties to another person;

- transferring him to fill an existing vacancy – even if he is not necessarily the best candidate for the job;

- altering his working hours;

- assigning him to a different place of work;

- allowing him to be absent during working hours for rehabilitation, assessment or treatment;

- giving him, or arranging for him to be given, training;

- acquiring or modifying equipment;

- modifying instructions or reference manuals;

- modifying procedures for testing or assessment;

- providing a reader or interpreter; and,

- providing supervision.

One of the most important aspects of the above is the obligation to consider alternative employment – even if Fred is not the best candidate for the job.

Example

> Mrs Archibald was a road sweeper. She became unable to work after a rare complication of surgery, and so could not fulfil her job requirements. Her employer interviewed her for an available administrative post but, even though Mrs Archibald could have done a competent job, chose to appoint a better qualified candidate. It therefore dismissed her. The House of Lords held that the employer had discriminated against Mrs Archibald by failing to make reasonable adjustments to allow her to remain in employment, as an employer is under a positive duty to discriminate in favour of disabled people – *Archibald v Fife Council [2004] UKHL 32.*

As long as you can demonstrate that you have considered the above steps, and there is nothing that can reasonably be done to enable Fred to remain in employment, you will be justified in dismissing him (under the *Disability Discrimination Act 1995*). It would be prudent to maintain some form of written record as to why none of the above are reasonably practical.

Dismissal procedure 2.30

By the time you have gone through the above steps you would have formed a preliminary view as to whether it is justifiable to dismiss Fred. In addition Fred will be aware that you are considering dismissal.

You will come to one of three conclusions:

- that it is necessary to dismiss Fred. This will often be the conclusion reached in cases of one long, ongoing period of absence, unless reasonable adjustments to the workplace will assist. It will be less common to reach this conclusion when Fred is frequently absent for short periods.

- that Fred is likely to carry on being absent in the future; however, it cannot be guaranteed and therefore he should be given a final chance. A tribunal would usually expect a reasonable employer to offer Fred a final chance even when he has taken long periods of absence in the past – remember, you are dismissing him due to the risk of future absences, not past.

- alternatively, that Fred is likely to return to work soon – whether with or without reasonable adjustments being made to the workplace – and is unlikely to continue being absent in the future. In this case it will be unfair to dismiss him.

The dismissal letter 2.31

If you have decided that it is necessary to dismiss Fred, then you should write to him accordingly and, under the new minimum dismissal procedures that came into force in October 2004, try to hold a meeting with him.

The letter should contain the following points:

- a brief description of the length and frequency of Fred's absences;

- a synopsis of your investigation into his illness (this is important because it might be the only proof before a tribunal that you have made efforts to determine whether Fred's illness is likely to be ongoing);

- that you have formed a preliminary view that his illness prevents him from carrying out his duties as an employee;

- that, after consultation with him (and, if appropriate, medical advisers – name them) there does not seem to be a reasonable chance of improvement;

- (if appropriate) that you have considered other options such as Fred working from home, having a part-time job or working flexitime, but those options would not work;

SICKNESS DISMISSALS (handwritten)

- (if appropriate) that you have considere   just-
  ments that can be made to the workplac   :d to
  dismiss Fred. Set out the options yo   plain
  (briefly) why they are not practical;

- that you would like to invite him   your
  preliminary conclusions. Set out a d   the
  meeting. If appropriate to the nature o: :d at
  home.

At the meeting, you need to discuss your prel   d. If
he tells you that he is going to return to work   dical
evidence), ask him if he has any explanatior   ltant
thinks differently. You may wish, as a final cha   (say,
a fortnight or a month) to come up with furi

If you decide to hold to your preliminary conclusion, then you should write to
Fred again after the meeting:

- summarising (again) the background;

- summarising the discussions you held at the meeting;

- stating that in the circumstances you have no option but to dismiss him
  with notice. See **CHAPTER 12** for any payments (such as notice pay) that
  you must make to him upon dismissal;

- stating that he has the right to appeal against your decision. If he wishes
  to appeal, he should put his reasons in writing to you within, say, seven
  days (note: the manner of requesting an appeal should be appropriate to
  the nature of Fred's incapacity). See **CHAPTER 11** for appeal procedures.

You should attach a cheque representing any accrued wages/holiday pay/
notice period.

It is important to note that the failure to invite Fred to a meeting will normally
make the dismissal *automatically unfair*. If it is impractical to hold the meeting at
your office (for example, if Fred cannot travel), consider holding the meeting at
Fred's home. If this, too, is impractical, it is better to have a telephone
discussion than no discussion at all. Ultimately, if Fred fails to attend the
meeting or a tribunal decides it was not practical to hold a meeting because of
Fred's condition, then the dismissal will not be *automatically* unfair (although
this does not mean it will be automatically fair – you still need to comply with
the other procedural requirements).

Giving a final chance   2.32

If, by contrast, you have decided that Fred should be given a final chance, then
you will need to set out the position in writing. The letter should contain the
following points:

- the first two points mentioned above (**2.31**), i.e. description of illness and your investigation;

- your concern that, at present, he seems unlikely to be able to continue fulfilling his role as an employee;

- a warning that unless he is able to resume normal attendance within a reasonable period (four weeks is suggested) then you will have no other option but to dismiss him and seek a replacement.

If he fails to respond   2.33

If Fred does not reply to your letter, and if he fails to resume his work within the allotted period, then you will be entitled to dismiss him. The dismissal letter should take the same form as the one set out above. If he responds that he did not receive the first letter, you will need to re-offer the final chance as set out above. You should make sure that, before dismissing him, you invite Fred to a meeting to discuss his absence (see **2.31**).

Dismissing due to lack of proper qualifications   2.34

It is not easy to claim that your reason for dismissing Fred is his lack of appropriate formal qualifications. This is for the simple reason that by the time an unfair dismissal action can be brought Fred will have been working for you for at least one year. Accordingly an employment tribunal will view with some scepticism a claim that Fred turned out to be improperly qualified.

If required qualifications change   2.35

As a matter of reality there are only two situations when it might be possible to dismiss Fred for reasons relating to his qualifications. The first situation is if the law relating to required qualifications changed. Thus if Fred was an electrical engineer, and a law came into being requiring all electrical engineers to gain a new qualification, then you (as a responsible employer) would encourage Fred to take the appropriate exam. If, however, he kept failing the exam (or refused to take it) then you would be justified in dismissing him for lacking the necessary qualification. Note that there is an overlap between the incapability reason in this example and the 'failure to comply with an enactment' reason for dismissing an employee (see **10.3**) – the most common example being a driver who loses his driving licence.

If the employee misled you   2.36

Secondly, you might be entitled to dismiss Fred if he misled you when he applied for a job. Thus if Fred was employed as a printer and it transpired that he did not possess the Guild qualifications that he had claimed to have, you might be entitled to dismiss him (provided you followed the appropriate procedure). This would be very closely linked to a dismissal for misconduct. You should be careful, however, that you are not perceived as acting disproportionately. Unless the fact of having the qualification is important to the continued performance of the job, if Fred can do the job you should allow him to continue with it (albeit, perhaps after issuing a written warning for misconduct).

In either of these scenarios, you will still need to comply with the minimum dismissal procedures (see **CHAPTER 4**) and ensure you have considered whether there is any suitable alternative employment you can offer. Failure to comply with either of these requirements will mean the dismissal will be unfair.

Chapter 3
How to Dismiss Someone for Criminal Acts Outside of Work

Introduction

Crimes outside of employment that affect employment will usually take the form of some violent or dishonest act.

It is uncommon to dismiss Fred simply because of a criminal act that he has committed outside of work. It may be that the criminal act is the last straw, or it may be that it makes you think that he is an undesirable person to have as an employee. It is only in certain circumstances, however, that a criminal act occurring outside of work justifies immediate dismissal, namely when it means that Fred becomes unsuitable to continue working, or other employees refuse to work with him.

Reasonable belief in guilt

It is important to note that for Fred's actions to qualify as criminal, he does not need to have been arrested by the police or convicted by a court. You are entitled to act on the basis that Fred has committed a violent or dishonest act if you have investigated the circumstances of the alleged act and formed a reasonable belief that Fred is guilty. If, with hindsight, it transpires that he was not responsible for the violent or dishonest act that you had blamed him for, you will not be criticised by an employment tribunal for acting unfairly provided you had investigated the matter fully at the time.

If Fred has been convicted and is in prison, or if he is in custody awaiting trial, then it may be that his contract of employment has been 'frustrated' and he is not allowed to claim unfair dismissal (in which case you need not be concerned about the mechanics of dismissal). This means that Fred's contract of employment is prevented from operating normally due to circumstances beyond your control – i.e. the fact that Fred is in prison. The courts have not laid down clear guidance as to how long Fred must be imprisoned for before the contract of employment becomes frustrated: however, a rule of thumb is that imprisonment of more than three to six months is likely to 'frustrate' the contract (and thus prevent Fred claiming unfair dismissal).

Meaning of 'crime' in this Chapter 3.3

Throughout this chapter the words 'crime' or 'criminal' are used as a convenient way of describing acts of violence or dishonesty. If Fred is referred to as a criminal, or his acts referred to as crimes, it does not mean that has been arrested by the police and prosecuted. It simply means that you suspect him of having committed an act which is technically illegal and involves elements of violence or dishonesty.

Three points to fair dismissal for criminal conduct 3.4

You will have to convince an employment tribunal on three points before it will declare a dismissal for criminal conduct outside of work to be fair:

(1)   that you had a genuine and reasonable belief that Fred had committed the criminal act (see **3.5**);

(2)   that the criminal conduct makes it difficult for you to continue employing Fred, due to its adverse affect on your business or the risk to your business of continuing to employ him (see **3.12**); and

(3)   that dismissal is a reasonable sanction in the circumstances (rather than, for example, issuing a written warning or suspending Fred for a period) (see **3.20**).

Stage 1: A genuine and reasonable belief that he had committed the criminal act 3.5

If Fred has been convicted of a criminal offence, then this step will be satisfied with little further investigation. A tribunal will accept that it is reasonable to believe that Fred is guilty of a crime if he has admitted it, or been found guilty of it, in court. But in the absence of a conviction, you will have to conduct your own investigation into whether you believe he is guilty.

If he is in custody, it may be that his contract of employment has become impossible to perform. If so, the law regards his employment as automatically terminated and Fred cannot claim unfair dismissal (see **3.2**).

If he has been charged and is awaiting trial, you may be justified in suspending him pending the result of the trial. Any suspension should be on full pay unless

Fred's contract of employment expressly provides that he can be suspended without pay. Suspension, however, may not be ideal (you may be short-staffed and still have to pay Fred his wages). In addition, an unreasonably long period of suspension (maybe as little as four weeks), particularly without pay, may entitle Fred to resign and claim that he has been constructively dismissed (see **17.2**).

The best approach, therefore, is not to await the result of the trial but to conduct your own investigation so as to enable you to form a view as to whether he may be guilty.

The evidence   3.6

When conducting your own investigation, the first stage is to consider what made you suspect that Fred had committed a criminal act. He may have come and told you about it, in which case it is clearly reasonable to believe that he had done it. You may have heard others gossiping, in which case you must speak to them to confirm that you had not misunderstood the allegations. Ideally, you should obtain signed statements from these people, but if they are reluctant to cooperate (and you should not press them too hard for fear of being accused of engineering evidence) you should make a written note of what they have told you whilst it is still fresh in your mind. Ensure that this note is dated and keep it safe – this is in case Fred later persuades them to retract what they have said.

Another reason for suspecting Fred of a criminal act is if you see his name in the newspaper being linked with a crime, or if you happen to know that Fred was in a particular place at a particular time and may be the culprit. In the absence of more concrete evidence it will be difficult to persuade an employment tribunal that your belief that Fred was guilty is reasonable. Accordingly you should be extremely wary of proceeding on the basis of speculation alone.

Put the reasons in writing and arrange a meeting   3.7

If you have sufficient information to believe that Fred may be guilty of a crime, then you should write to him, stating the following:

- that you believe he may have committed an offence of dishonesty, violence, etc. Specify the crime that you believe he may have committed, and set out the date(s) on which he is thought to have committed it;

- your reasons for believing that he has committed the crime. If the reason is gossip, state the names of the people from whom you heard the gossip.

This is important because the informant might dislike Fred and have fabricated the allegations. Although you might be unaware of any grudges between employees, Fred might be able to explain the allegations if you tell him who the informant was. An employment tribunal is unlikely to condone your failure to tell Fred who was making allegations against him (except in exceptional circumstances – see **4.8**);

- that this might have an effect on his continued employment with you. Explain why you think it may make his continued employment with the company difficult or impossible;

- a request to discuss the accusations with you. Include a date for the discussion in the letter, but make it clear that the date can be rearranged if inconvenient to him;

- that he is entitled to bring people, whether witnesses or a representative, with him to the meeting.

Explain the allegations   3.8

At the meeting, you must explain to Fred the precise nature of the allegations being made against him. Allow him to make any representations he thinks fit, and if he wishes more time to investigate the *matter* you should allow him extra time (unless there is a compelling reason not to, such as extreme urgency). Do not hesitate to question him on inconsistencies in his explanation – if he cannot explain away inconsistencies then you will be better able to justify your belief in his guilt.

Take notes at the meeting   3.9

As with all interviews, it is important to maintain an accurate record of what is said. Even if Fred admits the allegation, if he later denies that he admitted it and a tribunal believes him then you are worse off than if he had not admitted it to start with (because the tribunal will think that you are being untruthful). Accordingly you should have a witness in the room with you who should take a detailed note of the proceedings. If the note is legible at the end of the interview, invite Fred to read and sign it. If the note is not legible, type up a legible version immediately after the meeting and ask him to sign the typed version. You should normally let him have a copy of the notes.

Do not make a decision during the meeting as to whether Fred committed the crime. In particular, you must not inform Fred of your decision at the conclusion of the meeting, no matter how much he may ask you. A tribunal might think that an immediate decision is either arbitrary or predetermined. You should put your decision in writing to him if and when you reach Stage (3) (see **3.20**).

Weigh up the evidence 3.10

After interviewing Fred, you should consider the information that you have received from different sources and make up your mind whether you think Fred is guilty of the acts that have been alleged against him. You do not have to be certain beyond a reasonable doubt, but you must have reasonable grounds for your belief that he has committed the crime. Although a decision will not necessarily be easy, you simply have to make up your mind which version of facts you accept. If Fred has given an alibi or some other defence, you should take reasonable steps to investigate his story (making sure you keep a full record of all steps you take).

Your conclusions must be reasonable on the evidence 3.11

If your conclusion is that you think Fred is guilty then this will not be criticised by an employment tribunal even if it later turns out that Fred is innocent. Provided that you can prove to a tribunal that you have investigated the matter properly, have a genuine belief that Fred is guilty and that there are reasonable grounds for your belief, then any action you take as a result will not be unfair just because there was an incorrect assumption of guilt.

Stage 2: The criminal conduct must make it difficult for you to continue employing Fred 3.12

The ACAS Code of Practice on Disciplinary and Grievance Procedures, which is viewed by tribunals very much as the 'highway code' of employment law, sets out the general test for dismissing somebody for criminal conduct outside of work. It provides that:

> 'If an employee is charged with, or convicted of, a criminal offence not related to work, this is not in itself reason for disciplinary action. The employer should establish the facts of the case and consider whether the matter is serious enough to warrant starting the disciplinary procedure. The main consideration should be whether the offence, or alleged offence, is one that makes the employee unsuitable for their type of work. Similarly, an employee should not be dismissed simply because they are absent from work as a result of being remanded in custody.'

In order to fairly dismiss Fred for criminal conduct outside of work, you must be able to persuade a tribunal that you decided one of the following:

- that as a result of the criminal conduct, Fred has become unsuitable for his type of work; or

- that as a result of the criminal conduct, other employees will no longer work with Fred and so either his work (or their work) cannot be performed properly. Although this is not specifically mentioned in the ACAS Code of Practice, tribunals are normally willing to accept this as a fair reason for dismissal in appropriate cases.

Offences of dishonesty   3.13

These will usually fall under the first test, namely that Fred has become unsuitable for his type of work. This is often the case if Fred occupies a position involving a degree of trust (such as the handling of cash). If, however, you are going to use this as a ground for dismissal, do not delay in dismissing Fred – it is no use trying to dismiss Fred for an offence of dishonesty which you discovered a month ago. This is because a tribunal may decide that your continued employment of him during the month is inconsistent with a genuine belief that he has become unsuitable for the work.

Example

> A shop assistant at Heathrow Airport was accused of stealing £100 from the till. However, the employer allowed nine days to elapse between reconciling the till (when it discovered the discrepancy) and accusing the employee. Although the decision is not particularly clear, the Employment Appeal Tribunal's grounds for finding the dismissal unfair would have been, in part, the nine day gap whilst the employee remained on the till being inconsistent with a genuine belief or suspicion that she was dishonest – *Allders International v Parkins [1981] IRLR 68.*

A tribunal is more likely to support the dismissal of Fred if he is a high-ranking employee. This is on the basis that he should be all the more aware of the potential consequences of his dishonest acts.

Example

> A manager who had worked at C&A for 20 years was believed to be shoplifting at a shop down the road. It was held that the dismissal was fair because the employee, when knowing of the harm to a retailer that shoplifting can do, had nonetheless committed such an act, must

therefore have been indifferent to the needs of his employer, and it was therefore risky to retain her in employment – *Moore v C & A Modes [1981] IRLR 71.*

Adverse effect on business   3.14

It may also be possible to dismiss somebody for offences of dishonesty because of the adverse effect that the retaining of employees believed to be dishonest would have on your business. Examples include where Fred is engaged as a security guard, handles other people's money or deals with clients' confidential information.

Example

A shipwright who handled cargo onboard a ship was dismissed because of theft away from work. It was held that the dismissal was fair because it would adversely affect his employer's business if clients discovered that they employed a man convicted of theft to handle their goods – *Robb v Mersey Insulation Co Ltd [1972] IRLR 18.*

Unsuitability for job   3.15

You must, however, ensure that you can show a tribunal that Fred's dishonesty means that he is unsuitable for his job. Some offences of dishonesty will not necessarily satisfy this test. For example, if Fred was convicted of receiving stolen goods, then it would not necessarily mean that he had become unsuitable for his job as, say, a secretary or a builder.

Offences of violence (other than sexual misconduct)   3.16

Offences of violence will usually fall under the second test set out in **3.12**, i.e. that other employees will no longer work with Fred or find it difficult to do so. It will be comparatively unusual to find that, as a result of violence away from the workplace, Fred is no longer a suitable person to perform the type of job which he does (i.e. the first test) unless Fred is engaged in a position where physical restraint is particularly important (for example, a security guard or a nightclub bouncer).

Is it difficult for people to continue working with him?   3.17

You must be cautious against deciding on your own that other employees will find it difficult to continue working with Fred. A tribunal will need to be satisfied that your belief was reasonable. You will need to be approached by employees who say that they are uncomfortable working with Fred. If you suspect that they will find it difficult to work with Fred, but they have not approached you, you should be wary of how you approach them.

Keep your enquiries low key, and ask employees whom you feel comfortable approaching for their views and the views of their colleagues.

It is only if the other employees confirm to you that they feel it to be difficult to continue working with Fred that you may be able to dismiss him. You will still, however, have to satisfy a tribunal that dismissal was a reasonable sanction in the circumstances (see **3.20**).

Offences of sexual misconduct   3.18

Offences involving sexual misconduct committed away from the workplace will sometimes be capable of justifying dismissal, but will by no means invariably justify dismissal. Dismissal may be justified under both tests set out at **3.12** above, namely that it may mean that Fred can no longer perform his job properly or it may mean that other employees will no longer work with Fred.

It is not permissible to dismiss Fred because he is convicted of a sexual offence related to a specific sexual orientation (such as indecent behaviour between two men in a public place), as this would amount to discrimination on grounds of sexual orientation, unless you are confident you can persuade a tribunal that you would also dismiss (in this hypothetical situation) a man who had been found guilty of indecent behaviour with a woman in a public place.

Examples

A college lecturer, who taught mixed-sex teenagers between the ages of 16 and 18, was dismissed following a conviction for gross indecency with other men in a public toilet. The tribunal held that the dismissal was fair under both tests. Under the first test, the college was reasonable in deciding that a man who could not control himself in public ought not to be trusted with young persons. Under a slightly varied form of the second test, it decided that the school was justified in taking account of

> the views of parents who did not want the lecturer to continue teaching their children – *Gardiner v Newport County Borough Council [1974] IRLR 262, IT.*
>
> A BBC cameraman was dismissed following a conviction for indecently assaulting a 13-year-old girl. The BBC argued that it would have to be selective in the assignments on which it could send him in the future (i.e. avoiding assignments where he would come into contact with young children) and it would be unreasonable to expect it to do that. The tribunal accepted that the BBC's views were reasonable, and held the dismissal to be fair – *Creffield v BBC [1975] IRLR 23, IT.*

Does this affect his work? 3.19

However, sometimes Fred's sexual misconduct will clearly not affect his ability to do the job or render his workmates reluctant to work with him. If you dismiss Fred in such a case and Fred claims unfair dismissal against you, he will succeed.

Example

> A male employee was convicted of incest and dismissed as a result. A tribunal held that his employers acted unreasonably in dismissing him. The incest was an isolated incident and had nothing to do with the employee's work. He did not work with women, and the gang of men with whom he worked did not seem to mind. There was no suggestion of any of his workmates being exposed to physical or moral danger. Accordingly the dismissal was unfair – *Bradshaw v Rugby Portland Cement Co Ltd [1972] IRLR 46.*

Stage 3: Dismissal must be a reasonable sanction in the circumstances 3.20

By this stage you will have decided that Fred has committed an offence which either makes him unsuitable for his job or makes it difficult for his colleagues to work with him. Accordingly dismissal may seem like the most sensible course.

However a tribunal will want evidence that you have specifically considered whether dismissal is an appropriate sanction. In an extremely large company, it may be possible to transfer Fred to another department. Thus if he sexually molests a woman outside work, and his female colleagues are apprehensive about continuing to work with him, dismissal will be unfair if he could easily be asked to work from home or be transferred to a male-only environment.

Arrange a meeting 3.21

The best view to obtain as to whether there is a reasonable alternative to dismissal is Fred's. It he is unable to suggest any alternatives to dismissal or explain why dismissal is not justified, then you will have gone a long way towards establishing that the dismissal was fair.

You should ask Fred, in writing, to come to a meeting with you to discuss his future position in the company. The letter should state the following:

- the offence which you believe Fred to have committed, the fact that you are considering dismissal and the reason that you are considering dismissal. If you had a meeting with Fred to establish whether he had committed the offence, briefly summarise the reasons for your decision from that meeting;

- an invitation to Fred to discuss the situation with you. You should state that the purpose of the meeting is to see if there are any reasons why Fred's conduct should not give rise to dismissal, and whether there are any alternatives to dismissal that can be adopted; and

- an invitation to Fred to bring a representative to the meeting if he so desires.

Take full notes in the meeting 3.22

At the meeting you should ensure that a full note is taken (see **3.9** above). You must consider any alternative proposals to dismissal that Fred puts forward. Do not forget that he will have a different perspective on events and that his views, as the person who is most directly affected, should not be dismissed out of hand. If, however, after having considered his proposals you are not satisfied that they are feasible (and, more importantly, you are satisfied that it is reasonable to reject his proposals) then you will be justified in dismissing him.

Again, do not tell Fred the result whilst you are actually in the meeting. This is to avoid an accusation of having prejudged the situation, and so that your reasons can be set out in writing after having been properly considered. This is particularly important because your reasons for dismissal should be in written form to be seen by the tribunal (if necessary). If you state your reasons orally in the heat of a meeting, there is a risk that they may be misinterpreted by Fred, which might prejudice your position in tribunal proceedings.

Letter of dismissal 3.23

If, after the meeting, you are of the view that dismissal is a proper course to take, you will need to write a letter of dismissal. You must ensure that the letter contains the following points:

- that you write following your meeting, stating the date, with your decision;

- the act of violence or dishonesty that you believe Fred has committed. If he has been convicted, refer to the conviction. If your decision that he has committed an offence followed an investigative meeting with him, refer to the date of the meeting and your findings;

- that Fred's continued employment is not possible, and your reasons for concluding this. Identify whether you rely on criterion 1 (i.e. that Fred is no longer suitable to undertake his job) or criterion 2 (i.e. that other employees find it difficult to continue working with Fred). Set out the reasons for your conclusions;

- that you have considered the matters put forward by Fred at your recent meeting, but that you remain of the view that dismissal is the only appropriate action. If Fred suggested alternatives, set them out and explain why they are not appropriate;

- that Fred has a right of appeal from your decision. See **CHAPTER 11** on appeals.

The letter of dismissal should contain any monies that Fred is owed – see **CHAPTER 12** for what you must pay. You should not permit Fred to work out his notice period since a tribunal would view this as being inconsistent with a belief that Fred could not continue in his job, and thus your credibility at the hearing would be undermined.

References 3.24

Treat any requests for references that come in within the next three months with caution. It is common practice for employee's advisors to try to obtain a reference from an employer in the hope that the employer will not refer to the reason for dismissal within the reference. This will then be used against you at a tribunal hearing as evidence that your stated reason for dismissal was a fabrication.

You are under no legal obligation to provide references for ex-employees (unless you are in a particular industry where it is mandatory or expected to do so, for example financial services). Indeed, many large employers nowadays refuse to give any substantive reference due to concerns about being sued for negligence. Accordingly, if you are concerned about giving a reference but do not want to prejudice Fred's chance of obtaining alternative employment, it may be appropriate to give a reference in the form:

'Fred worked for this firm as a sales assistant between June 1992 and October 2002. It is this company's policy not to give any information on the capability or conduct of any employee. This should not be seen as an adverse reflection on Fred.'

If Fred is going to claim unfair dismissal against you, he must do so within three months of the termination of his employment (but see **18.9** below). If he was dismissed with notice then the three month period begins running from the expiry of the notice period. Accordingly, if you have not received an unfair dismissal claim form within three months, you are highly likely to be safe from a claim and can give such references as you please.

Note that if you give an unjustified bad reference through mistake or malice, Fred may have a claim against you for negligence or defamation.

Chapter 4
How to Dismiss Someone for Breaches of Discipline at Work

Introduction 4.1

Breach of discipline at work is probably the most common reason for immediate dismissal, as contrasted with dismissing Fred with notice. An immediate dismissal is often referred to by its legal description as a 'summary' dismissal. As you will see, however, you will not always be able to justify summary dismissal to a tribunal, and you must guard against over-reacting to Fred's breach of disciplinary standards. Although a tribunal will take account of the size and resources of your business when judging whether or not you have acted fairly, even the smallest business needs to follow a proper procedure when dismissing somebody for what may seem, on the face of it, a manifestly dismissable offence.

Breaches of discipline can cover all sorts of behaviour. Behaviour such as violence or theft at work will fall within this heading. It will also cover less serious offences such as smoking in breach of company policy, swearing, intoxication or personal use of the telephone. It can also cover more unusual conduct such as divulging confidential company information or harassing fellow employees.

The principal test which an employment tribunal will apply is to see whether your action was something which 'no reasonable employer would have done'. If the tribunal decides that no reasonable employer would have acted in the way that you did, then the dismissal will be unfair. It is important to note that this does not mean simply that you need to arrive at a conclusion (i.e. to dismiss) and be able to show that the conclusion was reasonable. Even if your conclusion is reasonable, but a tribunal decides that you reached that conclusion in a way which no reasonable employer would have done (for example, if you failed to hold a disciplinary hearing) then it will hold the dismissal to be unfair.

Reasonable responses: advantage of a clear disciplinary code
4.2

In deciding whether you have acted fairly, a tribunal will look at whether your actions fall within a band of reasonable responses which a reasonable employer could make. The tribunal will not criticise you for failing to act in a perfect or ideal way, provided your actions bring you within the band of reasonable responses. In other words, a tribunal should not find that a dismissal is unfair simply because the members of the tribunal might have acted differently in the same situation. They will, however, find the dismissal to be unfair if they conclude that your actions were such that no reasonable employer would have acted in that way.

Example

> A company dismissed an employee under its policy not to employ drug addicts. The Employment Appeal Tribunal held that although a more lenient employer might not have dismissed him, it was within the range of reasonable responses to have a policy against the employment of drug addicts, and thus the dismissal was fair – *Walton v TAC Construction Materials Ltd [1981] IRLR 357.*

Ideally, you should have a clear disciplinary policy setting out the type of conduct which you consider would warrant disciplinary action, and the potential consequences if the policy is breached. If such a policy has been brought to Fred's attention, and he then commits an act which is prohibited by it, you will have gone a long way towards showing that you have acted fairly in dismissing him. If your company does not have a disciplinary policy, one should be issued to all employees to cover yourself in future situations. Indeed, since October 2004 it has been a legal requirement that a disciplinary policy should be given to all employees within two months of commencing employment (before October 2004, this requirement applied only if you employed over 20 employees). An example of a disciplinary policy can be found in the sample written statement of particulars of employment in **APPENDIX 4**.

The benefit of a clear disciplinary policy is such that you can often dismiss somebody for breach of disciplinary rules without any prior warning if the offence and the consequence is spelled out clearly enough in the policy. This will be examined in more detail at **4.31** below.

Three points to establish fairness of dismissal
4.3

There are three stages as to which you must satisfy a tribunal before it will declare that your dismissal of Fred was fair. They are:

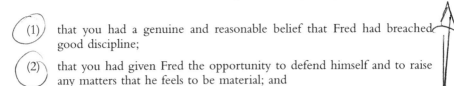

(1) that you had a genuine and reasonable belief that Fred had breached good discipline;

(2) that you had given Fred the opportunity to defend himself and to raise any matters that he feels to be material; and

(3) that dismissal is a reasonable response to Fred's actions (taking into consideration any mitigation or representations made by Fred).

As with dismissals for incapability, it is important to be able to prove that you have gone through each of these stages in case Fred brings a tribunal claim against you.

One exception must be mentioned. If Fred is a trade union official, you must not dismiss him (or issue written warnings) unless you have discussed the case with a senior trade union representative or a full-time trade union official. If you fail to liaise with a senior representative throughout the disciplinary process, it is highly likely that a tribunal will find the dismissal to be unfair. The reason for this requirement is to make it harder for an employer to dismiss someone who is involved in trade union activities by dressing up the dismissal as being for misconduct.

There is a certain degree of overlap with dismissals for criminal acts outside of the workplace (see **CHAPTER 3**). As before, each step needs to be addressed separately by you and thus will be discussed separately below.

Suspending the employee pending dismissal 4.4

Whilst you are going through the dismissal procedure, you will need to decide whether to suspend Fred pending the completion of your investigations. If the breach of discipline is so serious that you are considering dismissing him summarily, you will usually need to suspend him. If you fail to suspend him in such circumstances, you leave yourself open to the argument that, given you permitted Fred to remain at work whilst investigating the breach, it could not have been serious enough to warrant removal from the workplace and thus could not have justified dismissal. Avoid this argument by suspending Fred.

Always suspend on full pay. Until recently, it was permissible to suspend on no (or reduced) pay if the contract of employment gave you that right. But from 1 October 2004, the law has changed so that employers cannot suspend on no (or reduced) pay during the disciplinary process – and if you do (and you go on to dismiss Fred), the dismissal will be automatically unfair.

You must act reasonably diligently once Fred is suspended. If he is suspended on full pay for more than, say, three months, a tribunal is likely to say you are in breach of the obligation to conduct disciplinary hearings diligently: this will entitle Fred to resign and claim constructive dismissal (and effectively pre-empt your disciplinary decision).

Example

> The Post Office suspended three employees on suspicion of theft. It kept them on suspension, on full pay, for six months. They resigned and claimed that the Post Office was breaching their contract of employment by failing to proceed promptly with the disciplinary process. They won their claim of unfair constructive dismissal – *McLory v Post Office [1993] IRLR 159, ChD).*

Stage 1: A genuine and reasonable belief that the employee has breached discipline 4.5

You can be convinced, to different degrees, that Fred has committed a particular breach of discipline. The clearest example will be when Fred has admitted it after being caught in the act, for example if he is discovered removing money from the till or in the middle of a fight. If he admits the act, you should obtain some form of corroborating evidence (since there is always the risk that he will deny his admission at a tribunal).

Ideally, you should obtain a statement from Fred, but it is important to avoid intimidating him with procedure at this stage. The easiest way to obtain a statement is to ask Fred to set out, in writing, the circumstances surrounding the offence. If he declines to do so, on the basis that there are no mitigating circumstances and so nothing is served by setting out his acts in writing, invite him to sign a statement confirming that he has not committed any similar breach of discipline before. Do not tell him that if he signs such a statement, he will not be dismissed: this would be misleading and you would be found to have acted unfairly.

Fred may refuse to sign anything admitting his act if it is likely to give rise to a criminal prosecution (e.g. theft). If this is the case, you should make a full note as soon after his admission as possible, date it, and ensure it is kept safely.

There will also be situations where you have not actually caught Fred in the act, but where evidence is discovered which makes it almost inconceivable that he has not committed the breach of discipline. Thus, for example, stolen company property might be discovered at his house, or a letter may be discovered addressed to a competitor which he has signed. You should remember, however, that such strong evidence is not the same as proof, and it will not avoid the need to perform an investigation into the allegations and give Fred an opportunity to put his case. The scope of the investigation is, however, flexible, and you will not be criticised for undertaking a smaller scale investigation than in a situation where Fred's involvement is based on circumstantial evidence only.

Finally, you will encounter situations where there is very little to go on, and you either suspect Fred simply because you have eliminated everyone else, or

40

you know it must be one of a group of people who have been in breach of discipline, but you do not know which one. In the latter situation, as will be seen in paragraph **4.9**, it may sometimes be fair if you dismiss all of the employees who are under suspicion and do not pick arbitrarily between them.

Where guilt is clear   4.6

If Fred pleads guilty to a criminal offence in connection with the breach of discipline, or is found guilty by a court, then you will be entirely justified in treating this first step as fulfilled and moving on to the second stage. As set out above, where his guilt is clear you will not need to expend too many resources in investigating the breach of discipline. You must, however, still investigate the surrounding circumstances insofar as they may be material to stage iii, since there may be circumstances which cast a very different complexion upon the appropriate sanction even if Fred has pleaded guilty.

Example

A miner, during the miners' strike, was charged with assaulting a fellow employee. The NCB decided to dismiss him if he was convicted. The miner pleaded guilty on a technicality, namely that he had threatened violence (which is technically an assault) but maintained that there had been no physical contact. His dismissal was held to be unfair since the NCB failed to give him an opportunity to explain his conviction and, if he had been allowed to explain his guilty plea on a technicality, they might not have dismissed him – *McLaren v National Coal Board [1988] ICR 370*.

What evidence should you obtain?   4.7

The ideal evidence would be a signed admission by Fred that he had committed the breach of discipline in question. However, this will rarely be forthcoming.

As long as you can prove that you had a genuine and reasonable belief in Fred's guilt, you will satisfy the first step of the dismissal. Accordingly any evidence showing that Fred committed the breach of discipline in question should be sought, whatever its form. It is not necessary for the evidence to be technically admissible in ordinary courts, since all you are seeking to show is that you, not a court, had grounds to suspect Fred. Thus hearsay evidence, which is not admissible in a criminal court, would be perfectly acceptable so as to show you had reasonable grounds for believing Fred to have committed a disciplinary offence.

Common forms of evidence are as follows:

- statements from other employees setting out that they saw Fred committing the disciplinary breaches, heard him admitting to it or saw him in the relevant area at the relevant time. This will frequently be the case if Fred has used violence in the workplace and a complaint is made by the victim. You should obtain statements in writing (rather than by word of mouth) so that if the employee leaves your company before a tribunal hearing, you will still be able to prove that the statement was made. Such statements should be obtained as soon as possible so as to avoid the suggestion at a tribunal that memory has faded due to lapse of time;

- complaints by customers. This will often be the case if Fred has been acting in an offensive manner. Ideally the complaints will be in writing, but often they will simply be comments over the telephone on an informal basis. Often you may be reluctant, for fear of damaging your public image or client relations, to ask the customer to confirm the complaint in writing. You should, therefore, ensure that the customer's complaint is carefully noted by you immediately after it is made. If you delay noting the complaint for several days, you open yourself to cross-examination on the grounds of diminished recollection;

- video surveillance: If you have video evidence from a security camera, this will be very compelling evidence to put before a tribunal. Make sure that it is easy to identify Fred on the video – you do not want a tribunal deciding that you acted hastily in concluding Fred to be guilty because his face was not clear on the screen. You should allow Fred to watch the video and make a note of any comments or admissions that he makes as a result of the viewing. Be cautious if you are a public body employer (such as a local authority) – the *Human Rights Act 1998* states that you must balance your need to protect your own interests with the employee's right to respect for privacy. Most public body employers have procedures for surveillance – make sure these are complied with;

- till mismatches: The fact the money is missing from the till does not necessarily indicate dishonesty – it could instead be error (see **CHAPTER 2**). Assuming, however, that you suspect something sinister, the first task will be to identify who is responsible for the discrepancies. If only one person has used the till at the time that the discrepancies arose, then this will be clear. If, however, a number of employees use the till then you will have to revise your system so as to allocate one employee to each till or, alternatively, to count the cash whenever there is a change of personnel. You should keep careful records of cash in the till, and ensure that this is clearly checked against the till rolls. If you have to prove your case in front of a tribunal, it would be useful to have graphs or charts plotting the expected amount in the till against the real amount over a period;

- arrest/conviction by police: This is addressed at **4.6** above. Remember – the mere fact that the police arrest Fred does not mean that you have reasonable grounds for believing him to have committed the act in question. You still need to carry out your own independent investigation.

The problem of anonymous informers 4.8

Sometimes an employee may have given you information, but on condition that you do not disclose his/her identity to Fred. This can create a problem, since Fred is entitled to know who is making accusations against him so that he can explain away any grudges or improper motives on the part of the accuser. Provided the informer has a genuine reason for wishing to remain anonymous, such as fear of retaliation, the law permits you to conceal his/her identity providing the following steps have been taken:

- you must produce a statement from the informer setting out all material information. The statement should be in a complete form, including names and other identifying items (such as the informer being in the same room as Fred at a particular date and time). It should include information relating to:

    — the date and time of any observation or incident;

    — the opportunity and ability of the informer to observe clearly and with accuracy;

    — any circumstantial evidence, such as knowledge of a system or arrangement, or the reason for the presence of the informer and why certain small details are memorable; and

    — whether the informer has suffered at Fred's hands previously or has any other reason to fabricate his evidence, whether because of a personal grudge or otherwise;

- if the informants refuse to provide a statement, even on an anonymous basis, you should keep careful notes of what they have said to you;

- you must then undertake an independent investigation looking for evidence to corroborate or undermine the informer's evidence. In particular, you must be able to demonstrate to a tribunal that you have sought to establish, independently, whether the informer has a grudge against Fred. This can include tactful enquiries to other employees;

- you will then need to decide how vital the informer's evidence is. If the evidence is non-essential, less objection will be taken to preserving the informer's anonymity. If the evidence is central, and without it you cannot reasonably conclude that Fred is guilty of misconduct, you must make a choice. Some tribunals will be sympathetic to the problem of an anonymous informer, and will permit you to rely on his/her evidence. Others will not be so sympathetic, and will take the view that if your case cannot stand without such doubtful evidence, you cannot reasonably conclude that Fred is guilty. At the end of the day, you have to perform a balancing act between judging the informer's credibility (both in terms of the evidence he/she gives and in terms of his/her reasons for wishing to remain anonymous) and your desire to proceed with the disciplinary process.

What if it might be one of a number of people? 4.9

If you cannot tell whether it was Fred or another person who has been acting improperly, you may sometimes be justified in dismissing both or all of them. You will need to prove the following to a tribunal:

- that a breach of discipline has been committed which, if committed by an individual, would justify dismissal;

- that you had thoroughly investigated the situation so as to try to identify a culprit;

- that, after your investigations, it remained the case that there was more than one person who could have committed the offence;

- that you had identified the possible culprits, and that there were no circumstances distinguishing any of them so as to make it more or less likely that (s)he had committed the offence.

You will usually be able to dismiss two people if you cannot work out which one committed the breach (provided you have gone thorough a full process of interviewing both persons). As the number of suspects increases, however, you will find yourself harder pressed to justify dismissing all of them. This is partly on the basis that a failure to narrow the group down is indicative of a failure to investigate thoroughly, and partly on the basis that it becomes disproportionate to dismiss a large number of innocent employees to secure the dismissal of one guilty employee.

Example

> Money had disappeared from an employer's safe. The employer believed that the culprit was one of two people, but could not establish which one had committed the theft. The Court of Appeal held that it was fair to dismiss both in these circumstances because the employer had to take action to protect its financial position and it had done everything it could to identify one or other of the employees as the thief – *Monie v Coral Racing Ltd [1980] IRLR 464.*

Stage 2: Giving the employee the opportunity to make representations 4.10

By this stage you ought to be able to prove that you have formed a genuine and reasonable belief as to Fred's guilt. You should have evidence to back this up, whether taking the form of statements, your own notes of conversations or documentary evidence such as altered invoices (proving theft).

The next stage is to give Fred the opportunity to explain the relevant events. It may be the case that the evidence against him has been concocted by other employees, in which case he may be able to point out discrepancies that you had not appreciated. It may equally be that there is a perfectly innocent explanation for the evidence, for example he might have removed £50 from the cash register at the request of another manager.

Accordingly it is necessary to put these allegations to Fred and see whether he can provide an adequate explanation or show that he cannot have been guilty of the offences of which he has been accused.

Since October 2004, all employers have been obliged to follow minimum dismissal procedures (set out in full in **APPENDIX 1**). A failure to follow these minimum procedures, unless one of the specific exceptions applies, will result in any dismissal being automatically unfair. One of the minimum requirements is to invite Fred to a meeting and ensure he has time, in advance, to consider the allegations against him *and* the basis for those allegations (i.e. the reasons why you think he has committed a breach of discipline).

There are a number of exceptions to the rule that a dismissal will be automatically unfair if you fail to invite Fred to a meeting. These are considered in **APPENDIX 1**.

Opportunity to defend 4.11

Failure to invite Fred to a meeting will almost inevitably render a dismissal unfair, both because you will (normally) be in breach of the statutory minimum dismissal procedures and because your decision to dismiss will be regarded as hasty and premature. You will not persuade a tribunal that you have acted reasonably if you have not taken into account matters which Fred might have brought to your attention if he had been given the opportunity to defend himself.

Example

An employee took two packets of pork chops from her employer without paying for them. She was not permitted to explain, and she was

> dismissed immediately for theft. The dismissal was held to be unfair on the basis that a fuller investigation might have supported her claim that she had the intention to pay for them – *Wm Low & Co v MacCuish [1979] IRLR 458.*

You must guard against taking the view that Fred's guilt is so obvious that there is nothing he can say which will cause you to change your mind. Apart from the fact that this attitude will irritate a tribunal, it is extremely rare for an employer to be justified in deciding that there can be no explanation or mitigation which would have a bearing on his decision. A tribunal will decide that you have acted unfairly if you have reached a conclusion which it would have been reasonable to postpone until you have discussed the matter with Fred. It is worth remembering that some of the greatest miscarriages of justice appeared at the time to be clearcut cases. Do not fall into the trap of assuming that Fred cannot possibly answer your allegations or explain his actions.

Inviting the employee to a meeting   4.12

Whether or not he is suspended, you will need to invite Fred to an investigative meeting. It is at this meeting that he will be able to put forward his representations or explanations. Prior to the meeting, you should inform him of the nature of the allegations being made against him. He will probably be fully aware of the allegations, particularly if you have already suspended him. However, you should still set out all relevant information in one document so as to prove to a tribunal, some months down the line, that you were addressing your mind to the proper matters.

You should write to Fred, stating the following:

- matters have come to your attention which lead you to suspect that he has committed a breach of discipline (stating in full the breach or breaches);

- you would like to give him the opportunity of putting forward any explanation or representations;

- your reasons for believing that he had committed the breach (in outline). You should enclose copies of any statements in support of the allegation (unless anonymity or confidentiality is an issue – this is addressed at **4.8**). This is important because it gives Fred the opportunity to comment on any bad blood between him and those offering evidence against him;

- invite Fred to meet with you at a convenient date. Include a date, place and time, but be prepared to change it to suit Fred's reasonable convenience (particularly if he has been suspended and thus is not present at the workplace);

- he is entitled to bring a representative should he so desire, and any witnesses whom he thinks would be of help. See **4.13** for further information.

In advance of the hearing, you must also provide copies of any evidence you intend to rely upon (or intend to ask him about). This would include any documentary evidence (such as till rolls, letters of complaint from customers, or a copy of your company's no-smoking policy), a copy of your disciplinary policy, and any notes you have taken arising from interviews/meetings with other employees or customers.

Legal entitlement to a representative   4.13

Since 1999, employees have been entitled to be accompanied by a representative at all disciplinary meetings and appeal hearings. They are entitled to be represented by a workplace colleague or a trade union representative. However, if Fred wants to be represented by somebody else, such as a family member, it is usually sensible to permit his representative of choice to accompany him.

The representative is legally entitled to paid time off work in order to discharge his functions as a representative. If he is unable to attend the disciplinary meeting, the law states it should be adjourned for up to five working days (but only if the employee requests an adjournment – it is not up to the employer to suggest it, although it would be good practice to do so).

The importance of note taking   4.14

In exceptional cases, tribunals have held that it is fair to have the entire investigative stage conducted in writing. In other words, you would not hold a meeting, but would simply invite Fred's written representations on the evidence against him. This was always a risky way of approaching disciplinary matters – tribunals did not like it for three reasons. First, written representations are not interactive, i.e. Fred could not respond to new matters raised. Secondly, Fred may not have been as articulate in writing as he would have been face to face. Thirdly, you are less able to judge credibility when something is said to you in writing than when it is said face to face.

Since October 2004, it has become mandatory to invite Fred to a meeting to discuss the matters giving rise to the possibility of dismissal. You should only refuse to have a face-to-face meeting if you have a very good reason for doing so, for example, you have strong grounds for believing that Fred may be violent in such a meeting. The full list of exceptions to this requirement is set out in **APPENDIX 1**.

It is perfectly legitimate to hold the meeting off your premises or after normal hours, so as to avoid disturbing other employees. Indeed, it is *desirable* to hold the meeting off your premises if Fred is concerned about seeing other employees.

You should prepare carefully for the meeting. You must not allow yourself to become emotionally aroused or appear to be personally critical of Fred at this meeting. The purpose of the meeting is investigative, not disciplinary. The disciplinary meeting comes later.

A person should be present to take notes. This is important so that the tribunal can see, when it reviews the circumstances of the dismissal months down the line, that you permitted Fred to make full representations. It is equally important so that the tribunal can see whether Fred was able to come up with a proper explanation at the time, in case he claims at the hearing that he said something which he did not, in fact, say. If you have the administrative resources available, a secretary should take full shorthand notes and thereafter produce a transcript. If you do not have such resources available, you should take as thorough a note yourself as you are able – in particular, record any admissions that Fred makes or any explanations that he puts forward in respect of the allegations.

There is no need to use a cassette recorder. Although it may appear prudent to have a incontrovertible record of what was said, in practice it is unusual to hear tape-recorded evidence and it is unwise to have any aspect of the dismissal as being something out of the ordinary. Furthermore, Fred may argue at the tribunal that the fact you recorded the conversation indicates that you expected him to dispute the facts, and this therefore indicates that you had already partially made up your mind.

If you are not the person who will be taking the final decision on dismissal, he or she should, ideally, be present. Tribunals sometimes criticise employers when the decision-maker has not personally interviewed the employee being dis-missed. However, if you are part of a large organisation with clearly defined procedures, or if your dismissal procedure has been agreed with a trade union, then this is unlikely to present any real difficulty.

If Fred does not attend the investigative meeting, you should write to him pointing out that he missed the appointment and asking him to contact you within, say, three days to rearrange the meeting. If he fails to contact you, or if he does not attend the rescheduled meeting, a tribunal will say you are justified in assuming that he is refusing to co-operate in the investigative procedure.

Once you have given Fred the chance to attend the investigative meeting, but he has not done so, you will be in a stronger position when it comes to deciding whether or not he has committed the breach of discipline concerned. If he has had a reasonable opportunity to explain, but has not taken it, you are entitled to assume that there is no reasonable explanation and that your understanding of events is correct.

The investigative meeting   4.15

At the beginning of the meeting, you should formally introduce everyone in the room (unless to do so would be ridiculous) and explain their role in the hearing. If Fred is not represented, confirm that he does not want to have a representative present. If he states that he does want a representative, ask him who he wants and why the representative is not attending at that meeting (NB you would have said, in your letter, that representatives are permitted – see **4.12**). Provided he comes up with a reasonable explanation, you should permit one adjournment of the hearing so as to allow him to obtain a representative – see **4.13** above. He has a legal right to an adjournment of up to five days in order to secure the services of a representative. Remember: a tribunal will be concerned to see if you have allowed him a proper opportunity to explain his case, and if you have unreasonably denied him access to a representative then you may be found to have acted unfairly.

Explain the purpose and format of the meeting to Fred (or his representative). Emphasise that the hearing is investigative and is not to determine what sanction should be applied. Also state that you will not be giving a decision at the end of the meeting, but will take your time to consider what Fred has said.

The exact procedure to be followed is up to you. However, there are three essential elements to the hearing:

(a)   Fred should know exactly what disciplinary rules he is alleged to have breached, and what evidence exists against him. This information should have been supplied to him, in writing, in advance;

(b)   he should be given a full opportunity to state his case; and

(c)   you must act, and must be seen to act, in good faith.

If your company has agreed a disciplinary procedure with a trade union, then the procedure set out in the agreement must be followed. Although deviation from an agreed procedure will not automatically mean that a dismissal is unfair, it does give Fred the basis of a case and makes it much more likely that a lawyer or Citizens' Advice Bureau worker will advise Fred to take you to the employment tribunal. If you do follow an agreed procedure without any deviation, a tribunal is unlikely to find that you have acted unfairly unless you are regarded as having taken any decisions in bad faith.

Evidence against the employee   4.16

If you have been following the procedure set out in this book, you will have satisfied the requirement that Fred knows exactly what rules he is alleged to have breached. He should also know the evidence that exists against him.

If you do not have statements from other witnesses, go through the gist of any evidence coming from other employees, customers, etc. If Fred keeps interrupting, stop him and explain that he will have the opportunity to comment later. Do not let him cause you to lose the flow of what you are putting across.

If you rely on an informer's statement (see **4.8**), you should show Fred a copy (with any identifying elements omitted or blanked out). If Fred, or his representative, has any questions which they wish to put to the informer, you should adjourn the hearing in order for you to put such matters to him/her. This is an exception to the rule that Fred is not usually entitled to cross-examine witnesses – see **4.17**.

You should also show Fred any documentary evidence (such as till rolls, letters of complaint from customers, or a copy of your company's no-smoking policy) and confirm that he has had the opportunity to consider them. If Fred tries to destroy any incriminating evidence then, provided both you and your witness will attest to that before the tribunal, you will have gone a long way towards justifying any dismissal (on the grounds that you cannot continue employing someone who deliberately sets out to frustrate disciplinary proceedings and destroy company documents).

If you are relying on a rule in Fred's contract of employment which he has breached, or on a rule contained in a notice or a memo, show Fred a copy of the contract or memo and ask him if he received a copy. If he says yes, you are entitled to regard his conduct as all the more serious (since he has deliberately, or, at best, inadvertently, ignored a company rule). If he denies having received the memo, you may need to investigate whether he did receive a copy (e.g. check the circulation list).

The employee's opportunity to put his/her case
4.17

Once you have told Fred the nature of the case against him, you must allow him to explain the evidence or state his version of events. If Fred's version of events is radically different, and raises fresh issues which have not been considered (for example, if Fred says that he removed money from the till because he was instructed to do so by a supervisor) then you must investigate these new issues after the hearing by talking to (and, if appropriate, obtaining statements from) anyone who may be able to assist.

Fred may wish to challenge the truth of other people's statements. He could allege that evidence has been fabricated due to a grudge or to move suspicion away from the real perpetrator. If, of course, Fred has been caught red-handed then you may feel that no further investigation is necessary before making up your mind. However, if Fred's explanation is plausible, a tribunal will want to see that you have performed such further investigation as is necessary in order for you to be able to take an informed decision as to which version of events is correct.

Legally, you do not have to allow Fred (or his representative) to question the witnesses who are making allegations against him. However, a tribunal might be better disposed in your favour if you have permitted Fred to question a witness where there is a crucial conflict of evidence. If you allow such questioning, it will show to a tribunal that you are taking steps over and above what is actually necessary to secure a fair hearing for Fred. This may help you in case you have made any mistakes in your procedure. If, however, you do not want cross-examination of the witnesses (as it can lengthen the hearing substantially, and can also generate resentment by the person being questioned), you should not be criticised for refusing to let it take place.

Acting in good faith 4.18

You must act, and be seen to act, in good faith. There are two elements to this. First, you must not have made up your mind before hearing Fred's version of events. Just as importantly, you must not be perceived by others as having made up your mind! Do not tell Fred you do not believe what he is saying (although it is legitimate, and indeed good practice, to point out to Fred inconsistencies in his case and invite him to explain them). Do not be overly critical or judgmental during the investigative meeting – the time for criticism and discipline is during the disciplinary meeting (see **4.40**).

Secondly, and ideally, you should not be both witness and decision-maker. If you are the principal witness, let someone else conduct the investigative meeting and take the decision as to whether Fred has committed the breach of discipline. In a very small company, it may not be possible to separate yourself from the proceedings – if so, a tribunal will not criticise you on this basis. However, if your company has sufficient management resources, you should not allow the same person to be both witness and judge.

Example

An employee was dismissed following allegations of sexual harassment. The chairman and club secretary saw one of the incidents of harassment, and were witnesses during the investigation. The entire committee of the club, including the chairman and club secretary, voted to dismiss him. It was held that the dismissal was unfair because there was no good reason why they had to act in dual capacities and their position as witnesses must have affected their impartiality as decision makers – *Moyes v Hylton Castle Working Men's Social Club and Institute Ltd [1986] IRLR 482.*

51

You will see that the separation of witnesses and decision-makers is described as an 'ideal'. Tribunals have not been consistent in the way that they approach this point, and there are a number of cases where the courts have said that tribunals should take a practical view and realise that employers are capable of both witnessing events and judging them impartially. However, to make any dismissal as watertight as possible, it is prudent to avoid this type of dual role unless you are a small company and lack the resources to do otherwise.

Do not give a decision at the meeting 4.19

After you have permitted Fred to put his case, you should summarise his explanations. Ensure that a full note is taken of your summary so that you can demonstrate that you are taking into account everything that Fred has said. You should then tell Fred that you will consider his representations, make any further enquiries that are necessary, and give him a decision within the next few days. Do not tell Fred at that stage what your decision is, or even give an indication of the likely decision. If you do so, you run the risk of being accused of having pre-judged the situation.

Investigate further if necessary 4.20

Following the meeting, you should check the note that was taken and ensure that it is legible. If you have the administrative resources, have a transcript typed up. Ideally, send a copy of the transcript to Fred. If he does not challenge its accuracy at the time, a tribunal is less likely to believe him if he tries to challenge its accuracy six months later at a tribunal hearing.

If Fred has raised any fresh issues during the hearing (such as evidence coming from someone with a grudge, or suggesting an alternative culprit) you must undertake further investigation. The degree of investigation will depend on the nature of the new issues raised. If you do not investigate further, a tribunal is likely to decide that you have acted unfairly because you would have pre-judged the situation without being in possession of all the relevant facts. Make sure that you keep notes of the further investigations.

Once any additional investigation is complete, you need to decide whether you consider Fred to have committed the breach which is alleged. You must weigh up the statements and the evidence which go against Fred together with Fred's explanation, and decide what you think happened. You do not have to be sure that Fred committed the breach of discipline – you simply have to decide whether it is more likely than not that Fred did commit the breach of discipline.

If Fred takes you to an employment tribunal, you will not need to show a tribunal that you were right in deciding that Fred had committed the breach of discipline. You simply need to show that your decision was a reasonable one.

This is a very important distinction from your point of view since, if further evidence appears after (and if) you have dismissed Fred showing that he could not have done what you thought, it will not affect whether Fred's dismissal was fair or unfair. Provided you have conducted a proper investigation, and provided that your conclusion was one which a reasonable employer might reach, a dismissal will be fair (as long as the other requirements set out in this chapter have been complied with).

Breach of discipline may not have been committed 4.21

If you decide that Fred probably did not commit the breach of discipline complained of, or if you feel that you will not be able to justify such a decision to an employment tribunal and do not want to take the risk of a claim being made, you should confirm this in writing to Fred. State that you accept his explanation, that you will not be taking these disciplinary proceedings any further and that although the investigation will be kept on file for administrative purposes it will not be held against him in any way. Be gracious – if you write a letter stating that 'we think you did it but cannot prove it' you are placing yourself at risk of allegations of bias if you need to bring other disciplinary proceedings against Fred in the future.

Arranging a formal disciplinary meeting 4.22

If you have decided that Fred did commit the breach of discipline complained of, and you wish to proceed with the disciplinary procedure, you will need to arrange a formal disciplinary hearing. You should put your decision to Fred in writing. Your letter should contain the following:

- A statement that, on weighing up the evidence/statements and considering Fred's explanations, you find that he committed the breach of discipline in question. Set out your reasons in brief.

- That you want to hold a disciplinary meeting. Inform him that the purpose of the meeting is to consider what disciplinary sanction is to be imposed. If you are considering dismissal (see **4.23** below for whether dismissal is an appropriate or a possible sanction) you must specifically state this and tell Fred that he should be prepared to put forward any reasons why dismissal is not appropriate.

- A statement of the time and place and, as before, tell Fred that if the date is inconvenient it can be rearranged. Tell him of his right to a representative (see **4.13**).

- A statement that he is entitled to appeal against your finding that he committed the breach of discipline in question, but that the appeal procedure will not come into operation until after the disciplinary meeting. Inform him that you will set out the mechanics of appealing at that time.

Note that the minimum dismissal procedures, breach of which renders a dismissal automatically unfair, only require employers to hold *one* meeting with the employee. However, it is far better practice to hold split meetings (one to investigate the facts, one to deal with sanction), and this approach should be followed unless you are a small company (and it is artificial to hold two meetings). If you are intending to only hold the one meeting, make sure you deal with *both* investigation *and* sanction at that one meeting.

Stage 3: Dismissal must be a reasonable response to the employee's actions
4.23

You are normally not entitled to dismiss Fred for a first offence unless the breach of discipline is severe (often referred to as 'gross' misconduct). Offences involving theft or other forms of dishonesty will usually justify immediate dismissal. Offences involving violence may do so, depending on the degree of violence used – if you dismiss an employee with 20 years' good service with your company because of a one-off minor fracas, a tribunal will probably find that 'the punishment exceeds the crime' and that you have acted unfairly. By contrast, if a perpetually troublesome employee becomes aggressive and engages in violence, you may well be justified in dismissing him for a similar lapse.

The distinction between a first breach of discipline and subsequent breaches is a fundamental one for the purpose of deciding whether dismissal is an appropriate sanction. Accordingly the two scenarios are examined separately.

First offences
4.24

The ACAS Code of Practice on Disciplinary and Grievance Procedures states: 'Never dismiss an employee for a first disciplinary offence, unless it is a case of gross misconduct.' However, tribunals are less rigid in deciding whether a dismissal for a first offence is fair or unfair than the ACAS Code suggests. As with determining whether Fred actually committed the breach of discipline, a tribunal is not concerned with whether *it* would have dismissed Fred for an offence, but whether the decision to dismiss was a reasonable one in all the circumstances. The law states that if some employers would have dismissed in a particular set of circumstances, but other employers would have only issued a warning, you should not be held liable for unfair dismissal simply because some employers might have acted less stringently.

In general, you should issue a warning (rather than dismiss) for first offences. You can, however, dismiss Fred for a first offence in three situations:

(i)   where he has committed an act of gross misconduct;

(ii) where you have good reason to believe that warnings will be ineffective; or,

(iii) where Fred has been made aware, in advance, that the breach of discipline in question would lead to his dismissal.

The above three situations are discussed in turn below.

(i) Gross misconduct   4.25

This is not as straightforward as it sounds. Gross misconduct usually describes conduct which is so serious that immediate dismissal is warranted. This is, of course, a circular definition. One of the advantages in dismissing an employee for gross misconduct is that you do not need to pay him/her any pay in lieu of notice (as you are obliged to do when dismissing for other reasons – see **CHAPTER 12**). And in limited circumstances, involving exceptionally serious gross misconduct, tribunals are not obliged to find that a dismissal is automatically unfair if the full dismissal procedure has not been followed, provided that a less onerous (known as the 'modified') dismissal procedure has been complied with.

The courts have always refused to lay down a definition of gross misconduct or to set out categories of offences which amount to gross misconduct. This is because each case has to be considered on its own facts, and a tribunal simply has to decide whether an employer has acted reasonably in dismissing for a particular offence. Laying down firm categories would limit a tribunal's ability to consider each case on its own facts, and accordingly the courts have avoided doing so.

However, if you dismiss Fred for one of the following reasons, tribunals are generally sympathetic to employers' claims that the acts amounted to gross misconduct and thus warranted dismissal for a first offence:

- *Violence*: violence in the workplace will usually justify immediate dismissal. However, the three factors which a tribunal will take into account (in addition to the fact that violence has occurred) are:

  — *Whose fault was the violence?* If Fred was acting in self-defence (albeit that he struck the first blow) or was so strongly provoked that violence is understandable, then a tribunal may find that a reasonable employer would have issued a warning, and that your dismissal of Fred was unfair. You should have come to a view on whose fault the violence was during the investigative stage, and a tribunal will have little sympathy for you if you say that you did not know or were not interested in who was at fault.

—   *How long has Fred been employed?* If Fred has been a good employee for many years, you run the risk of a tribunal finding that you acted unreasonably in dismissing Fred. This is because the hypothetical reasonable employer would have realised that the violence was a one-off incident and issued a warning rather than resort to dismissal.

—   *The nature of the workplace*: any degree of violence may be unacceptable in an office environment, whereas a certain degree of physical banter would be accepted as the norm on a building site. Your reasonable response, as an employer, has to take into account whether Fred's behaviour has crossed the line from appropriate to unacceptable.

If you have considered the above factors, and think that there are no extenuating circumstances, then dismissal may well be an appropriate sanction (subject to representations made by Fred at the disciplinary hearing).

- *Theft*: This will almost always justify dismissal, other than in first offences of petty theft (such as stealing a few stamps). The dishonest removal of cash, even if only a small sum, will almost always amount to gross misconduct.

- *Entering into competition with employer*: A tribunal will not regard preparatory steps for setting up in competition with an employer as being gross misconduct unless there is a clear prohibition on such conduct in Fred's contract of employment. It is not sufficient to say that Fred should have known that competition is not permitted if it does not appear in his contract. However, if matters go further than preparation, and Fred actively engages in conduct which is detrimental to your business, you will be justified in treating such actions as gross misconduct. Note that applying for jobs with your competitors is not gross misconduct, or indeed misconduct at all, since an employee is under no legal obligation to remain employed by you. An exception to this rule is if Fred's contract contains a clear clause prohibiting him from working for other employers in a particular area, or from using confidential company information. Such clauses are subject to very complex legal checks to determine whether they are enforceable, and if you are contemplating dismissal on grounds of Fred entering into competition you should seek proper legal advice.

- *Intoxication*: Unless alcoholic intoxication is accompanied by aggravating factors, such as extreme rudeness to customers or violence, it is unlikely to be regarded as gross misconduct by tribunals. If, however, your company has a clear rule prohibiting alcohol then Fred's intoxication may fall within category (iii) below (see **4.31** onwards).

- *Drugs*: If Fred is under the influence of illegal drugs, then his conduct will usually amount to gross misconduct and you can readily dismiss him for a first offence.

Example

> Miss O'Flynn worked for an airline. She tested positive for cannabis during a random drugs test. She admitted having smoked cannabis the previous weekend when off-duty (and this was sufficient to yield a positive result on the drugs test). The Employment Appeal Tribunal said that the employer had acted fairly in dismissing her, even if she was not under the influence of drugs when at work, because they had a clear drugs policy and Miss O'Flynn had breached it – *O'Flynn v Airlinks EAT/0269/01.*

- *Matters particular to your business*: Some businesses may have particular standards which, if breached, will justify dismissal without warning even though they do not fall within conduct usually regarded as gross misconduct. At the end of the day, a tribunal has to decide whether you acted reasonably in dismissing for a first offence in the absence of express, prior warnings or notices. The disciplinary breach must be fairly substantial to satisfy this test. They will often relate to conduct affecting health and safety, as shown by the following example.

Example

> An employee tied down a lever on an automatic lathe in a factory, thereby removing an important safety device. Although the employment tribunal was not certain that this breached any of the employer's rules, it decided that the employer had acted fairly in dismissing him because the conduct endangered the health and safety of all other workers and it was fair to dismiss for a first breach – *Martin v Yorkshire Imperial Metals Ltd [1978] IRLR 440.*

Is gross misconduct a reasonable label?   4.26

Note that the decision as to whether something amounts to gross misconduct is an objective one – i.e. the tribunal will decide whether the hypothetical reasonable employer, in the same situation, would regard Fred's actions as gross misconduct. The fact that you have labelled Fred's actions as being gross misconduct will not assist if, as a matter of reality, it did not amount to gross misconduct.

Example

> An employee failed to use the correct procedure when ringing up a
> £1.46 purchase on the till. This fell within the employer's definition of
> gross misconduct and she was dismissed as a result. The tribunal held that
> the employer had not acted reasonably because this was a one-off lapse,
> and the fact that an act was labelled as gross misconduct did not
> necessarily mean that the dismissal was justified – *Laws Stores Ltd v
> Oliphant [1978] IRLR 251.*

Consistency in applying rules is vital **4.27**

It is vital that you are consistent in treating particular acts as gross misconduct.
In other words, if someone else has committed the same breach of discipline
on an earlier occasion and you did not dismiss him, a tribunal will find that you
have acted unreasonably and arbitrarily in dismissing Fred for the same breach.
Any such dismissal is almost certain to be found unfair.

If, however, you can show that the earlier person would have been dismissed
were it not for particular exceptional circumstances that do not exist in Fred's
case, then you will not be acting arbitrarily and will be able to justify your
different treatment of the two employees.

Dismissal for first offence if gross misconduct is established **4.28**

If you can establish that Fred's act amounts to gross misconduct, you are
justified in dismissing him for a first offence unless he can produce extenuating
or mitigating circumstances sufficient to displace the presumption that dismissal
is a reasonable response. The disciplinary hearing, and your actions subsequent
to that, are considered below at **4.40**.

(ii) Where warnings will be ineffective **4.29**

If a first offence does not amount to gross misconduct, then you cannot dismiss
Fred for it unless he has specifically been made aware that such conduct might
lead to dismissal. The appropriate course of action is to issue a warning to Fred
that if he continues to act in that way then he will be facing dismissal.

Occasionally, however, it is clear that any such warning will be futile, for
example from Fred's employment history.

Example

> A college lecturer was dismissed, following a reorganisation of teaching duties, because he had objected to the reorganisation, become uncooperative and argumentative with the head of the college and tried to involve students in the dispute. The college argued that a warning would have been futile. Although the lecturer said that he would have ceased being disruptive if he had received a warning, the tribunal held that a warning would have made no difference to his conduct and found that dismissal was an appropriate sanction – *Farnborough v Governors of Edinburgh College of Art [1974] IRLR 245*.

Importance of warnings **4.30**

Note that your belief and assertion that a warning will be futile does not necessarily mean it would be futile. You will need to be able to justify your position to a tribunal. If you are unsure, and do not want to risk paying compensation to Fred, take the safe route and issue a warning for a first offence.

It is important to be able to show that you considered whether a warning would be effective before coming to the conclusion that dismissal is appropriate. It is not a defence to say, at the tribunal hearing, that you did not think about it at the time but upon reflection you do not think a warning would have made any difference (although such an argument, if proven, may have some effect on the level of compensation – see **CHAPTER 13**).

Bear in mind, however, that if Fred has a history of such action, he should have received warnings before (in which case you should be considering dismissal for subsequent offences – see **4.36**). If you have failed to give him warnings in the past he has a legitimate expectation that his ongoing breaches of discipline will be overlooked by you. If that is the case, a tribunal will view a dismissal as arbitrary (because it is contrary to past practice) and thus unfair.

Example

> An experienced machine operator was dismissed for disobeying an instruction to help a new, inexperienced assistant. She had similarly refused in the past. However, in the past the employer had taken a more relaxed attitude and had not issued warnings. The tribunal held that the dismissal was unfair because the employee had a legitimate expectation that her conduct would not lead to dismissal, and that the employer should have first warned her that he would no longer tolerate her attitude – *Hackwood v Seal (Marine) Ltd [1973] IRLR 17*.

(iii) The employee has been made aware that the breach of discipline in question will lead to dismissal 4.31

The presumption a tribunal adopts is that it is unfair to dismiss an employee for a first offence unless he has committed an act of gross misconduct. Instead, a reasonable employer should give a clear warning that dismissal is likely if the employee does not cease acting in the way that he has been doing.

The rationale behind requiring an employer to give a warning is so that the employee is made fully aware that the employer views his conduct as serious enough to warrant dismissal. Tribunals take the view that in the absence of such a warning, it is unfair to dismiss an employee for minor matters. However, once such a warning has been given and the employee is aware of the weight which the employer attributes to his conduct, it becomes reasonable to dismiss him if he continues to act in a way which he knows is contrary to the employer's instructions.

It follows that if the employee is aware, even on a first offence, of the weight that an employer attaches to particular matters, yet nevertheless disregards rules prohibiting him from acting in that way, it may be reasonable to dismiss him for such a first offence. In essence, the rule will act as a substitute for a prior formal warning.

The employee must be aware of the rules 4.32

The rule must have been brought to the attention of the employee before his wrongful act took place. It is no good trying to persuade a tribunal that a dismissal is justified because of a rule that Fred was unaware of, since he cannot be at fault for disregarding something he does not know about.

Example

An employee missed a morning's work as a result of a hangover brought on by excess drinking at his firm's Christmas party. Because the same thing had happened (with different employees) the year before, the employer had agreed with the trade union that such misconduct would lead to instant dismissal. However, this was not communicated to the employee. The tribunal found that the dismissal was unfair because the employee had not received any notice or warning that such conduct would lead to dismissal – *W Brooks & Son v Skinner [1984] IRLR 379.*

Ideally, the rule should be contained in Fred's contract of employment. If he does not have a written contract, or if the contract does not contain such a rule, it will be sufficient if you can show that Fred was aware of the rule.

Ideally, he should have seen the rule in writing (for example, in a memo or a notice pinned to a notice board). It is dangerous to try to persuade a tribunal that someone had informed Fred orally of the rule, since a tribunal may not accept such evidence if it is contested by Fred, or may conclude that insufficient weight was given to the rule if it was simply mentioned in conversation.

Needless to say, if such a rule does not exist then you will not be able to rely on it for the purpose of dismissing Fred for a first offence. You may, however, wish to consider imposing such a rule for future occasions. This can easily be done in a memo circulated to all staff. Ensure, however, that the new rule is not contrary to any of the current terms of employment (e.g. a unilateral change in working hours) since this would entitle your employees to resign and claim constructive dismissal.

You will need to be able to prove that Fred was familiar with the rule. It is irrelevant whether he was thinking about the rule at the time he committed the offence; all you need to prove is that the rule had been brought to his attention. If the rule is contained in Fred's contract, which he (presumably) would have signed, then you will have no difficulty showing a tribunal that Fred was aware of the existence of the rule.

If the rule was contained in a memo, or a notice, you should ask Fred during the disciplinary meeting (see **4.16**) if he was aware of it. If he denies having been made aware of it, or denies having received the memo, you will have to take a calculated risk as to whether you want to proceed with the dismissal, and risk a tribunal finding that Fred was not familiar with the rule and thus that dismissal was a disproportionate sanction for a first offence. The alternative is to issue a formal warning to Fred in respect of his conduct and dismiss him should he offend a second time.

Rule must be unambiguous   **4.33**

The rule must be clear and unambiguous. It must state exactly what conduct is prohibited in a clear and concise fashion. A tribunal is unlikely to find that it is reasonable to dismiss for a first offence of breaching a rule when the rule is not, itself, clear. Accordingly a rule saying that 'any employee who is guilty of misconduct will be dismissed' will be disregarded by a tribunal because it is so wide as to be meaningless. The conduct which is warned against must be spelled out in the rule with precision and clarity.

Furthermore, the rule must explicitly state that breach will lead to dismissal. In the past tribunals have shown a tendency to find that a rule which simply says that breach 'may' lead to dismissal is not sufficient to place the employee on notice that breach will result in their dismissal. This is a peculiar approach, since any reasonably intelligent employee understands the meaning of the phrase 'breach of this rule may lead to your dismissal'. Nevertheless, there have been a number of cases where tribunals have said that this is inadequate and that an absolute form of wording is required before the employer can rely on the rule to justify dismissal for a first offence. Although tribunals are becoming more realistic about the precise wording of the sanction to the rule, there remains a slight risk in dismissing somebody in reliance on a rule which is not written in absolute terms.

Rule must have been enforced in the past   4.34

The rule must have been rigidly enforced in the past. If you have waived the rule or sanction for other employees, a tribunal will say that Fred could not have been certain that his conduct would lead to dismissal, since it had not led to dismissal for others, and thus it is unreasonable for you to arbitrarily impose a heavier sanction for a first offence that you have done in the past.

Example

> A company had a no-smoking policy due to high fire risks. The employees were aware of this rule: however, in practice employees who were caught smoking were simply given casual warnings. The employee in this case was dismissed following being caught smoking. The tribunal held that the dismissal was unfair because he had been lulled into a false sense of security due to the more casual approach taken by the employers in the past both with himself and with other employees – *Bendall v Paine & Betteridge [1973] IRLR 44.*

If, however, you can point to particular mitigating circumstances in the prior case where you did not dismiss, you can probably explain your previous failure to dismiss and thus show that your conduct is not inconsistent or unreasonable.

Is it reasonable to enforce the rule this time?   4.35

Even if the rule is clear and it has been rigidly enforced in the past, you must still form the view that dismissal is a reasonable sanction in all the circumstances of the case. Even when rules justifying dismissal exist, tribunals will regard rigid adherence to them as unfair if the hypothetical reasonable employer would have formed the view that dismissal was not warranted due to the particular circumstances of the case. You therefore have to be sure that you can justify your adherence to the rule to a tribunal.

Subsequent offences   4.36

If Fred has committed disciplinary offences in the past, which have resulted in warnings rather than dismissal, you will usually be justified in dismissing him for further breaches that would not, on their own, warrant dismissal.

The ACAS Code of Practice on Disciplinary and Grievance Procedures states:

'First formal action – misconduct

Where, following a disciplinary meeting, an employee is found guilty of misconduct, the usual first step would be to give them a written warning setting out the nature of the misconduct and the change in behaviour required.

The employee should be informed that the warning is part of the formal disciplinary process and what the consequences will be of a failure to change behaviour. The consequences could be a final written warning and ultimately, dismissal. The employee should also be informed that they may appeal against the decision. A record of the warning should be kept, but it should be disregarded for disciplinary purposes after a specified period (e.g. six months).

…

Final written warning

Where there is a failure to improve or change behaviour in the timescale set at the first formal stage, or where the offence is sufficiently serious, the employee should normally be issued with a final written warning – but only after they have been given a chance to present their case at a meeting. The final written warning should give details of, and grounds for, the complaint. It should warn the employee that failure to improve or modify behaviour may lead to dismissal or to some other penalty, and refer to the right of appeal. The final written warning should normally be disregarded for disciplinary purposes after a specified period (for example 12 months).

Dismissal or other penalty

If the employee's conduct or performance still fails to improve, the final stage in the disciplinary process might be dismissal or (if the employee's contract allows it or it is mutually agreed) some other penalty such as demotion, disciplinary transfer, or loss of seniority/pay …'.

This sets out what ACAS regards as ideal personnel management, namely a written warning, then a final written warning, and only then moving to dismissal. However, the law does not require employers to act in this ideal fashion, but only to act fairly and reasonably. There are three situations to be considered, as set out below:

(i)   where the previous episode of misconduct resulted in a formal warning;

(ii)   where the previous episode of misconduct did not result in a formal warning; and,

(iii)   where the previous misconduct is of a different nature to the present misconduct (for example, where Fred's earlier misconduct concerned timekeeping whereas the present misconduct concerns rudeness to customers).

(i) Where a formal warning exists   4.37

Notwithstanding the provisions of the ACAS Code of Practice (see **4.36** above), tribunals do not generally require employers to have gone through a written warning and then a final written warning prior to dismissal. Nor do tribunals require employers to give a verbal warning before a first written warning. Whilst tiered warnings represent good industrial practice, you are unlikely to be found to have unfairly dismissed somebody if they have had one clear warning before dismissal (unless the old, or the new, breach of discipline involved something minor).

As with all dismissals, the essential requirement is that your decision to dismiss must be reasonable. It will not be reasonable to dismiss Fred for a first offence unless it falls into one of the categories described above. However, if Fred has received a formal written warning in respect of his conduct, yet continues to act in a way which you have forbidden, it will only be in the rarest of circumstances that a tribunal will say that you have acted unreasonably in dismissing him (the main exception being if his 'offence' is trivial – see below).

The formal warning must have made it clear that dismissal was a likely, or a possible consequence if Fred erred again. The courts are not concerned with whether the prior warning was oral or in writing, provided it was clear and made the consequences of repeat performance obvious. However, you should be wary of relying on an oral warning (unless you made a note of the warning in Fred's personnel file at the time) since Fred may deny ever having received the warning. It is always best to put these things in writing.

Do not rely on very old warnings as justifying dismissal. An employee who commits a minor offence when he starts employment, works well for ten years and then slips up again is entitled to different treatment to that received by an employee who has committed the same offence twice within six months. A general rule of thumb is that verbal warnings should be disregarded after six months, and written warnings after twelve months. The ACAS Code of Practice, which suggests a first written warning should be disregarded after six months, again represents best industrial practice and no tribunal will criticise an employer for relying on a written warning for up to twelve months.

Provided that the offence which Fred has repeated is not trivial (trivial offences being those such as making personal telephone calls, using vulgar language away from customers, failing to follow a technical company procedure such as sick reporting procedures, or smoking in a non-smoking area) then a tribunal is unlikely to say that your decision to dismiss Fred falls outside the band of reasonable responses which you could make. Accordingly, if you have performed a full investigation and held a proper disciplinary hearing, your decision to dismiss Fred will be upheld if he takes you to an employment tribunal.

If the offence was trivial, you will not be entitled to dismiss Fred after just two offences. A tribunal would consider that a reasonable employer would, in such circumstances, issue a stern final written warning (see **4.45**) and that dismissal at this stage would be excessive. You should, therefore, issue one more warning and only dismiss Fred if he breaches your rules once again.

(ii) Where a formal warning does not exist   4.38

Even if Fred has committed the offence before, if you did not formally warn him that his conduct breached good discipline then you cannot dismiss him for repeating the offence. If you issued a verbal rebuke, this may be sufficient to be a formal warning if you made it clear at the time that a repeat of the offence was likely to result in dismissal (see **4.37**) but it is dangerous to rely on it as there may be doubt about exactly what was said.

The reason for not being able to dismiss Fred is that a tribunal will say that, by not warning him on the prior occasion, you lulled him into a false sense of security and thereby his conduct must be viewed as less, not more, culpable than the last time. Accordingly, since you did not dismiss him after the first offence, it can hardly be reasonable to dismiss him following the second offence in respect of which he is less blameworthy.

Since you are not able to dismiss Fred, you should use the opportunity to protect your position so that if he offends a third time, you will be able to dismiss him lawfully. This will involve issuing a stern formal letter warning him that you regard his conduct as extremely serious and that, although you waived disciplinary proceedings the first time, you are not prepared to carry on doing so and that if he repeats his actions again he will be dismissed. See **4.45** for more details on the contents of formal written warnings.

(iii) Where the misconduct is of a different nature   4.39

You are entitled to dismiss Fred due to his conduct even if his previous misconduct has been of a different type. Thus, for example, if Fred receives a warning for ignoring safety procedures and then, one month later, commits a completely unrelated offence, you may still rely on the first warning to justify dismissal. This is because it will, subject to it being otherwise reasonable on the facts of each individual case, be within the band of reasonable responses to dismiss an employee who has engaged in more than one act of misconduct even though they are of a different nature.

However, if the two acts are completely dissimilar, and are not closely linked in time (within, say, six months of each other), then a tribunal may find that on the facts of the individual case it would not be reasonable to rely on the warning for the first offence as justifying dismissal for the second offence. You may be safer issuing another warning. Should Fred then offend again, you will be in a much stronger position to justify his dismissal to a tribunal (given that there will be two warnings on record and he will therefore have a well-documented history of misconduct).

The disciplinary meeting   4.40

Tribunals tend to be more concerned about going through the correct procedure during the investigative, rather than the disciplinary, stage of effecting a dismissal. Nevertheless, it is important that you adhere to the various procedural requirements for two reasons. First, you will want to ensure that the sanction you impose is a proper one and is proportionate to the offence. Second, you do not want to leave any holes for Fred to exploit during a tribunal hearing.

Having two meetings – one investigative, one disciplinary – is good practice but is not *necessary* to ensure the dismissal is fair. Large employers routinely have policies which allow for two meetings; smaller employers tend not to. It is perfectly legitimate for employers to decide to hold one meeting only, at which the investigation *and* discussion of the potential sanction takes place. You must ensure, if going down this route, that the meeting (and the information given in advance of the meeting) complies with the mandatory minimum dismissal procedures set out in **APPENDIX 1**, as you will not get a second chance to put things right.

Fred is again entitled to be represented at this meeting – see **4.13** for further details.

It is again important that you have somebody present at the meeting to take notes, or take as full a note yourself as is possible.

There are two approaches to adopt, depending on whether you are contemplating dismissal. If, having considered the matters set out above, you are of the view that dismissal is likely to be an unreasonable response then you need not follow the same approach as you would do if dismissal were contemplated. At the end of the day, however, you must take a commercial decision as to the best way forward for your business, bearing in mind the risk and the sum of money involved if Fred succeeds in proving unfair dismissal to a tribunal (see **CHAPTER 13**).

Dismissal *is* being contemplated   4.41

If dismissal is being contemplated, you should state when calling the meeting that you are considering dismissal. Ask Fred if there are any extenuating or mitigating circumstances that he wishes to put forward.

If Fred asserts that he did not commit the act of misconduct, tell him that you have already decided that he did, that he had the chance to make representations on his guilt during the investigative stage, and that this meeting is solely concerned with the disciplinary sanction. You should also tell him that he will have a future opportunity to appeal against your decision that he has committed the act of misconduct (see **CHAPTER 11** on appeals).

Allow Fred to put forward any matters that he considers to be relevant. Even if you think that his arguments are immaterial, allow him to have his say.

It is often useful to ask questions like 'if you were me, what would you do?' or 'do you understand that the company cannot continue employing people who verbally abuse customers?' It is surprising how many employees capitulate in the face of questions like this, and agree that dismissal is appropriate. This has a powerful psychological effect, since it may inhibit them from claiming against you once they have admitted that dismissal was reasonable. Further, if you have taken a proper note of their responses, it will go down well with a tribunal that Fred did not challenge your proposed actions during the disciplinary meeting.

Once Fred has put his point of view forward, you should tell him that you will consider his comments and put your decision to him in writing. Do not give him any indication of your likely decision at this stage.

Dismissal is *not* being contemplated   4.42

You may not be contemplating dismissing Fred, and prefer to issue a warning, or you may simply have decided to issue a warning due to the risk of a tribunal finding a dismissal to be unfair. If this is the case, you should tell Fred at the beginning of the meeting that you do not intend to dismiss him but are considering issuing a formal warning. Ask him if he has any representations to make. If he denies having committed the offence, tell him that the question of guilt has been decided, is a matter for appeal and it is not why you are holding the meeting.

It is unlikely that Fred will want to prolong a meeting which he will find very embarrassing. Once he realises that you do not wish to dismiss him, he will probably want to finish the meeting as quickly as possible and may well agree that a warning is appropriate. It is for this reason that holding a formal disciplinary hearing is useful – it will mean that you are in a stronger position to dismiss Fred should he re-offend if he agreed to a formal warning in respect of the present offence.

Deciding on an appropriate disciplinary sanction   4.43

There are a number of sanctions you can impose. They are as follows:

- *Dismissal*: If you decide to dismiss, you will need to be certain of your reasons and certain that you can justify the decision to dismiss as reasonable in the circumstances. If you have followed the guidelines set out in this book and considered all the relevant factors, you should be confident that you can justify a dismissal.

- *Demotion/transfer*: Be very careful if the demotion or transfer involves a reduction in salary or prestige (as will almost always be the case). It will entitle Fred to resign and claim constructive dismissal (although he will not succeed if you could have reasonably dismissed him for the offence). If his offence does not justify dismissal, you run as much risk in reducing his salary as you do in dismissing him.

- *Suspension without pay*: This is only permissible if Fred's contract of employment specifically authorises it. If you suspend without pay when the contract of employment does not authorise you to do so, Fred can claim constructive dismissal on the ground that you are in breach of your contractual obligation to pay him wages.

- *Suspension with pay*: On first thought, this may appear more of a reward than a disciplinary sanction. It may have an impact, however, if Fred is denied the opportunity of earning commission or overtime, or where the suspension itself would embarrass Fred amongst his colleagues – and thus encourage him to conform with disciplinary rules in the future.

- *Formal warning*: This will be the most common sanction imposed when you are not resorting to dismissal.

- *Fine*: You are not permitted to fine Fred, except in very specific circumstances where his fault has led to a discernible financial loss for your company and he has agreed to your right to make deductions from his wages in writing before he started employment. Avoid this – if you fine him when you are not entitled to do so he can resign and claim constructive dismissal (see **CHAPTER 17**).

- *Informal warning*: An unlikely sanction since this will be a simple reprimand of the type which may occur during the ordinary course of a working day. If you have been through the full investigative and disciplinary procedure, it is likely that the offence warrants something more than an informal warning.

Consider the options and any mitigating circumstances 4.44

Although you will have formed a view as to the appropriate sanction, if it is dismissal you should specifically consider other options and think about why they are not appropriate. Thus in a case of aggression towards customers, you may think that demotion is not appropriate because Fred would still come into contact with customers, that suspension without pay is not appropriate because his contract does not authorise you to do that, and that you had already issued a formal warning and thus a further warning is unlikely to be of any effect.

Do take into account Fred's explanations. If he says that the reason he was late for work was because of a death in the family, a tribunal is not going to uphold dismissal as a reasonable sanction. However, it will often be the case that Fred's mitigation is immaterial to your reasons for dismissal. Thus if he seeks to justify 'borrowing' money from the petty cash box on the basis that he was temporarily short of money, this would not be relevant since you are dismissing him for dishonesty and the reason for his dishonesty has little bearing on your decision.

The purpose in considering other options is one of justification at a later date – if you tell a tribunal that you actively considered alternate sanctions then they are more likely to condone your decision to dismiss as reasonable than if you admit that you had not considered other options at all.

If you are a very large employer, it may be worthwhile having a form printed listing alternative sanctions and containing space for you to fill in why they are not appropriate. This will be useful from an evidential point of view at any tribunal hearing. If you are not a large employer, having such a form will appear artificial and peculiar to the tribunal and thus it would be unwise to use one.

The necessary elements of both a formal warning letter and a dismissal letter are set out below.

Warning letter 4.45

It is important that the warning letter is clear and to the point. It should state that continued misconduct, or a repetition of the offence, is likely to lead to dismissal. The letter should contain the following points:

- you write further to your meeting on [date], at which you discussed the appropriate sanction for the offence. Identify the offence in a few words, but do not go into detail – this will have been done in your previous letter following the investigative meeting;

- if Fred agreed that a formal warning was appropriate, reference should be made to this in the letter. In any event, state that the letter constitutes a formal warning that, if there is a repetition of the offence or continued misconduct, Fred is likely to be dismissed unless there are exceptional extenuating circumstances;

- state that he has a right of appeal from the warning, and that his appeal should be sent to the appropriate person in writing within, say, seven days (see **CHAPTER 11** for more details on appeals); and

- if Fred has been on suspension, inform him of the date that you expect him to resume work.

It does not matter whether you hand the letter to Fred or post it to him. You should, however, ask him to sign a copy of the letter as an acknowledgment of receipt and return it to you. This is important because, should you dismiss Fred in the future, you will need to prove that he had received the formal warning.

Dismissal letter 4.46

If Fred is suspended, you can justify sending a letter to him at home. However, if he has continued working during your investigations, a tribunal will regard it as callous (and thus indicative of an unreasonable attitude) if you simply send him a letter of dismissal by post. It is both courteous, and good industrial practice, to inform him verbally that he is being dismissed and either hand him the letter or tell him that you will confirm the dismissal in writing within 24 hours.

If you are dismissing Fred for gross misconduct, you do not need to give him any notice pay. Indeed, for various legal reasons (which fall outside the scope of this book) it is actually detrimental to your case to give any notice period. Accordingly the dismissal should be instant (or, to use the legal word, summary).

If the dismissal is not for gross misconduct, you need to give an appropriate notice period. **CHAPTER 12** deals with the number of weeks' notice that you are legally obliged to give to Fred. You have three options as to how to deal with Fred's notice period:

(i)   require him to continue working during the notice period;

(ii) require him to remain on your company's books, but to remain at home and not work for any other persons (this is known as 'garden leave'); or

(iii) pay a lump sum in lieu of notice. Depending on the terms of his contract and the way the letter is phrased, this sum can be paid free of tax. Note, however, that this option may sometimes prevent you relying on restraint of trade or confidentiality clauses in Fred's contract. If such clauses exist, and you wish to rely on them, you should seek specific legal advice.

Contents of letter 4.47

Your letter should state the following:

- that you write further to your meeting on [date], which you called in order to determine whether dismissal was justified as a result of Fred's conduct. Identify the conduct in one or two sentences;

- if you are dismissing Fred as a result of gross misconduct, that his actions amount to gross misconduct. If you are dismissing him following breach of a rule or a previous warning, identify the source and/or date of the rule or the warning and state that your decision has been taken against the background of the rule or the warning;

- if appropriate, that you have considered suspension or demotion, but that you are of the view that they would not be appropriate. State that your business interests prevent the continued employment of Fred and give a reason (such as you are losing customers as the result of Fred's conduct, or that his drinking problem is affecting the quality of his work);

- if the dismissal is for gross misconduct, that Fred is summarily dismissed and that he is not entitled to notice pay. Otherwise, state which one of the options in paragraph **4.46** applies and, if appropriate, enclose a cheque or say that a cheque will follow; and

- that Fred is entitled to appeal within, say, seven days. If he wishes to appeal, he should set out his reasons in writing in a letter to the appropriate person. See **CHAPTER 11** for more details on appeals.

Say nothing further 4.48

If Fred contacts you after receiving the letter, be polite but firm. Do not say anything that might prejudice your case at the tribunal (such as you were not sure that it was him who was stealing, but you had to sack someone to protect your own job).

References 4.49

See the discussion of references at **3.24**.

Dismissing for computer/internet misuse: a particular study

Introduction
4.50

Computer and internet misuse is becoming an increasingly common reason for dismissing employees. In July 2002, a survey by *Personnel Today* magazine suggested that almost 70% of all dismissals were associated with online pornography. It is helpful to deal with the particular issues that may arise in this situation as a separate study.

Two main issues arise may arise from Fred's misuse of computers and the internet:

(a) drain on productivity – time spent surfing the net is time *not* being spent working, leading to a reduction in productivity. In addition, dissemination of personal emails and attachments may reduce the overall efficiency of your network;

(b) potential liabilities – if Fred downloads pornography or racially charged material (particularly if he forwards it on), your company may be exposed to liability for harassment. Likewise, Fred may inadvertently defame somebody by posting gossip to a web forum, or sending emails to friends, which your company may find itself liable for.

Internet and email policies
4.51

You will have difficulty dismissing Fred for computer and internet misuse unless you have a written, internet policy (which Fred would have been aware of) expressly prohibiting the conduct Fred has been engaged in, and which warns dismissal is likely to result from any breach of the policy.

A typical policy might be:

Email facilities and internet access are provided for business use only, although we will not object to your occasional use of these facilities for personal purposes.

Please be aware that we may monitor your use of Email. This is to ensure that the Email system is not being misused by:

(a) sending defamatory or harassing Emails, which could incur liabilities for us;

(b) you sending or receiving excessive numbers of Emails (preventing you from working properly during your working hours);

(c)   you receiving executable programmes as attachments to Emails (which, if received unsolicited, you must delete without opening) which might contain viruses; or,

(d)   entering into contracts which have not been authorised by a director of the company.

You must not download, store or view any material which might be considered to be offensive, pornographic or discriminatory. You are reminded that computer systems maintain a log of which websites you have visited, and the company may examine this log as part of monitoring to ensure compliance with this policy.

In addition, you must not send (which includes forwarding) any Email which contains offensive, pornographic or discriminatory content.

Breach of the above policy will result in disciplinary proceedings. We will regard a serious breach as gross misconduct, which is likely to result in your dismissal.

Dismissals for breach of policy   4.52

If Fred has been download offensive material, or spending excessive time on the internet, it is normally prudent to give a written warning before dismissal (if it is a first offence). Nevertheless, if the email policy is sufficiently specific and the breach is a significant one, you are likely to be able to persuade a tribunal that you were acting reasonably in dismissing Fred.

Examples where dismissals were held to be fair

Dismissals will tend to be fair where the downloaded material is particularly offensive or voluminous *and* where a policy exists prohibiting such conduct. Alternatively, a dismissal is likely to be fair if there is an element of dishonesty involved, for example obtaining access to the computer system by deception.

Example

Mr Parr was dismissed when his employer, a local authority, discovered he had been accessing pornographic pictures and videos on the internet at work. He admitted it was true but claimed he found himself on the site by mistake, had initially 'got stuck' there, and was re-visiting it only because he was disturbed by the prospect that entry could easily be made by children. His employers disbelieved him and dismissed. A tribunal upheld the dismissal as fair on the grounds there had been a full investigation and Mr Parr was guilty of violating an established code of conduct – *Parr v Derwentside District Council (Newcastle Upon Tyne employment tribunal, 23/3/98, case 2501507/98)*.

Example

Mr Joinson was a trade union shop steward who was entitled to access his employer's computers to obtain engineering information only. His daughter, who had wider computer access, worked for the same company. Mr Joinson used his daughter's password to access information which could be of use to him in his trade union activities, and against the interests of the company. He was dismissed for gross misconduct. The EAT held that if an employee deliberately used an unauthorised password in order to enter a computer to gain access to information to which he was not entitled, that would of itself gross misconduct which would *prima facie* attract dismissal as a penalty – *Denco Ltd v Joinson [1991] IRLR 63*.

Example

Mr Thomas was a lead personnel officer with the London Borough of Hillingdon. The employer had a clear policy stating that it would dismiss employees who accessed pornography at work. Mr Thomas did precisely that, and was dismissed. The Employment Appeal Tribunal overturned a tribunal's decision that the dismissal was unfair, saying that if Hillingdon reasonably believed that accessing pornography was a dismissable offence, then it should not be criticised for following its own reasonable policies – *Thomas v London Borough of Hillingdon EAT/1317/01*.

Examples where dismissals were held to be unfair

Dismissals for internet/computer misuse will tend to be unfair where there is a lack of a clear procedure or policy prohibiting such conduct, or where the breach was minor. In such a case, you should issue a clear written warning to Fred, enabling you to dismiss him if there is further inappropriate conduct.

Example

Mr Dunn was dismissed when his employer discovered he had been accessing and printing off pornographic material. He was summarily dismissed after a very brief interview. The dismissal was found to be unfair, on the basis that there was no clear breach of company policy which would automatically warrant dismissal. However, Mr Dunn's compensation was reduced by 50% to reflect his contributory fault – *Dunn v IBM (UK) Ltd (Croydon employment tribunal, 1/7/98, case 2305087/97).*

Example

Mr Rodrigues used a colleagues' password to access data which he did not personally have access to via computer, but which he could have properly obtained over the telephone. The dismissal was found to be unfair, as BT's computer policy did not make it clear that breach would result in dismissal and, in any event, the sanction was considered unreasonable and excessive given the minor nature of the breach – *BT plc v Rodrigues (unreported, EAT 20/2/95).*

Chapter 5
How to Dismiss Someone for Concealing Criminal Offences

Introduction   5.1

CHAPTER 3 dealt with situations where Fred committed a criminal offence away from work. CHAPTER 4 dealt with situations where Fred may have committed a criminal act at work. Sometimes, however, you may discover that Fred has prior criminal convictions that he failed to disclose when you first employed him. If it is a very minor conviction (such as a driving offence) you would be unwise to dismiss him, since a tribunal would almost certainly find that your action is disproportionate (unless a clean driving licence is an essential element of Fred's employment).

Can you dismiss?   5.2

In order to dismiss Fred for concealing a conviction, it is essential that he must have actively misled you. If there is a space on your application form for criminal convictions, and he has failed to disclose the offence, this will suffice. If, however, you did not ask him about convictions during the selection process, he will not have concealed the offence and you cannot dismiss him on that basis.

Unless the offence is trivial, a tribunal will uphold your decision to dismiss Fred for deliberate concealment of a criminal offence before starting work. This is particularly so if Fred is employed in a position of trust.

Example

Mr Torr was a guard for British Rail. When he applied for the job, he stated that he had not been convicted of any criminal offences. In fact, he had been convicted of two offences; the first involving a prison

> sentence of three years (16 years before his job application) and the second involving a prison sentence of nine months (six years before his application). Eighteen months into his employment, the first conviction was discovered and he was dismissed. The Employment Appeal Tribunal decided that the dismissal was fair, even though the conviction was 16 years old, since the job of a guard involved supervision over a train, its passengers and freight and it could not be entrusted to a person who dishonestly concealed a criminal conviction – *Torr v British Railways Board [1977] IRLR 184*

There are three steps which you must go through before you can dismiss Fred:

(i)   ensure that there actually is a conviction;

(ii) ensure that the conviction was not 'spent' at the time Fred applied for employment;

(iii) give Fred the opportunity to explain why he failed to disclose the conviction.

(i) Ensure that there actually is a conviction   5.3

This sounds self-evident. However, if Fred claims unfair dismissal and then denies the conviction, you will have to prove that he had been convicted of an offence. Presumably you would have been told by someone about Fred's conviction – thus the easiest way to verify it is to ask your informant about his source.

As a matter of reality, most employees will admit to a conviction if confronted with it (since they believe that the conviction can be verified with the police). This is a misapprehension – the police will not disclose details of convictions to the public, or even to an employer. Accordingly you may place yourself at risk if you dismiss Fred on the basis of unsubstantiated or unconfirmed allegations of concealing a conviction.

Certain types of employer can obtain disclosure of an employee's spent *and* unspent convictions from the Criminal Records Bureau (http://www.crb.gov.uk). This is only available in connection with jobs which are exempt from the *Rehabilitation of Offenders Act 1974* (see **5.4** below), such as doctors, accountants, nurses, lawyers, prison officers, traffic wardens, police officers or people dealing with children or vulnerable adults.

The Criminal Records Bureau is due, at some point, to make certificates available to individuals (which employers can ask to see) containing details of unspent convictions. Although this service was meant to commence in 2002, at the date of writing (September 2004) the CRB has not yet begun providing this facility.

If Fred admits the conviction, make sure that his admission is recorded in writing (so that a later denial to a tribunal will carry little weight). The best place to do this is in a letter inviting Fred to explain why he failed to disclose the conviction.

(ii) Ensure that the conviction is not spent 5.4

Under the *Rehabilitation of Offenders Act 1974*, convictions become 'spent' after a certain period of time. If a conviction is spent at the time he applied for his job, Fred is regarded as a 'rehabilitated person' and is entitled, by law, to withhold details about the conviction from you. If you dismiss Fred because of a concealed spent offence, the dismissal will be unfair and you may have to pay considerable compensation to him.

The rehabilitation periods are as follows:

- over 30 months' imprisonment – no rehabilitation period; the conviction will never become spent;

- imprisonment between 6 and 30 months – 10 years;

- imprisonment for less than 6 months – 7 years;

- fine or probation – 5 years;

- conditional discharge or binding over – 1 year or, if longer, the duration of the order.

The above periods should be halved if Fred was under 18 when he committed the offence.

(iii) Give an opportunity to explain failure to disclose the conviction 5.5

Once you have established that Fred has an undisclosed, unspent conviction, you must give him the opportunity to explain why he failed to disclose it. You can also use this occasion to allow him to put forward reasons as to why he should not be dismissed.

You should write to Fred, making the following points:

- you have discovered that he concealed a conviction at the time he applied for his job. Set out what the conviction was and, if you know it, the sentence he received. If Fred has admitted the conviction to you, make reference to his admission in the letter;

- you consider the deliberate concealing of a conviction to be a very serious matter;

- you would like him to come to a meeting to explain why he failed to disclose the conviction. State the date, time and place of the meeting. Inform him that he can have a representative present if he wishes;

- in view of the seriousness of his actions, you are considering dismissal and he should use the meeting as an opportunity to put forward reasons why dismissal would not be an appropriate response.

Procedure at the meeting 5.6

At the meeting, you should follow the same procedure as for investigative meetings when dismissing someone for breaches of discipline (see **4.12**). Do not forget to invite Fred's comments on whether dismissal is an appropriate response (see **4.41**). Do not tell Fred your decision during the meeting.

The decision to dismiss 5.7

Once the meeting has concluded, you will need to decide whether Fred has produced a reasonable excuse for failing to disclose his conviction. There are a number of excuses regularly used. These range from 'oh – I didn't realise it included convictions for shoplifting – I thought it was just for violence' to the unlikely 'I forgot about the conviction'.

A tribunal is unlikely to criticise you for disbelieving Fred's excuse that he forgot about a conviction. A conviction for a criminal offence is not the sort of thing that slips people's minds, particularly if their focus has been triggered by the question 'do you have any convictions?'

If, however, the question asked at the selection stage was 'do you have any criminal convictions which might affect your suitability for the job', rather than the wider 'do you have any criminal convictions?', you may have to accept an excuse from Fred that he did not think a particular conviction relevant. This is a question of fact and degree – if the job is a security guard and Fred has been convicted of theft, it is clearly relevant and you will be justified in rejecting his excuse. It is important therefore that your application form includes such a question.

Most frequently, you will simply face a lack of cooperation from Fred. If he fails to put forward an excuse for concealing the conviction, you should have little difficulty justifying his dismissal to a tribunal, subject to the following point.

Is dismissal an appropriate sanction? 5.8

Once you have satisfied yourself that Fred lacks a valid reason for concealing the conviction, you need to decide whether dismissal is an appropriate sanction. Provided your view is reasonable, a tribunal will uphold the dismissal if Fred later complains of unfair dismissal.

Dismissal will usually be appropriate if Fred has deliberately concealed an unspent offence. The fact that an offence was near, but not quite at, its rehabilitation date when you employed Fred will not assist him. The courts have made it clear that there is no obligation on an employer to extend the social policy behind the *Rehabilitation of Offenders Act 1974* by discounting offences which are not yet spent under the Act.

If, however, the offence was a very minor one then a tribunal may say that dismissal was an unreasonable response. Usually, minor offences will become spent fairly quickly and thus the fact that it is not spent means it is likely to be a more serious offence. If Fred has had warnings for incompetence or misconduct, you will be on stronger ground even if the offence is minor, since it is more reasonable to dismiss a 'bad' employee for concealing a minor offence than it is to dismiss an able, otherwise trusted employee.

You will not be able, in these circumstances, to dismiss Fred without notice. Therefore you can either require him to work out his notice period, or pay him money in lieu of notice – see **4.46** for further details.

The dismissal letter 5.9

If you decide that dismissal is reasonable, you should write to Fred setting out the following:

- further to your meeting on [date], you have considered the reasons he gave for failing to disclose his conviction. State, briefly, his explanation and explain why you do not accept it;

- although you have taken into account his comments about dismissal and (if appropriate) his long/good working record, you are of the view that his continued employment is not possible because he secured the employment only by deliberately concealing details of his past conviction;

- you are dismissing him. State whether you are requiring him to work out his notice period or paying him in lieu of notice;

- Fred is entitled to appeal within, say, seven days. If he wishes to appeal, he should set out his reasons in writing in a letter to the appropriate person. See **CHAPTER 11** for further details on appeals.

The letter can either be handed to Fred or posted to him at home.

Chapter 6
How to Dismiss Someone for Refusing to Obey Instructions

Introduction   6.1

Although Fred may not have committed any disciplinary offences, and may be perfectly capable of doing his job properly, you may wish to dismiss him for failing to obey instructions. Such instructions can include telling Fred to enter credit card transactions in a certain manner, or imposing a 'no-smoking' policy on the whole office. It will only be in the rarest circumstances that you can dismiss somebody for a one-off failure to obey instructions; more usually, you will need to give them at least one – and often two – clear warnings.

As with all dismissals, it is necessary to follow a careful procedure or you risk a tribunal finding that you have acted unfairly.

Fred's refusal to obey instructions can arise in two different ways, namely:

(i)   a refusal to carry out tasks which Fred ordinarily does; and

(ii) a refusal to carry out new tasks which did not previously form part of his ordinary working day.

There are also more fundamental instructions which Fred may be reluctant to follow, such as changing job locations (which may or may not require a move of home) or changing from a day-shift to a night-shift. Each of these will be considered in turn.

(i) Refusal to carry out tasks which are usually undertaken   6.2

This will usually be a valid reason for imposing disciplinary sanctions. If Fred is refusing to complete tasks which fall within his usual remit, you are entitled to take action to compel him to do so. If he continues to refuse, dismissal may become an appropriate sanction.

Common examples of this may be where Fred refuses to work with a particular colleague because of friction or a grudge, or where he decides that he does not wish to use safety equipment. You must be in a position to show that your instruction is both lawful and reasonable. It will be lawful if it is a task which Fred is required to do under his contract of employment. This is usually a matter of inference and practice; however, if you have a job description sheet (of which Fred has a copy) then any task appearing on that sheet will fall within those which he is contractually obliged to do.

If there is no job description sheet, or if the task is not included on that sheet, then a tribunal will almost always find that an instruction falls within Fred's contract of employment if it is something that he has been required to do (and has done) in the past, or if it is something that employees of his job description in other companies are asked to do.

The instruction must also be reasonable. Although you may be contractually entitled to insist that Fred operates a particular piece of machinery, it will not be reasonable to require him to operate it if the safety mechanisms are broken. If you dismiss him for disobeying an unreasonable order, even if it is technically within his contractual duties or job description, a tribunal is likely to find that the dismissal was unfair.

(ii) Refusal to carry out new tasks   6.3

Again, the central issue, in determining whether or not you can discipline Fred, is whether the instruction was a lawful and reasonable one. If the task is one which you have not required Fred to carry out before then you may have greater difficulty showing that Fred is contractually obliged to do it (unless it is contained within a job description).

Are the new instructions lawful? The law recognises that an employer's require-ments change (for example, you may need Fred to work in a different department or use new safety equipment). Accordingly, you are allowed to alter Fred's job description (for unfair dismissal purposes) if you can show that there is a 'sound, good business reason' for doing so. Note that you must establish a 'sound, good business reason' – if it is simply 'desirable' it may not be enough.

What is meant by a 'sound, good business reason'? There is no straightforward answer to this question, and thus you should be confident that you can justify to a tribunal that you are acting reasonably. If the new instructions do not affect Fred's financial circumstances (such as requiring him to work additional hours but giving him a *pro rata* pay increase so that it does not detrimentally affect his pay) and you can show that the changes are good for your business then a tribunal is likely to say that you are entitled to make the changes to Fred's job description.

Sometimes issuing Fred with new tasks will be as the result of a general, widespread business reorganisation. Dismissing as the result of a business reorganisation is dealt with in **CHAPTER 8**.

Is the new instruction reasonable?   6.4

This is a question to be decided in each case. It would probably not be reasonable to instruct a senior employee to clear the dustbins, even though it is in your business's interests that someone empty them. If your instruction is unreasonable, then Fred will have a good claim for unfair dismissal if you dismiss him following his non-compliance with it.

Fundamental instructions   6.5

Fundamental changes, such as changing shifts or moving work locations, can sometimes justify dismissal if Fred refuses to comply. Unlike the above two scenarios, however, if the change is fundamental then you are more likely to be able to dismiss Fred for his initial non-compliance (rather than having to go through a warning stage before dismissal).

The first point to consider is whether Fred's contract of employment entitles you to give the relevant instructions. It is necessary to have an express clause; you will not be able to imply one should it not have been specifically agreed or set out in writing. Many contracts of employment contain a 'mobility clause', allowing you to require Fred to move to anywhere within the United Kingdom. Such a clause will entitle you to dismiss Fred if he refuses to move.

If there is no express right to issue the fundamental instruction in Fred's contract, you will need to show that it is reasonably necessary for your business interests to make the change to his contract. This is discussed further in **CHAPTER 8**. Note that if you want Fred to move his place of work, you may have a redundancy situation – see **CHAPTER 7** for further details.

Tribunals will be more sympathetic to you if you dismiss Fred for his refusal to comply with a fundamental instruction than if he is dismissed for failing to comply with a mundane, everyday instruction. This is because fundamental instructions are, by their nature, usually far more central to the business's interest and thus a tribunal will be more inclined to find that you were justified in taking the action that you did.

The first failure to obey instructions   6.6

Usually, you will not be entitled to dismiss Fred following his first failure to obey instructions (unless it is a fundamental instruction). Your approach should therefore differ depending on the type of instruction in question.

Non-fundamental instructions 6.7

In this situation, you should issue Fred with a formal warning. Write to him, and state the following:

- that you are concerned about his failure to comply with your instruction(s) on [date]. Set out what the instruction was, and briefly refer to the circumstances surrounding Fred's refusal;

- any effect Fred's conduct had on health and safety, on customer relations or on the profitability of your company. This will justify the weight that you place on compliance with instructions;

- the reason, if not covered by the above, why it is important that Fred comply with the instruction;

- that your company requires its employees to comply with reasonable instructions, and that in failing to do so Fred is in breach of his contract of employment;

- in the circumstances, you are giving Fred a formal warning that continued disobedience, whether of this or any other instruction, may lead to his dismissal;

- that he has a right of appeal against the warning. If he wishes to exercise the right, he should do so in writing within, say, seven days (see **CHAPTER 11** on appeals).

You should ask Fred to sign a copy of the letter as evidence that he received it – it is not uncommon for employees to claim, at tribunal hearings, that warning letters were never sent.

Fundamental instructions 6.8

You should write to Fred, stating the following:

- the actual instruction and the fact that he has failed to comply with it. If you have discussed the matter with him, and he has indicated an ongoing disinclination to comply, state the date and gist of the conversation;

- either that he is obliged to comply with the instruction under his contract of employment (and, if appropriate, quote the relevant section);

- or that it is necessary, in the interests of your business, that he comply with the instruction. Give a brief (one sentence) explanation of why it is in the business's interests to require Fred to act in this way;

- a time limit within which Fred will have to comply with the instruction. Often, in this type of situation, it is better to give a time limit within which Fred will have to confirm that he will comply. The time limit must be a reasonable one – it would be unreasonable to insist, for example, that Fred agrees to move to a new place of work 200 miles away within 24 hours;

- that if Fred does not comply with the instruction he will be dismissed.

If he still does not comply 6.9

If Fred complies with your instruction, or indicates that he will do so, then your goal will have been achieved. If he states, after having received the letter, that he has no intention of complying you should still allow the time limit to elapse, but can then miss out the next stage and proceed to the dismissal (see **6.14**).

If the time limit elapses and Fred has not responded positively, you should write one further letter to him setting out the following:

- you write further to your previous letter, and note that Fred has failed to comply with the instruction by the date set;

- you are giving him one final chance to comply (or to agree that he will comply); if he does not do so within, say, 48 hours then he will be dismissed.

Again, if Fred complies with this final letter you will have achieved your goal. If not, you can proceed to dismissing him (see **6.14**).

Subsequent failures to obey instructions 6.10

If, after having received one warning for failing to obey instructions, Fred continues to disobey your orders then you may be able to dismiss him at this stage. It will depend on the type of instruction he has disobeyed, the time gap between the two incidents and whether his subsequent refusal is related to the first one. If you cannot justify dismissal (and this is addressed in more detail below), you should give a second warning.

If, after having received two warnings for failing to obey instructions, Fred continues to disobey your orders then you will be able to dismiss him (except in exceptional circumstances).

Can you dismiss after just one warning? 6.11

If Fred's second refusal to obey instructions is in connection with a fundamental instruction going to the basis of his work (such as changing working hours, as above) you should follow the same procedure as in **6.7** above.

If neither instruction has been a fundamental instruction, you need to satisfy yourself that it would be reasonable to dismiss Fred in the light of just one prior warning. In general, for it to be reasonable all three of the following tests must be satisfied:

- the instructions must have been important ones or, more accurately, not trivial ones. They must be related to the way in which he performs his work (or the type of work which he undertakes). An example of a trivial instruction, which would not justify dismissal at this stage, would be not wanting to take a lunch break at a particular time;

- there must not have been a long time gap between the two refusals. As a rule of thumb, if the two refusals occur within one month of each other you can probably justify dismissal. If the time gap is longer you should issue a second warning before dismissing;

- the two refusals must be connected. This can be satisfied either by Fred refusing to obey the same instruction after having received a written warning, or by him refusing to obey instruction 'B' because he had received a warning for refusing to obey instruction 'A' – in essence, if he is objecting through spite over the first warning.

In the absence of all three tests being satisfied, it would be dangerous to dismiss Fred based on one warning only. You should issue a second warning (see **6.7**) and then re-consider dismissal if he offends a third time.

Smoking: a special case   6.12

A common situation where Fred refuses to obey instructions is where you have brought in a 'no-smoking' policy. In such circumstances, assuming Fred has been made aware of the policy, you should issue him with a formal warning (as above) if he is caught smoking.

If he re-offends, you will need to consider relocating him to a suitable environment where smoking is permitted. If there is no appropriate place where he can continue working as a smoker, or if he refuses to be relocated, you will be justified in dismissing him. Your dismissal letter should follow the format set out below at **6.19**.

Can you dismiss after two or more warnings?   6.13

You will rarely be criticised for dismissing Fred after two warnings. There are only two scenarios where a dismissal might be found to be unfair:

- if there has been a long time gap between the warnings. In general, any warning over twelve months old should be disregarded. If, however, almost twelve months have elapsed since the last warnings (and thus Fred has been on 'good behaviour' for a long time) you are much better off issuing another warning since a tribunal might find that you are acting unreasonably in relying on old warnings for comparatively minor matters;

- if the instructions in question have been trivial ones, such as refusing to bring the milk in or make coffee, a tribunal may find that you are using Fred's refusal to comply as a sham to hide the real reason for dismissal. If it forms this view, the dismissal will be unfair. If you genuinely want to dismiss Fred for failing to make the coffee, this is likely to be symptomatic of a more general breakdown of the relationship between Fred and other members of staff. Consider dismissal because of personality clashes – see **10.4** below.

Dismissal procedure   6.14

Since a failure to obey instructions is a form of misconduct, you need to follow a similar procedure to that involved in dismissals for misconduct. You should write to Fred, stating the following:

- that you are concerned about his failure to obey instructions. Set out the incident in question and refer (briefly) to any discussions you have had about it;

- that this is not the first time that he has failed to obey instructions. Refer to the previous warning letter(s) and state that he was warned on that occasion that repeated failure to comply might lead to his dismissal;

- that you cannot justify continuing to employ somebody who persistently refuses to obey instructions;

- you would like him to meet you to discuss reasons why he should not be dismissed. State a date, time and place for the meeting, but say that it can be changed if it is not convenient for Fred. Tell him he can bring a friend or representative to the meeting – see **4.13** for more information about representatives.

If Fred fails to attend the meeting, you should reschedule it once. If he fails to attend a second time, you can dismiss him without further enquiry (unless he provides a good reason for the second failure to attend). Use the dismissal letter set out at paragraph **6.19** below, but amend it so that it refers to Fred missing the meetings.

The meeting   6.15

At the meeting, you should have someone present to take notes. If you are a small company, you can take notes yourself (although it is never ideal to do so since it is difficult to think, talk and write at the same time).

Explain the purpose of the meeting to Fred. Tell him that you are not happy about his failures to obey your instructions, and that you find it difficult to see how you can continue employing someone who disregards instructions. Ask him whether he understands your position, and whether he understands that it goes against the interests of your business to carry on employing him. If he agrees with you, it will place you in a strong position should he then turn around and claim unfair dismissal.

If he does not agree, ask him why he failed to obey the most recent instruction. If he tries to discuss an earlier warning for disobeying a previous instruction, explain to him that he had the right to appeal against that warning when it was first issued and it is too late to challenge it now.

Unless he has a very good reason for refusing to obey the instruction, you can continue with the dismissal process. His belief that your instruction was bad for the business, or detrimental to customer relations, will not be a good reason – you are the manager and it is for you, not him, to decide policy. He cannot substitute his decision for yours and then disregard instructions to do what he is employed to do.

Safety of customers or other employees will, if justified, usually be a good reason and will prevent you from dismissing Fred (indeed, sometimes dismissing Fred in connection with him taking steps during a health and safety emergency will mean the dismissal is automatically unfair – see **18.2**). Likewise, if Fred has received conflicting instructions from two managers, and he is not at fault in failing to clarify those instructions, he cannot be dismissed for failing to comply with one of the two sets of inconsistent instructions.

Note that if Fred's reason for refusing to obey an instruction is that he believes the instruction is unlawful (whether he is right or wrong), or that your company is in breach of a legal obligation (including health and safety obligations), then you run the risk of a tribunal finding that you dismissed him (should you eventually do so) because he raised legitimate complaints about the legality of your business – often referred to as 'whistleblowing'. If this occurs, you ought to seek professional legal advice before dismissing.

He has a good reason for disobeying   6.16

If you decide that he has a good reason for not obeying your instruction, tell him that you accept his explanation and that you will take no further action. Write a letter to him confirming your decision.

He does not have a good reason for disobeying   6.17

If he does not have a good reason for non-compliance, you move on to consider the sanction. Do not inform Fred at this stage that you do not accept his explanation – it is better to do so in writing when you can choose your words with care.

Tell him again that you are considering dismissal. Ask him if there are any facts of which you are not aware which might influence your decision. Feel free to question him on anything he puts forward – if his explanation contains inconsistencies it will assist with justifying a decision to dismiss to a tribunal.

Conclude the meeting by telling him that you will consider what he has said and put your decision in writing. Do not give an answer, or even a preliminary indication, at that stage (otherwise you may face the allegation at a tribunal that you had already made up your mind).

Is it reasonable to dismiss?   6.18

You then need to consider whether or not it is reasonable to dismiss Fred. If he refuses to comply with a fundamental obligation, or if he has refused to obey reasonable orders in the face of warnings for prior disobedience, a tribunal is likely to find that a decision to dismiss is reasonable unless Fred has provided an explanation which justifies his disobedience.

The dismissal letter   6.19

If you decide to dismiss Fred, you must do so with notice – you will not be able to dismiss him summarily. You should write to him stating the following:

- that you refer to your meeting on [date];

- you have carefully considered the matters that Fred put forward. State, briefly, what Fred's main points were;

- *either* that you do not accept his explanation/excuse (and state the reason for disbelieving him);

- *or* that you accept his explanation but, on weighing it up against the (repeated) failure to comply with instructions, do not think that you can continue utilising Fred's services;

- (if appropriate) that you have considered demotion or suspension, but you do not think that they would be appropriate. State that your business interests prevent Fred's continued employment and give a reason (such as you are spending an inappropriate amount of management time on him, or are losing business);

- that in the circumstances, you are dismissing him. State either that he is required to work out his notice period, and that his last day of employment will be [date]; or that you do not require him to work out his notice and will pay him ___ weeks' salary in lieu of notice (see **4.46** for further details);

- if, before his notice period expires, he changes his mind and agrees to comply with the instruction, you will withdraw the dismissal;

- that he has a right of appeal against your decision within, say, seven working days. If he wishes to appeal, he should set out his reasons in writing in a letter to the appropriate person. See **CHAPTER 11** for further information on appeals.

Say nothing further 6.20

If Fred contacts you after receiving the letter, be firm but polite. Ask him again to comply with the instructions. Do not be drawn into a debate about the correctness of your decision to dismiss, but instead ask him to use the internal appeal procedure.

Likewise, be careful about offering references during the course of the next three months. See **3.24** for further discussion of this point.

Chapter 7
Dismissing for Redundancy

Introduction   7.1

This is a complex area of law. You stand more risk of being found to have made
an error on procedural matters when you dismiss for redundancy than when
you dismiss for any other reason. There is also a close overlap with dismissals for
business reorganisation (see **CHAPTER 8**). Note that if Fred is dismissed
because of a business reorganisation but he is not technically redundant, you do
not have to pay him a statutory redundancy payment (although many
employers choose to do so anyway).

This part is important: the word 'redundancy' has a specific legal meaning.
Non-lawyers, employers and employees often use the word 'redundancy' to
describe a dismissal where there is no blame to be placed at the employee's feet,
i.e. when there is no misconduct or incapability involved. This is wrong, and
you will fall foul of a tribunal if you make this mistake.

You can only dismiss for redundancy in specific circumstances. These are set
out below. If there is a redundancy situation, a dismissal will still be unfair if
you select Fred to be dismissed based on particular grounds (see **7.27**), or if
you fail to have a period of consultation with Fred and his colleagues before
the dismissals. A dismissal may also be unfair if you select Fred for redundancy
based on personal characteristics (such as he is too loud) rather than objective
criteria (such as timekeeping and length of service). Finally, a dismissal for
redundancy may become unfair if you fail to consider whether there is any
alternative employment that can be offered to Fred.

If you are making large-scale redundancies, you would be wise to seek specific
advice from a solicitor specialising in employment law. In particular, if you are
proposing to make 20 or more employees at one establishment redundant
within a period of 90 days or less then special rules will apply. These special
rules are not addressed in this book and you must seek proper legal advice.

Definition and procedures   7.2

This chapter is divided into two sections. The first section is an analysis of
when you can declare redundancies. The second section sets out the procedure
that you must follow when making Fred redundant.

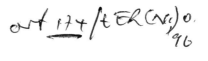

When can you declare redundancies? 7.3

There is a very precise definition contained in *section 139* of the *Employment Rights Act 1996*. This provides that an employee is taken to be dismissed by reason of redundancy if:

'the dismissal is wholly or mainly attributable to:

(a)   the fact that his employer has ceased or intends to cease:

     (i)   to carry on the business for the purposes of which the employee was employed by him; or

     (ii) to carry on that business in the place where the employee was so employed, or

(b)   that the requirements of that business:

     (i)   for employees to carry out work of a particular kind, or

     (ii) or employees to carry out work of a particular kind in the place where the employee was employed by the employer,

has ceased or diminished or are expected to cease or diminish.'

What does that mean? Essentially, you can declare redundancies in two types of situation, namely:

(a)   when you are planning to close down your business, or the part of your business for which Fred works, at the location where Fred is employed to work; or,

(b)   where your business no longer needs as many (or any) employees to carry on a particular kind of work.

Situation (a) 7.4

This is relatively straightforward. If you are closing down your business, or the department Fred was employed in, or the location where Fred was employed, then his position becomes redundant.

You may have heard, in the past, debate about the effect of mobility clauses on this type of redundancy (a mobility clause is a clause in Fred's contract that lets you relocate him across the country). However, even if such a clause exists, it is no longer an impediment to declaring redundancies.

Example

> Noel Murray worked on one of two production lines in the slaughter
> hall of a slaughterhouse run by Foyle Meats. Business declined and the
> company decided to close one of the production lines. Mr Murray was
> amongst the 35 or so employees selected for redundancy, after proper
> consultation with unions involved, and was dismissed on 27th March
> 1995. He claimed he had been unfairly selected for redundancy, because
> under his contract he could be required to work in any department and
> so the company was wrong to have selected people for redundancy solely
> from those who worked in the slaughter hall. The House of Lords
> rejected their claim, saying their dismissal was clearly attributable to the
> closing down of the slaughterhouse, and thus it was a redundancy –
> *Murray v Foyle Meats Ltd [1999] IRLR 562.*

Situation (b) 7.5

This can occur where you have a drop-off in business, or re-organise your
company, and thus need fewer employees to cope with your business
requirements. It might also occur where you are replacing employees with
mechanical or computerised methods of working, and there is therefore a
reduction in the need for human employees to carry on doing those particular
tasks.

Be careful to distinguish this situation from other types of business reorganisation. If you decide to change your administrative staff to a night-shift, you have
not reduced the need for employees to carry out work of a particular kind (i.e.
administrative work) at that place of business, and accordingly any dismissals of
employees who refuse to change hours will not be due to redundancy. It will,
instead, be due to a business reorganisation (which will not entail paying a
redundancy payment).

You can make Fred redundant even if he has not been doing the kind of work
which you have less of a need for employees to do. The test to apply is twofold,
namely:

- have the requirements of your business for employees to carry out work
  of a particular kind ceased or diminished (or are they expected to cease
  or diminish)?

- if so, is the need for Fred's dismissal caused wholly or mainly by that state
  of affairs?

If the answer to both questions is 'yes', and if you have followed a proper
procedure throughout, then you will be able to dismiss Fred for redundancy.

Example

> A company which employs six production machines, each with its own operator, decides it only needs five machines and resolves to make one person redundant. A fork-lift truck driver who delivers materials to the machines is selected for redundancy, on a 'last in, first out' basis since he is the most junior employee, and one of the machine operators is transferred to be a fork-lift truck driver. The Employment Appeal Tribunal held this would be a redundancy since there was a reduction in the need for employees to do a particular kind of work (i.e. operate the production machines) and the fork-lift truck driver had been dismissed as a direct result of this, even though he was not one of the employees directly affected – hypothetical scenario discussed in *Safeway Stores v Burrell [1997] IRLR 201*.

Even if the business decision is legitimate, follow correct procedures 7.6

One important point is that a tribunal will not question your business decision to close down a particular location or dismiss employees due to a reduction in work. Provided your decision is not manifestly unreasonable, or a sham designed to dismiss employees by an illegitimate route, tribunals take the view that they should not interfere in business decisions. Accordingly the commercial reasons for closure will not be investigated and you need have no concern about confidential information finding its way into a public hearing.

Example

> An employer decided to close down its entire night-shift. An employee complained of unfair dismissal on the grounds that there was no need to do this. The tribunal decided that it was not entitled to consider the manner in which an employer decides to cut down the workforce, and refused to decide whether the redundancies were necessary – *Guy v Delanair (Car Heater) Ltd [1975] IRLR 73*.

It may, however, still be necessary for you to show that a redundancy situation existed. Thus you may be required to provide basic evidence to a tribunal to show that you did make a business decision to downsize, rather than you have simply decided to dismiss Fred (and, often, others as well) and wrongly attached the label 'redundancy'.

Proper procedures 7.7

When dismissing for redundancy, the need to follow a proper procedure cannot be overemphasised. Going through the procedure is time consuming and thus costly. It is less costly, however, than paying an unfair dismissal award to somebody who no longer works for you. This is particularly the case when making multiple redundancies (when the cumulative cost of several awards can be substantial).

In essence, a tribunal will consider that even if a redundancy situation did exist, an employer would not be acting reasonably in making the decision to dismiss a particular employee unless he had considered all alternative options and consulted the employee first. The most frequent, and expensive, error that an employer can make is to assume that consultation would not make any difference. Other than in exceptional cases, which are addressed below at **7.18**, the failure to warn and consult with employees will render a dismissal unfair. Ignore this requirement at your peril!

Procedures for instituting redundancies 7.8

In essence, the procedure falls into three stages:

Stage 1: Consultation

Stage 2: Selection

Stage 3: Consideration of alternative employment

If mistakes occur during stages 1 or 3, a tribunal might find that any dismissal was technically unfair, but that a dismissal was inevitable anyway. It those circumstances, any award will be limited to the pay that Fred would have earned if he had remained employed a few weeks longer whilst you went through the proper procedures. Similarly, if stage 2 (i.e. your selection procedure) is unfair, the tribunal might find that under a proper selection procedure there was a 60% chance that Fred would have been chosen for redundancy – in which case any award will be reduced by 60%. This is discussed further in **CHAPTER 13**.

Redundancy procedure – stage 1 – consultation 7.9

Once there is a redundancy situation and you begin contemplating redundancies, it is necessary for you to consult or warn the workforce. This is to allow them the opportunity to put forward solutions to avoid job losses. Although some solutions that employees (or a trade union) suggest may be unworkable, a dismissal is likely to be unfair if you fail to warn and consult.

The first issue is whether you need to involve a trade union. This is straightforward – either your business recognises a trade union or it does not. You recognise a trade union if you negotiate with the union for collective bargaining purposes. If you do recognise a trade union, you should warn and consult the union in addition to individual employees (see **7.22** below). If you choose to consult with one and ignore the other, you face criticism from an employment tribunal.

If you are dismissing over 20 employees within 90 days, special rules apply (which are outside the scope of this book), including holding a workplace election for employee representatives. It is advisable to consult a specialist employment lawyer to avoid falling foul of some very complex rules, penalties for breach of which are up to 13 weeks' pay for each employee at risk of redundancy.

Consultation with individual employees   7.10

As stated above, a tribunal will almost always find a redundancy to be unfair if you failed to warn and consult the employees in advance. Four questions arise out of this:

(i)   How long before dismissal should the consultations take place?

(ii)   Which employees should you consult?

(iii) What should the consultations consist of?

(iv)   Is there ever an exception to the need to consult?

(i) How long before dismissal should the consultations take place?   7.11

The answer to this is: the longer, the better. The period over which consultation takes place will depend to a large extent on the size and administrative resources of your business, and on the urgency of the need to make redundancies. If a consultation period is very short (say, less than one week) then you risk a tribunal deciding that you were simply paying lip-service to the need for consultation.

If you are a small-to-medium company and are not making multiple redundancies, you should have little problem if you allow a one-week consultation period for redundancies. Larger companies, or small companies making multiple redundancies, should try to allow at least two weeks. If you are able to give greater warning, you should do so.

You may be able to persuade a tribunal that it was reasonable to allow a shorter period if there is a good reason for not providing a lengthy consultation period. Examples might be where an announcement that your business was closing down, or having cash-flow problems, would harm your business. Do not deceive yourself into using this reason when harm would be minimal – tribunals are quick to ferret out false labelling by employers or claims that the company's finances fall into categories which they do not.

(ii) Which employees should you consult? 7.12

You should consult all employees who fall into the pool from which you will be selecting those to be made redundant. In other words, you should consult everyone 'at risk' of redundancy.

Identifying a proper pool is important, as the following illustration shows. Assume that Fred works as a grade 1 mechanic. You obtain new equipment which results in you needing to employ fewer grade 2 mechanics. If your pool of potential redundancy candidates consists of grade 2 mechanics only, you will not have the option of dismissing Fred. If, however, your pool of redundancy candidates includes all grades of mechanics then, once you have established the need to make redundancies, you will be at liberty to dismiss Fred if he meets (or fails) the selection criteria.

Working out the pool of redundancy candidates can be fraught with risk. This is because, in practice, some tribunals view this particular step as an exception to the rule that tribunals should not interfere when an employer has acted reasonably (even though they should not do so).

You are unlikely to be criticised if you select any of the following as your pool of candidates:

- all those who work at a particular location, when you are closing down that place of business;

- all those in a particular division or sub-division, such as plastic manufacturing or telephone sales, when you are ceasing to carry on that part of the business;

- all those who carry out work of a particular kind, such as drivers, when your need for drivers has diminished.

Consult even when everyone is being made redundant 7.13

There are two occasions where you might be looking to make everyone from the pool redundant. This will happen if:

- you are closing down a place of work or a particular type of work; or

- if the type of work which you are dispensing with is done by a very small number of people, you may wish to make all of them redundant.

Even when this is the case, you should still go through the consultation procedure. This is because the employees might have sensible suggestions for re-employment. The failure to consult may render a dismissal unfair even when it is seems obvious that redundancy would take place (although any compensation would be low).

'Bumping' employees   7.14

It is generally regarded as acceptable to 'bump' employees. This means that if you needed to make a salesman redundant, but wanted to dismiss Fred (a buyer) instead, you could move one of the existing salesmen to Fred's position as a buyer and dismiss Fred in his place.

It should be noted that, despite the comment above, there is some very small doubt (arising from a one-off court case which said the opposite, which has never been expressly overruled) that bumping is *not* permitted. However, in practice tribunals recognise that bumping is accepted industrial practice and – even if bumping was technically not regarded as redundancy – it would almost certainly be regarded as some other substantial reason for dismissal (see **CHAPTER 10**), which would be fair provided the normal redundancy procedures were followed.

(iii) What should the consultations consist of?   7.15

The first step is to write to all the candidates for redundancy. The letter should be formal. It should contain the following points:

- that you anticipate having to make redundancies in the near future. State the anticipated number of redundancies and, in brief, the reason for making redundancies;

- unless the pool is obvious, such as when you are closing down an entire place of work, set out in one sentence how you identify the pool of candidates for redundancy. State that Fred is a member of the pool;

- your timescale. State that you will be meeting with employees individually (and, if appropriate, as a group) and specify a time for such a meeting. State the anticipated date that the redundancies will take effect. If you are also consulting with the trade union, mention this;

- that the purpose of the meeting(s) is to discuss ways of avoiding redundancy and an examination of whether it may be possible to find alternative employment;

- invite voluntary redundancies. Paragraph **12.17** onwards deals with redundancy payments; it is common for voluntary redundancies to be rewarded with an enhanced pay package. Make it clear, however, that if more people apply for voluntary redundancy than you actually intend to make redundant, that it will be your choice as to who is offered redundancy. State that anyone who wants to apply for voluntary redundancy should do so in writing by a certain date.

Public meetings 7.16

It is your choice whether to have individual meetings with each candidate, or whether to hold an initial meeting en masse. If you choose the latter, make sure that you give everyone the opportunity to speak. Public meetings are not necessary, but they have the advantage that there is an undeniable record of consultation. The disadvantage is that these meetings have the potential to become confrontational and emotive. Even if you have a public meeting, you still ought to hold one-to-one consultation meetings with individual employees.

At the meeting(s), you must stay in control. Your employees will be concerned about their future. The more agitated they become, however, the more likely they are to develop a grudge and complain to an employment tribunal.

During the meeting(s), explain to your employees the reasons for deciding to make redundancies. Be candid with them – they are less likely to complain to an employment tribunal if they recognise you are telling the truth. If you have been able to find alternative employment (see **7.30**) then you must offer it (this should be confirmed in writing). If not, ask them if they have any suggestions.

You should tell your employees of the selection criteria you are intending to adopt and, if applicable, discuss their ratings with them – see **7.25** which discusses selection criteria and scores. Although in the past some tribunals have viewed this latter step as unnecessary, there is now a movement towards fuller consultation to the extent of giving employees the opportunity to comment on individual ratings. Further, some employees lodge complaints to the tribunal for no other reason than they want to know why they were selected for redundancy. If you tell them voluntarily, you may avert their claims. Do not, however, disclose or discuss anybody else's 'scores'.

Once you have held the consultation meetings, you will be able to take a decision on whom to select for redundancy. If your employees have made any sensible suggestions as to possible reorganisation of the business or re-employment for themselves, take these suggestions seriously. If you do not adopt them, ensure that you will be able to justify to a tribunal why you, as a reasonable employer, have not adopted suggestions that would enable you to avoid dismissals.

Individual meetings   7.17

You should also hold individual redundancy consultation meetings with all employees who you have provisionally selected for redundancy. At the meeting, you should:

- go through the reason for the redundancies (this should have already been explained in the letter);

- explain the selection criteria (if appropriate) and, if you have used a selection matrix (see **7.25** below), go through Fred's ratings;

- offer him the opportunity to comment on those ratings, or on his provisional selection. If he makes legitimate points on the ratings (for example, reminds you of a successful piece of work he did which warrants an overall higher rating than you initially gave), agree to adjust the rating;

- discuss with him whether there is any suitable alternative employment available for him in the company (see **7.29–7.43** below);

- ask him if there is anything else he would like to raise.

As always, make sure a full note is taken of the meeting: this is important evidence if he later brings a tribunal claim against you.

(iv) Is there ever an exception to the need to consult?   7.18

Until October 2004, there were two main exceptions to the need to consult – where consultation would be futile, and where delay would be fatal to the business. Both of these were difficult to establish and often resulted in tribunals saying the employer had acted unfairly.

The new position   7.19

Since October 2004, it has become mandatory to hold a meeting with the employee who is at risk of dismissal. Unless one of a small number of exceptions apply, a failure to hold a meeting will *probably* render a dismissal automatically unfair. The word 'probably' is used because the new legislation is not clear on whether a one-to-one meeting is required, or whether a group meeting is sufficient. It would be prudent to assume that a one-to-one meeting is required.

The exceptions to the need to hold a meeting are set out in **APPENDIX 1**. The three of most relevance to redundancy meetings are:

- where it is not practical to hold a meeting within a reasonable time, e.g. where the employee is on long-term sick leave;

- where the employer has reasonable grounds to fear the employee will be violent or damage property during a meeting; and

- where the employer's business suddenly ceases to function because of an unforeseen event, with the result that it is not practical for him to employ *any* employees. This exception is very narrowly drawn and will very rarely apply.

There is also an exception where the employer is dismissing more than 20 people for redundancy within a 90-day period; but, as stated earlier, you should take specialist legal advice in this situation as complex rules relating to consultation apply.

Reasons for a failure to consult   7.20

If in doubt, consult. The risk entailed in a failure to consult is considerable. Most employers who fail to consult do so for one of four reasons:

(a)   they are unaware of the need to consult and do not seek legal advice;

(b)   they find the entire process of consultation embarrassing, and want to avoid awkward confrontations with long-standing employees (who may also be friends). Imagine, though, the position if your roles were reversed. Would you prefer to have several weeks' warning of impending dismissal, and the opportunity to seek employment elsewhere? Or would you prefer to receive a letter one morning telling you that you need not report to work next Monday? Provided it is handled with tact, a sensible employee will be grateful for the consultation rather than resent you for it;

(c)   they hope it will not come to redundancies. But this avoids both legal and moral responsibility. Either redundancies will occur or they will not. If they do occur, you will have established your position up front and enabled yourself to dismiss your employees fairly. If they do not occur, you are no worse off for having undertaken a consultation exercise;

(d)   they think that none of their employees will claim against them. This is a dangerous assumption. The absence of warning and consultation will make an employee more, not less, likely to seek advice on their rights. A chat in a pub, followed by a visit to the local Citizens' Advice Bureau or a solicitor, will very rapidly start the ball rolling.

Advantages of consultation   7.21

There are two distinct advantages in warning your workforce of impending redundancies. First, every person who volunteers for redundancy is one less employee who may claim for unfair dismissal. Secondly, some employees might use the consultation period to search for employment elsewhere. If they find employment elsewhere, and resign to take it up before you have formally notified them that they have been selected for redundancy, they will be unable to claim unfair dismissal (since they will not have been dismissed, and thus cannot have been unfairly dismissed).

Consultation with a trade union 7.22

This section assumes that you recognise a trade union for the purpose of collective bargaining. If you do not, this section can be ignored.

If you are dismissing less than 20 employees within a period of 90 days then, provided you have fully consulted your employees, you can probably get by without consulting a trade union. If you are dismissing 20 or more employees within a period of 90 days, then special rules apply which fall outside the scope of this book. Consult a solicitor.

Nevertheless, if you do recognise a trade union, it will impress a tribunal if you have taken these additional steps since it will enhance your image as a reasonable employer.

There is another practical reason for consulting with a trade union. If the employees who belong to the union believe that they have been unfairly dismissed, they will seek help from the union. If the union perceives itself as having been snubbed or ignored by you, it is more likely to provide financial or legal assistance for claims against you.

The corollary of this is that if the trade union has been involved throughout, has been fairly consulted and any agreements have been honoured by you, it is far less likely to advise employees that they have a claim against you (or, indeed, to fund any such claims).

Communicating with the trade union 7.23

Write to the trade union at the same time as warning/consulting the employees. Explain the need for redundancies and invite a representative to a meeting to discuss whether there are any alternatives to redundancy, and how the selections for redundancy should take place (see **7.25**). Take their views into account, but do not forget that employment law requires consultation, not obedience. If you are able to agree selection criteria with the union, it is almost inconceivable that a tribunal will decide that the procedure is unfair.

Once you have agreed the selection criteria, the trade union should not be involved in applying the criteria. It is for you to assess employees and determine which ones are to be selected for redundancy. It is important to retain firm control over this – you must avoid any accusations of delegating the decision on who should be dismissed to somebody outside your organisation. In reality, few trade unions will want to be involved in the actual selection since it entails favouring some members over others.

Further, once you have applied the selection criteria and identified those to be made redundant, you should not reveal the employees' scores to the union. There can only be one reason for such a request – the union is fishing for evidence that you have, or have not, applied the criteria in a way which they would consider fair. There is no obligation on you to disclose this information. Do not fall into the trap of doing so.

Redundancy procedure – stage 2 – selection   7.24

You have identified the pool of potentially redundant employees. You have invited volunteers for redundancy, and may have had some responses. You are now in the position where you have to select a pre-determined number of people from a pre-determined pool. These people will be dismissed by you. Who do you choose?

There is no golden rule, other than the fact that in selecting people for redundancy you must use objective, rather than subjective, criteria. In other words, you must use criteria that can be judged objectively, such as length of service or frequency of absence, rather than criteria that depend largely on the views of the person doing the judging (such as friendliness to customers).

During the 1970s and 1980s, trade unions and employment tribunals regarded the vital (and, often, only) factor in redundancy selection as length of service. Redundancies would be fair only if the most junior people were dismissed before people with longer service records, irrespective of how good they were or the disadvantage of leaving a company with an older workforce and bereft of young talent. This principle is commonly known as 'LIFO' (which is an acronym for 'last in, first out'). An occasionally acceptable alternative was 'FIFO' ('first in, first out') which had precisely the opposite effect.

In the last decade, trade unions and tribunals have begun to appreciate that length of service should not be the conclusive factor in determining who is to be selected for redundancy. It can, however, remain an important factor. The reason for requiring an objective system of selection is to ensure that an employer does not use the excuse of redundancy to dismiss employees whom he would be unable to dismiss legally in more salubrious times.

Choosing the criteria for selection   7.25

If you have agreed selection criteria with a trade union, you should apply them to the pool of employees in the same way as if you had chosen the criteria yourself.

As stated above, the criteria must be objective. Provided that the criteria are objective, are reasonable (e.g. hair colour of employees, although objective, is not a reasonable factor to take into account in selecting for redundancy) and are applied in good faith a tribunal will uphold your selection.

It is common nowadays to use a combination of several criteria. A table can then be built up of employees' scores under the various criteria, and those with the lowest totals are the ones selected for redundancy. This is shown in the example below.

	Years of Service	Attendance Record	Technical Expertise	Disciplinary Record	Productivity	TOTAL
Fred	6	4	5	4	3	22
Jeremy	12	2	3	4	4	25
Catherine	6	5	5	5	2	23
Jennifer	2	4	1	4	4	15
Key: 5 Excellent 4 Good 3 Above average 2 Satisfactory/requires training 1 Unsatisfactory/requires training						

In this example, if it were necessary to select two of the pool of four for redundancy, Fred and Jennifer would be the two selected since they have the lowest total scores.

Simple and objectively fair selection   7.26

Theoretically, you can use as many criteria as you like and perform 'weighting' exercises (i.e. give more importance to some factors than others). This will not, however, impress a tribunal. A tribunal wants to see a simple, easily implemented and objectively fair method of selecting people for redundancy. A technical and convoluted scheme indicates too much forethought and may be interpreted as an attempt to fix the criteria so as to arrive at a pre-determined result.

Factors never to be used in selection   7.27

There are a number of factors that must not be used in selecting your employees for redundancy. If your decision to dismiss is caused by, or is based upon, any of certain prescribed reasons then it will be automatically unfair. The reasons are set out, at length, in the employment legislation but broadly fall into the following categories:

- involvement with health and safety matters;

- pregnancy, birth of a child or exercising rights to maternity leave (see **7.43** for the position if a woman otherwise selected for redundancy happens to be pregnant or on maternity leave);

- being unable to work due to incapacity arising out of the birth of a child;

- any allegation (including bringing proceedings) that you have infringed any of his/her rights conferred by the employment legislation (note: not all the employment legislation falls within this category – but even if you select somebody because they have asserted you infringed one of their non-protected rights, a tribunal is unlikely to consider this reasonable behaviour);

- any involvement in, or membership of, a trade union (or, likewise, non-membership of a trade union).

These reasons are set out in more detail at **18.2**. In addition, if the selection process has been influenced by any factor relating to gender, race, sexual orientation, disability, religion or belief, you may be found to have discriminated against some employees. Discrimination claims fall outside the scope of this book and you should seek legal advice before acting if you think there is potential for a discrimination claim.

Discuss scores with employees during consultation   7.28

The degree of consultation over selection will vary depending on the size of your business and the inevitability of dismissal. If you are going to be making all the pool candidates redundant, any consultation over the method of selection will not need to be as thorough as if you are making a small number of people from within the pool redundant (where the selection criteria, and the scores under those criteria, will be vital).

During the consultations with individual employees, you should tell them what their provisional scores are under the various headings. Invite their comments. If they have a good explanation for a low score, for example if their 'attendance' score is low due to a recent illness which is unlikely to recur, you should reconsider the provisional score in the light of their explanation. Keep careful notes of any comments made by the employees during these meetings. This will be evidence that you did consult properly and, just as importantly, will be evidence of what was (and thus what was not) raised by the employees during the consultation. When assessing scores for attendance, you should disregard any absences arising from a female employee's pregnancy (i.e. maternity leave and pregnancy-related sickness absences).

Redundancy procedure – stage 3 – alternative employment
7.29

After the selection stage you should have established the identity of those to be made redundant, whether by reason of selecting the whole pool (as when you are closing down a location) or because you have drawn up a table and chosen those with the lowest scores. The final stage is to consider alternative employment for each of those employees.

Consider alternative employment
7.30

No matter how fair your selection and consultation procedures may be, an employment tribunal is likely to find a dismissal to be unfair if you have not considered whether you can redeploy any of your redundant employees. This requirement is justified on the basis that a reasonable employer would not dismiss an employee due to redundancy if he can redeploy him elsewhere. The need to consider alternative employment is mandatory even for small business (although, in such cases, there will usually be no possible alternative employment available).

What alternative employment must you consider?
7.31

Do not fall into the trap of thinking that employment is not suitable because it entails a demotion or a reduction in wages. If there is any position, unless manifestly unsuitable, which Fred would be reasonably capable of doing, you should offer it to him. He may reject it – but it should be his decision and not yours. If you decide that a job is available, but you do not think Fred has the necessary attributes to fulfil it, make a note as to why he is not suitable and keep the note on his personnel file.

In addition to determining whether there are any alternative positions at your company, you must also take steps to ascertain whether there is any available employment at any associated companies. This means you should contact any subsidiaries or parent companies, as well as any other subsidiary of your parent companies and ask them to investigate whether they have any suitable positions available. If they do not respond to you, ensure that you chase them up (and keep a record of doing so) so that you can establish that your original request was not simply a sham.

If a job is available which Fred is capable of doing, you must offer it to him. This is for four reasons:

- if suitable employment is available and you do not offer it to him, the dismissal will be unfair;

- if he accepts the job, you will not have to pay him a redundancy payment;

- if he unreasonably refuses a suitable job, you are not obliged to pay him a redundancy payment (see **7.39**);

- if he does not accept the job and claims unfair dismissal, the fact you have offered him alternative employment will assist your case and, in any event, may reduce any award he receives if the dismissal is found to be unfair (see **13.15**).

If the individual is disabled within the meaning of the *Disability Discrimination Act 1995*, you are under an obligation to give him/her priority over other suitable candidates when considering who should be offered alternative employment (see **2.29**). Also, if the redundant employee is a woman who has been absent on maternity leave, then she is entitled to 'trump' all other employees and be offered any available suitable alternative employment at the date she otherwise would have returned to work following the end of her maternity leave.

If no alternative employment can be found   7.32

Do not merely consider alternative positions for Fred. Also ensure that you have a contemporaneous record of doing so. The best way to do this is to combine it with consultation (which is also an ingredient in making the redundancy dismissal fair). Write to Fred in the following terms:

- that, further to (your meeting on [date]) or (your letter dated [date]), you regret to inform him that he has been selected for redundancy;

- you have reviewed the position within the company and, after full consideration, are sorry to say that there are no suitable alternative vacancies available for him. If you have contacted associated employers, state this, identify the companies you have contacted and state that your efforts have not been successful;

- that if he has any suggestions as to possible redeployment, or if he is aware of any vacancies elsewhere that you could recommend him for, that he should contact you as soon as possible;

- alternatively, if he would like to meet to discuss the situation further, he should contact you to arrange a convenient time (if you have not already invited him to a meeting under **7.17**, you should make this a clear invitation to a meeting and suggest a date and time);

- that you will continue reviewing the possibility of alternative employment; however, if nothing comes available, that his last day of work will be [date]. This will normally be at least his notice period away (see **12.11**) – otherwise you will have to pay him in lieu of notice;

- that he has a right to appeal against your decision. If he wants to appeal, he should write to you, setting out the reasons, within (say) seven days. See **CHAPTER 11** on internal appeals.

You should also give details in this letter as to how his redundancy pay will be calculated. This is discussed further at **12.17**.

Consider suggestions   7.33

If Fred does make any suggestions, you must consider them carefully. If his suggestion is impracticable, write to him and explain your reasons for rejecting it. If he has suggested another position within your company and you are unsure as to his suitability, you may wish to consider employing him on a trial basis. The failure to try Fred in a position which he may be suitable for might make an otherwise fair dismissal unfair.

Once Fred's employment has terminated, assuming you have been unable to find any alternative employment, you should pay him his full redundancy entitlement together with any contractual redundancy entitlement or pay in lieu of notice (if appropriate). Err on the side of caution and overpay, rather than underpay in borderline cases, to avoid unnecessary grievances.

If alternative employment is found   7.34

If you have managed to find alternative employment for Fred then, unless the job is essentially the same as he was already doing (which might be the case if you have closed down one place of work and moved Fred to a nearby location to do the same job), he is legally entitled to a four-week trial period during which his right to a redundancy payment is unaffected.

You should write to Fred in the following terms:

- that, further to (your meeting dated [date]) or (your letter dated [date]), you regret to inform him that he has been selected for redundancy;

- you are able to offer him alternative employment within the company (or with an associated company – state its name). State the job title and description, the salary and any other relevant details. If you have a written job description or contract of employment, enclose it with your letter.

- inform him of the date that his existing job will disappear. This will often be at least his notice period away (see **12.11**), otherwise you may have to pay him in lieu of notice if he does not take up the new job;

- tell him of the start date for his new job. This must be within four weeks of the old job finishing, although if the old job finishes on a Friday, Saturday or Sunday then you are entitled to an extension until four weeks on the following Monday. Note that you need not pay him during these four weeks;

- that he is entitled to a four-week trial period in order to decide whether the new job is suitable;

- ask him to confirm in writing, within seven days, that he will accept the new job. If he does not do so, you should speak to him and get him to write out, in your presence, an acceptance or a rejection of the new job (subject to the trial period).

Do not try to make the job offer conditional on not having a four-week trial period. This will render the alternative employment unsuitable (since it deprives Fred of a right to which he is legally entitled) and will make the dismissal unfair.

If the job is not accepted 7.35

If Fred does not accept the job, you should continue searching for alternative employment for him until he is dismissed. You may not, however, be obliged to pay him a redundancy payment if he has unreasonably refused suitable employment. This is discussed further at **7.39**.

Make sure that you do actually offer Fred any alternative position, even if he has told you in advance that he will not accept any further employment with you. If you fail to make a specific job offer, there will be no offer of employment that Fred has unreasonably refused. Accordingly you will still have to pay a redundancy payment.

The trial period 7.36

Fred is entitled to a four-week trial period in which to assess his new job, unless the new job is identical, for all practical purposes, to the old one. If, during this four-week period, he decides that he does not want to continue with the new job, he is entitled to resign and will be deemed, legally, to be in exactly the same position as if you had offered him the new job after he was selected for redundancy and he had not accepted it.

If Fred resigns after the four-week trial period, then the resignation will be deemed to be an ordinary resignation and he will not be entitled to a redundancy payment. Further, unless he can bring himself within the rules for constructive dismissal (see **17.2**), he will have resigned in the ordinary way, thus not have been dismissed and will be unable to claim unfair dismissal.

The four-week trial period means four calendar weeks, rather than four working weeks. Accordingly if your place of work closes for a week, this will not suspend the running of time for the purpose of calculating the four week trial period.

Example

> An employee was made redundant. His trial period for his alternative employment started on 21 December 1986. His workplace closed for seven days over Christmas. He resigned on 19 January 1987. The tribunal held that the four-week period continued to run over Christmas, even though the workplace was closed, and thus it had expired on 18 January 1987. The employee's resignation was therefore one day outside his four-week trial period and he was not entitled to a redundancy payment
> – *Benton v Sanderson Kayser Ltd [1989] ICR 136.*

Extending the trial period   7.37

It is possible to extend the four-week trial period. This can only be done by agreement in writing before Fred starts work in the new position, and it can only be done if the purpose of the extension is to allow time for retraining Fred. The agreement must also specify the terms and conditions of employment that will apply if Fred stays on after the trial period. Unless these conditions are complied with, the extension of time will not be valid and Fred will lose his right to a redundancy payment. It is apparent that there is little incentive for an employer to suggest, or agree to, such an extension.

Continuity of employment   7.38

If Fred remains in employment after the trial period, he is deemed for all practical purposes never to have been dismissed (even if there was a break in his employment of up to the permitted four weeks between the old job and the new job). In particular, his length of employment will not be re-set to zero by the new job, but will continue as if uninterrupted, for the purpose of establishing whether Fred has been working for one year (so as to gain employment rights) if you try to dismiss him in the future.

Unreasonable refusal of suitable alternative employment   7.39

If Fred declines the new position, whether during his trial period or when the job is first offered to him, then the termination of his employment is still regarded as being caused by the redundancy (rather than by his refusal to take up the new job).

However, Fred may disentitle himself to a redundancy payment if two criteria apply. These criteria are:

- that the alternative employment offered was suitable for him; and,

- that his failure to accept it was unreasonable.

If this exception applies, Fred will not be entitled to any redundancy payment (although he may still be entitled to pay in lieu of notice if you did not give him sufficient notice when telling him of his final day of work – see **12.11**).

If your redundancy selection was fair, then the fact that you rely on this exception to avoid making a redundancy payment will not make an otherwise fair dismissal unfair. If you withhold a redundancy payment on the basis that Fred has unreasonably refused a suitable job offer, this is not something which goes towards the fairness or unfairness of the dismissal. The worst that can happen if, in reality, you are not entitled to withhold payment is that Fred will successfully claim against you in the employment tribunal for the redundancy payment that you would have paid him anyway. In such circumstances, you will be no worse off.

There is a certain amount of overlap between the above two criteria – some factors will be relevant both to the suitability of the new job and whether Fred is acting unreasonably in declining it. However, tribunals will address the two criteria separately, and so it is sensible to deal with them in a similar way.

Suitability of alternative employment 7.40

Employment will be 'suitable' for Fred if, objectively, it is similar in terms of pay, duties, hours, responsibility and status. Note that the new job does not have to be 'equal' to the old one in order for it to be suitable. The pay can be slightly lower, the responsibility slightly less. The basic test is that the overall package must be appropriate for somebody of Fred's skills, abilities and working history.

Examples

Headmaster, with many years of experience, offered a job in a mobile pool of teachers with his pay frozen at his current level. The drop in status made the new job 'quite unsuitable' – *Taylor v Kent County Council [1969] 2 QB 560.*

Nightworkers offered double-day shiftwork. This was held to be unsuitable – *Morrison & Poole v Ceramic Engineering Co Ltd [1966] 1 ITR 404.*

Old job had compulsory overtime; the new job had no overtime. This was held to be unsuitable – *O'Connor v Montrose Canned Foods Ltd [1966] 1 ITR 171.*

Employee required to move from Bournemouth to Bristol, but was given an increased salary to compensate. This was held to be suitable – *Gotch v Guest [1966] 1 ITR 65.*

Additional daily journey time of between one and four hours depending on traffic held to be unsuitable – *Bass Leisure Ltd v Thomas [1994] IRLR 104.*

Note that the number of jobs you offer to Fred is immaterial – suitability is concerned with quality of alternative employment, and not with the quantity of jobs offered.

Unreasonable refusal of suitable employment   7.41

If you consider that the employment was suitable for Fred, the next step is to decide whether he acted reasonably or unreasonably in refusing it. This is a subjective test – i.e. the question is whether Fred himself is acting reasonably, not a hypothetical employee. The factors here will often be more personal and, indeed, you may sometimes be unaware of the factors which cause Fred to decline a new job. However, as mentioned above, if you do withhold his redundancy payment, the worst that can happen is that a tribunal orders you to pay it. It will not result in a finding of unfair dismissal against you.

The main factors which will be taken into account are the following:

- *other employment*: if Fred has already obtained another job, particularly if there has been delay before your offer of alternative employment was made, he will usually not be acting unreasonably in declining your alternative job offer;

- *hours*: if the new job entails a fundamental change of hours, such as moving to a night-shift, it is likely to be reasonable to refuse it;

- *location*: if the new job entails moving to a new part of the country, it will probably be reasonable to refuse;

- *genuineness of offer*: if Fred has genuine grounds for believing that your offer is a sham, designed to prevent him claiming a redundancy payment, or if he reasonably believes that your company is in dire financial straits and may be unable to pay him, he may be reasonable in declining the new job.

Examples

Employee had been employed for five years in Newcastle. He had two children at the local schools, one of whom was about to sit GCE exams and the other the 11-plus. He was offered a three-year contract in Glasgow, to be followed by a job in Leeds. It was held that his refusal to move was reasonable – *Bainbridge v Westinghouse Brake and Signal Co Ltd [1966] 1 ITR 89*.

Offer of new position made at 3.30pm on Friday, but not confirmed in writing until 9.00am Monday. An answer was required by 10.30am on Monday and, at 11.30am, the position was given to somebody else. It was held that the refusal was reasonable – *Barratt v Thomas Glover & Co. Ltd [1970] 5 ITR 95*.

Firm moved from Essex to Devon. The employment offered might not have been suitable, but the employee refused even to go and inspect the new location (without giving any proper explanation). It was held that the refusal was unreasonable – *Douce v F Bond & Sons Ltd [1966] 1 ITR 365*.

Starting to recruit again 7.42

Redundancy dismissals only occur, in general, when you need to reduce the size of the workforce. This is inconsistent with recruiting from outside to fill positions (unless the new jobs are of a different nature from those from which you are dismissing people, and could not reasonably be considered suitable alternative employment).

If you are justifying a redundancy dismissal to an employment tribunal, a question you are almost guaranteed to be asked is whether you replaced Fred or whether you recruited anybody else to fill any new positions. If you have replaced Fred, you will have great difficulty persuading the tribunal that the strict definition of redundancy applies (see **7.3**) and you are highly likely to be found to have unfairly dismissed Fred.

As a rule of thumb, you should not replace Fred for at least three months – preferably six. If you do decide to re-open his job, you should offer the job first of all to Fred. If you do not do so, a tribunal is likely to draw the inference that the entire redundancy procedure has been a sham, and that you had a concealed reason for dismissing Fred which you dressed up as a redundancy situation. Although Fred normally has to bring an unfair dismissal claim within three months of being dismissed, there are two exceptions when a tribunal will let him have a longer period. These are:

● if he reasonably believes, on the day the three months expires, that you are still following a dismissal procedure (which normally means if he reasonably believes you are still dealing with his appeal) – in which case, he has an extra three months (six in total) to bring his claim; or

- if it was not reasonably practicable to bring a claim before he became aware of the replacement.

Extensions of time for bringing unfair dismissal claims are discussed in more detail at **18.9**.

A special case: women on maternity leave   7.43

Employers are understandably cautious about dismissing women who are absent on maternity leave, as it always involves the risk of a claim for sex discrimination and perhaps even adverse publicity.

There is no rule that says a woman on maternity leave cannot be selected for redundancy. Inevitably, a tribunal will be particularly concerned to check that your selection criteria are genuine and were properly applied. In other words, a tribunal will want to be satisfied that you have not tweaked the selection criteria, or the scores awarded under those criteria, to engineer the dismissal of a woman on maternity leave *because* of her maternity absence. But provided you are confident you can justify the scores you apply to the woman, then you should not feel as though you cannot dismiss a woman on maternity leave.

Be cautious, though, if the woman is the *only* employee who is being made redundant. In that situation, tribunals will be sceptical about whether you have invented a claim to a redundancy situation as a sham, to dismiss the employee. They will want to examine whether you have absorbed her duties amongst other employees, and whether you have subsequently recruited to cope with the additional work caused by increasing others' workloads.

If using 'attendance' as a factor in selection, you must disregard the effect of the woman's maternity absence (and absence because of pregnancy-related sickness). The best way to do this is to look at the 12 months (or whatever period you use) *before* she commenced her maternity leave and, when writing to her to warn her of potential selection for redundancy (or at the meeting, if she attends), going through any absences whilst pregnant and asking her if they were pregnancy related. If they were pregnancy related, ignore them.

Finally, there is a special rule relating to the offer of suitable alternative employment. Employers should look at alternative employment for women on maternity leave *both* at the date of the redundancy process (as with other employees) *and also* at the date she would have been due to return to work at the end of her maternity leave. If there are any suitable vacancies available at the date she would have been due to return to work – even if this is months after the redundancy process, she *must* be offered that job. In other words, a woman due to return from maternity leave trumps other employees when it comes to being offered a suitable vacancy, even if they may be better suited to the job than her.

Chapter 8
Business Reorganisation/Changing Employment Conditions

Introduction 8.1

When reorganising your business, you may wish to make changes to Fred's duties or terms and conditions of employment. The most common changes include reducing his pay, changing his working hours, introducing confidentiality or non-competition clauses or changes to job title.

Bear in mind that there is a close overlap between business reorganisations and redundancies. You are advised to consider **CHAPTER 7** to ensure that what you propose to do does not fall within the definition of redundancy.

Legally, you are not entitled to make any changes to Fred's terms and conditions of employment unless he agrees. A contract of employment cannot be changed by you alone, just as Fred cannot change it alone (for example, awarding himself a pay rise). If you therefore make changes, or threaten to make changes, to Fred's contract of employment, he is entitled to resign and claim constructive dismissal.

Having a claim of constructive dismissal brought against you is not fatal – if you have acted fairly and it is necessary in your business's interests to make the changes to Fred's terms and conditions of employment, then the constructive dismissal should be found to be fair. Constructive dismissal, as a general concept, is considered at **17.2**.

Fair dismissal, actual or constructive 8.2

In order for a dismissal (whether actual or constructive) to be fair, you must establish that the reason for the dismissal is either capability (**CHAPTER 2**), conduct (**CHAPTERS 3** to **6**), redundancy (**CHAPTER 7**), contravention of a statutory provision (**10.3**) or 'some other substantial reason'(*Employment Rights*

Act 1996, s 98). Changes to Fred's terms and conditions of employment because of business reorganisations, are capable of amounting to 'some other substantial reason'.

Correct procedure 8.3

Ideally, you should make the change to Fred's terms and conditions by obtaining his consent. Provided that there is a formal agreement between you, it will be binding on him and he will not be entitled to resign and complain about it later. The agreement need not be in writing (although it is prudent to record it in writing).

Alternatively, if Fred declines to consent, you may have to implement the change by delivering an ultimatum. If Fred then refuses to agree, you can dismiss him (provided you go through the correct procedure). If he resigns and claims constructive dismissal, you will have a defence to the claim.

Obtaining consent to the change 8.4

Ideally, you should try to obtain Fred's consent to the change. A mere acquiescence is insufficient: you need to show that you have provided 'consideration' for Fred's agreement to the change. The 'consideration' can take the form of a nominal pay rise, a slight reduction in working hours, an increase in holiday entitlement or even you giving up some of the original changes you were pressing for. In essence, it has to be something to Fred's benefit or your detriment.

Because of the need to provide consideration when obtaining Fred's consent to a change in his terms and conditions, it is common practice to combine the changes with an annual or half-annual salary review. Employees do not have an entitlement to a salary increase each year (although if you give everyone else a salary increase but not Fred, he may claim constructive dismissal on the grounds that you are treating him arbitrarily and unfairly).

If you are able to combine the change to his terms and conditions with a salary increase, you should write to him in the following terms:

- that you are making a number of changes to the organisation of your business, and that you wish to make the following changes to his terms and conditions of employment. Set out the change carefully – if you are introducing a non-competition or confidentiality clause, ensure the text of the clause is set out;

- that you seek his consent to the change. If he accepts the change, you propose to increase his salary to £x or increase his holiday entitlement to y days per year. It is not anticipated that there will be any other salary increases in the next year;

- if he accepts the change, sign and return a copy of the letter. The salary increase will take effect from date.

If Fred does sign the letter, you will have covered yourself and he will be unable to complain of the changes at a later date.

If Fred is unwilling to consent   8.5

If the job involves a pay cut or a loss of prestige, Fred may be unwilling to consent to the changes. In that case, you have to impose the changes upon him. Provided this is done in a fair manner, and provided you can establish a sound, good business reason for imposing the change, you will be able to satisfy the tribunal that the dismissal was fair if Fred resigns and claims constructive dismissal.

Imposing the changes   8.6

If Fred will not consent to the changes, or your business is in financial difficulties and you cannot afford to offer Fred a pay-rise or increased holidays, you may need to impose the changes to his terms and conditions of employment upon him.

When can you impose changes?   8.7

You cannot impose changes on Fred just because you feel like it. You need to be able to establish that there is a 'sound, good business reason' for the change.

Example

> A small number of secretaries employed by the National Farmers' Union received commission as well as a normal salary. This caused tension because they believed their overall package was less than other secretaries employed by the NFU. Accordingly the NFU decided to end the commission element and brought their salary structures into line with other secretaries. The Court of Appeal held there had been a sound, good business reason for this reorganisation, and the dismissal of Mr Hollister (who had refused to sign the new contract) was fair – *Hollister v National Farmers' Union [1979] IRLR 238.*

You do not need to establish that your business is on the edge of insolvency and that it will collapse if the changes are not made. You do, however, need to show that there is a good reason for adversely affecting Fred's rights – merely increasing business profitability on an already profitable business is unlikely to be enough, particularly if the changes to Fred's contract involve a financial detriment to him.

In essence, the more detrimental the changes are to Fred, the more fundamental the business justification must be. By contrast, when the proposed changes do not act to Fred's financial detriment (such as changing, without increasing, the hours worked), it will be easier to justify them. It will also be easier to justify changes if other employees have agreed to them (which is why it is important to seek consent before trying to impose the changes).

If the changes involve increased working hours for Fred, you may have difficulty persuading a tribunal that you are acting fairly unless you offer Fred a *pro rata* wage increase.

Bear in mind that an assertion by you that you have a sound, good business reason for the changes to Fred's contract will not be enough. You will need to provide evidence to satisfy the tribunal – this might take the form of accounts, business plans, profitability projections or management consultant appraisals.

Examples

An employee's contract stated he had to work during day-time hours. He was asked to work a night-shift one week in six and refused. The tribunal thought that there was a proper reason for the change and held the dismissal to be fair – *Knighton v Henry Rhodes Ltd [1974] IRLR 71.*

Ms Moreton worked during school term-time only. She was asked, and given 12 months' notice, to work during school holidays as well as during term-time since it was necessary for her employer's business. She refused. The tribunal held that there was a fair business reorganisation, thus Ms Moreton's claim for unfair dismissal failed – *Moreton v Selby Protective Clothing [1974] IRLR 269.*

Imposing the changes   8.8

Provided you can justify the business reasons for the changes, there is no real procedure that you need to go through when imposing the changes on Fred. You should write to him in the following terms:

• that further to your last letter, you note that he has not responded. If you have sought to introduce changes for other employees, and they agreed, state this (although do not mention any other employees by name);

122

- despite the fact that he has not replied, you consider it necessary for business reasons to introduce the changes to his terms and conditions. Set out the precise changes you are proposing again;

- if you offered a pay rise, or other benefits, state that you intend to stand by the additional benefits you were previously offering to him;

- the proposed changes will apply from date;

- invite Fred to a meeting to discuss the reasons for, or the effect of, the changes.

What happens next 8.9

What happens next is up to Fred. He can do one of three things, namely:

(i)   comply with the changes;

(ii) continue working but refuse to comply with the changes; or

(iii) resign.

(i) Fred complies with the changes 8.10

If he complies with the changes, your problem is solved. Ask him to sign a sheet of paper, or a new statement of terms and conditions of employment, which reflects these changes.

(ii) Fred continues working but refuses to comply 8.11

If he continues working, but refuses to comply with the changes, you are entitled to dismiss him whilst simultaneously offering him a new job on the new terms and conditions. Provided you can establish a good, sound business reason for the changes, a tribunal will rule such a dismissal to be fair. The procedure to adopt should be similar to that set out in **CHAPTER 6** (dismissing for refusing to obey instructions).

(iii) Fred resigns 8.12

If he resigns, claiming constructive dismissal, then you should succeed at a tribunal (provided you can establish a sound, good business reason for the changes), arguing *either* that he was not constructively dismissed (in other words, that he jumped before he was pushed) *or* that the constructive dismissal was fair, for the reasons discussed above. From October 2004, employees are (normally) unable to claim constructive dismissal unless they have sent you a written grievance and allowed 28 days to elapse before issuing a tribunal claim.

Chapter 9
Dismissing when Taking Over a Business or Contract

Introduction 9.1

Like redundancies, this is an area of law that is fraught with hazard. The rules relating to dismissing employees when you take over a business are governed by a European Directive which was incorporated into English Law by the *Transfer of Undertakings (Protection of Employment) Regulations 1981 (SI 1981 No 1794)* – commonly known by its acronym as 'TUPE'. These Regulations have generated more appeals and more complexity than any other area of employment law.

TUPE is due to be updated shortly, but the DTI has not (at the date of writing in September 2004) published the new rules.

If you are taking over a business which employs more than a small number of people (say, over 2 or 3 employees), and you are considering dismissing them or changing their terms and conditions of employment, it is highly recommended that you seek advice from a specialist employment solicitor. This chapter can do no more than set out when complex issues of employment law are likely to arise. It deals with two separate situations, namely:

- dismissing employees when buying a business; and
- dismissing employees when taking over a contract.

Both of these scenarios may be governed by the rules contained in TUPE. Before turning to the practical steps to take in these situations to minimise liabilities or dismiss employees, it is sensible to consider an overview of the law relating to transfers of businesses or contracts.

Overview of TUPE 9.2

In essence, TUPE provides that where an 'undertaking' (see **9.3** below) is transferred from one business to another, all of the employees formerly employed by the first company are automatically transferred along with the undertaking, so that they become employed by the second company. If either the first or the second company tries to dismiss them because of the transfer, the dismissal will automatically be unfair (except in particular circumstances, namely where there is an economic, technical or organisational reason for the dismissal).

In addition, after the transfer the employees remain employed on the same terms and conditions as before the transfer. Accordingly, the new company cannot change the employees' contract of employment (including their hours or pay). If they do, the employees are entitled to resign and, subject to lodging a formal grievance and waiting 28 days, claim constructive dismissal.

The effect of TUPE is that when you buy a business, or take over a contract, you may often find yourself legally responsible for all the employees who worked for that old business or on that contract.

What is an 'undertaking'? 9.3

The *TUPE Regulations* only apply to transfers of 'undertakings'. The courts are constantly changing their minds on what is meant by an 'undertaking'. There are no hard and fast rules – simply a number of indicators – and it quite conceivable that one employment tribunal would consider a certain takeover to include an 'undertaking', whereas on the same facts another tribunal would not consider there to have been a transfer of an 'undertaking'.

Essentially, for there to be an 'undertaking' there has to be a recognisable economic entity transferred. If you buy a high-street printing shop – purchasing the premises, the machinery, the stock, the name and the goodwill – you would have purchased an entire economic entity. Accordingly TUPE will apply and all of the printing shop's employees will automatically transfer to your employment. If you dismiss any of them (which, since they have been automatically transferred to you, includes not providing them with work and a salary), you are deemed to have automatically unfairly dismissed them (unless you can bring yourself within the defence at paragraph **9.6**).

Very frequently, however, it is not clear cut as to whether there has been a purchase (or transfer) of an economic entity. The core question is whether the business remains the same business, but in different hands. The following factors are often considered by tribunals in deciding whether an undertaking has been transferred:

- whether you carry on business in the same manner as before;

- whether there has been an assignment of goodwill or book debts;

- whether there has been an assignment of stock;
- whether you have taken over the old business's premises or trading name;
- whether you have taken over outstanding contracts/work in progress/customers;
- whether you are taking on a significant number of staff from the old employer.

If the answer to any one of these questions is 'yes', there is a risk that a tribunal will find that a transfer of undertakings has occurred. If the answer to more than two or three of the questions is 'yes', it is likely that a tribunal will find that a transfer of undertakings has occurred.

TUPE can apply to contracts as well as whole businesses

9.4

It is not necessary for you to take over an entire business for TUPE to apply. If you take over a contract, and the contract forms an economic entity in its own right (by being a separately identifiable part of the seller's business), then TUPE may apply and you may find yourself liable for all the employees that the seller employed to deal with the contract.

Example

A health authority contracted out cleaning services to company A. When the contract was re-tendered, company A lost the cleaning contract and company B won it. Many of the employees of company A were taken on by company B, which had provided its own cleaning equipment, management and materials. The Court of Appeal held that there was a transfer of undertakings, since the provision of cleaning services amounted to a separate undertaking in its own right. Since company B had reduced the wages of the cleaners it took on, they claimed constructive dismissal and were held to have been unfairly dismissed – *Dines v Initial Healthcare Services [1995] ICR 11.*

Note that for TUPE to apply, there must be a specific undertaking which transfers. It is unlikely that the transfer of a short-term, one-off contract, as contrasted with a longer-term contract involving a series of activities (such as an annual cleaning contract), would be sufficient to amount to a TUPE transfer. Thus if you run a printing shop and take over one of a competitor's contracts, or even one of a competitor's main clients, but the contract/client does not form an separate economic entity for your competitor in its own right, the TUPE rules are unlikely to apply and you will not be obliged to take on any of his employees.

What happens when TUPE applies? 9.5

When TUPE applies, all the employees who had been employed by the seller/previous contractor are automatically transferred into your employment. If you fail to provide work, you are deemed to have dismissed them. If you change any of their terms and conditions of employment, including pay, they are entitled to resign and claim constructive dismissal. If you dismiss any of them, whether directly or constructively, any such dismissal is automatically unfair if the transfer is the reason (or principal reason) for the dismissal. Justifications such as redundancy, capability or conduct do not apply if the true reason for the dismissal is the transfer.

It is only those employees 'assigned to' the transferring contract/business who are deemed to become your employees. Usually it will be clear which employees are assigned to a contract; however, sometimes difficulties occur if a particular employee divides his time equally between two contracts, or is on a temporary assignment.

Example

> Mr Bademosi worked as a security guard for 21 years at a site owned by Cable & Wireless. For a period of one year, he was transferred to work at a magistrates' court. A month before he was due to return to the Cable & Wireless site, his employers lost the contract to provide security services at the magistrates' court. The question was whether Mr Bademosi was 'assigned to' the magistrates' court contract. The Employment Appeal Tribunal stated that, looking at the global picture – rather than the moment in time when the TUPE transfer occurred – he was *not* assigned to the magistrates' court and therefore his employment did not transfer under TUPE – *Securiplan v Bademosi (EAT/1128/02).*

Exception to the TUPE rules: economic, technical or organisational reason 9.6

There is one defence to the dismissal being automatically unfair. If you can establish that the dismissal was for an 'economic, technical or organisational reason entailing changes in the workforce' (*regulation 8(2)* of the *TUPE Regulations*), then the dismissal will be potentially fair provided you can show that you have gone through a proper procedure of consultation and consideration as to who should be dismissed. This is a very useful exception to the TUPE rules and should be carefully investigated to see if an economic, technical or organisational reason can apply.

What is an economic, technical or organisational reason?   9.7

There are no real guidelines as to what amounts to an economic, technical or organisational reason: however, the words are ordinary words and are treated as bearing an ordinary meaning. It is unlikely to be enough to dismiss somebody for 'economic' reasons because it would increase the profitability of your business – this would apply to most transferred employees and would destroy the purpose of TUPE. Instead, you would probably need to establish some fundamental business need, perhaps falling short of a risk of insolvency but going beyond mere convenience.

It is important to note that the 'economic, technical or organisational reason' must be one which entails a change in the workforce. The reason must be one which requires change in the numbers of, or nature of, the workforce. If there are technical reasons for no longer employing Fred, but the reasons do not entail a change in the workforce, then this defence will not apply.

Example

> Mrs Green was employed as a manager of a care home. The care home was sold to a new owner, Mr Elan. Mr Elan decided to take over Mrs Green's job, but there was no overall reduction in the number of employees. Mrs Green argued her dismissal was unfair, because there was no 'economic, technical or organisational reason entailing a change in the workforce'. The Employment Appeal Tribunal disagreed: there was a change in the *structure* of the workforce (i.e. introducing an owner/ manager), even if the total number of employees remained the same. Accordingly, Mrs Green failed in her claim of unfair dismissal – *Green v Elan Care Limited, unreported, EAT 4/3/02.*

Final point to note   9.8

You cannot avoid the effect of TUPE by requiring the seller of the business to make redundant or dismiss employees for other reasons prior to the transfer. The courts have said that any dismissal in anticipation of such a transfer is void, and the employees will still transfer over to your employment. As a result, you will be liable for their automatic unfair dismissal.

Example

> One hour before a business transfer, all the staff were dismissed by the insolvent vendor (and told they would not receive any notice pay or

outstanding holiday pay). Immediately after the sale, the new owner began hiring (different) replacement employees. The House of Lords held that the *TUPE Regulations* applied to employees who were unfairly dismissed immediately before the transfer in an attempt to avoid the Regulations – thus all the dismissed staff's employments transferred to the new business owner and they could sue the new business for unfair dismissal – *Litster v Dry Forth Dock and Engineering Co Ltd [1989] IRLR 161.*

Dismissing employees when buying a business 9.9

There are two methods of buying a business:

(a) purchasing the shares of the company, so that the company remains the same but you become the new owner. This can only be done with limited companies: if you are buying a firm or a sole trader's business, you can only use method (b) below;

(b) purchasing the assets and liabilities of the business but, if it is a company, not the company itself.

Method (a): Buying a company by purchasing its shares 9.10

When you buy the shares of a company, there is no transfer of undertaking. Legally, there has not been any transfer of an economic entity – the business was there in its existing form before you purchased the shares, and it remains in the same form after you have purchased the shares.

Accordingly, TUPE does not apply. You do not need to worry about dismissals being automatically unfair, or about establishing an economic, technical or organisational reason for the dismissal.

However, the fact that you have purchased the shares of a company does not give you an immunity from general unfair dismissal law. The normal rules apply, namely that you have to have a valid reason for dismissal and have to act reasonably. You will therefore need to come within one of the other reasons for dismissal such as capability, conduct, business reorganisation or redundancy, and follow the dismissal procedures set out in those chapters.

Method (b): Purchasing the assets and liabilities of a business   9.11

When you purchase the assets and liabilities of a business, and take over its goodwill, there will almost always be a transfer of an undertaking. In this situation, any dismissals caused because of the takeover will be automatically unfair unless you can establish an economic, technical or organisational reason for the dismissal entailing a change in the workforce.

Hint

> When negotiating the purchase, if you do not want to take on certain employees, see if you can negotiate an indemnity or contribution from the seller in case you are found to have unfairly dismissed them. Any such indemnity should be backed up by personal guarantee otherwise, since you are taking all the assets of the business, the seller may have no assets against which to enforce an indemnity.

Either way, TUPE applies   9.12

Presumably, prior to purchasing the assets and liabilities of the company, you will have formed an idea as to which members of staff you wish to retain and which you wish to dismiss. Note that this chapter gives guidance as to an appropriate procedure to adopt for dismissing employees fairly provided you can establish an economic, technical or organisational reason for doing so. There is no method of avoiding the protection that employees receive as the result of TUPE: i.e. you must still persuade a tribunal that there was a genuine economic, technical or organisational reason warranting the dismissals. If you cannot satisfy this requirement, you will be found to have unfairly dismissed those employees you have not kept on.

Step 1: Identify the changes you need to make in the workforce   9.13

A tribunal will not be impressed if you try to persuade employees that their employment has not transferred to you. If you deny that Fred has become your employee when you take over the business he used to work for, it will be extremely difficult to persuade a tribunal later that you have acted fairly even if you can establish an appropriate economic, technical or organisational reason.

This is not to say that you should admit that Fred's employment has transferred to you if you are unsure that it has, since in such circumstances you may well be found to have voluntarily employed Fred. If the position is not clear, you should consult a solicitor specialising in employment law.

Letter to employees 9.14

The first thing to do, therefore, is write to all employees who were employed by the old business. This can be done after contracts are signed but before the date of the takeover. Your letter should state the following:

- their old employer has sold the business to you. State your full name (or the name of your firm/company) and, if a company, your registered address;

- the date on which the transfer will happen and that, from that date, they will all be employed by you;

- their terms and conditions of employment will remain the same after the transfer of employment;

- any employee is entitled to object to their employment being transferred. If they do object, they should contact you in writing. Note that there is no obligation to tell an employee of his right to object; however, if any employee does object, his employment will not be transferred and thus you cannot be found to have unfairly dismissed him. It is not necessary that his objection be in writing: however, if the objection is verbal only it may cause difficulties if he subsequently denies having objected to the transfer;

- as a result of the transfer, some organisational changes are going to be made to the company. Set out in one or two sentences the reasons for the changes (fuller reasons will come later). State that it is possible/probable that some jobs are going to be lost;

- if you wish to do so, invite volunteers to object to being transferred and offer a compensation package for such volunteers;

- you are available to discuss the above (giving contact details) and, in any event, you would welcome any written comments or suggestions on how to avoid job losses.

Contact trade union 9.15

If the company you are buying, or your company, recognises a trade union, you should contact the trade union and discuss with it methods of avoiding job losses and selecting employees for dismissal. The advantages of doing this are set out at **7.22**. This consultation should be ongoing throughout the entire dismissal process. The vendor should also have involved the union previously, whilst the vendor was negotiating the sale of the business.

Make sure vendor informs and consults with workforce   9.16

Although not strictly anything to do with unfair dismissal (with which this book is concerned), there is an obligation on the vendor to provide information to a trade union, or elected employee representatives, about a contemplated transfer and the impact it has on the workforce. A failure to do this can involve a payment of up to 13 weeks' pay for each employee and – for those employees who have transferred to your company – the liability to pay this will transfer to you. If you are unsure whether the vendor is complying with his information and consultation obligations, it is important you seek professional advice.

Plan changes carefully   9.17

Once you take over the business, you should decide exactly what changes need to be made. Remember you will have to justify any dismissals as falling into a economic, technical or organisational category entailing a change in the workforce. Take these words seriously – an employment tribunal will. If you have board or management meetings, discuss the changes that need to be made at a meeting and ensure that full minutes are taken. If you own your own business and do not have board meetings, draw up a business plan detailing the precise changes that you wish to make to the structure or organisation of the business. Do not identify people who are to be dismissed at this stage. Ensure that the business plan is dated.

Note that you will not be able to dismiss all (or some) of the old employees and replace them with new employees selected by yourself: this is because such dismissals are unlikely to be capable of being categorised as economic, technical or organisational reasons and, in any event, are unlikely to be regarded as fair by a tribunal.

Step 2: Select the employees to dismiss   9.18

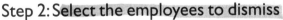

Once you have decided what changes are to be made, and the number of people who are to be dismissed (and, if appropriate, from what department), you should write again to all employees in the following terms:

- now that the transfer has taken place, it is necessary to make a number of changes within the workforce. Set out your reasons in one or two paragraphs and explain why jobs are going to have to go;

- if you are consulting with a trade union, refer to this in your letter and state the name of the trade union representative with whom you are consulting;

- your provisional position is to dismiss *x* number of people from each department in which you intend to make dismissals;

- again, if you wish to do so, invite volunteers and offer a compensation package;

- state that if there are an insufficient number of volunteers, you will have to select candidates for dismissal. State your selection criteria (see **9.19** below).

What selection criteria should you use?   9.19

If you need to select people for dismissal, what selection criteria should you use? If you have been consulting with a trade union, you should agree selection criteria with the union. Provided these criteria are properly implemented, a tribunal will accept them as being fair and reasonable. See **7.24** above for further details.

If you have not been consulting with a trade union, or cannot agree selection criteria, you must choose your own. It is crucial that the criteria be objective – see **7.25** for more details on choosing selection criteria.

There is one difference between selecting employees for dismissal when taking over a business, and when making redundancies in your own business. In the latter case, you will know the employees and be able to judge them within the framework of the selection criteria. With new employees, particularly if the old company did not keep detailed personnel records, it will be much harder to make assessments. In such circumstances, you may have to fall back on basic criteria such as 'LIFO' (last in, first out), 'FIFO' (first in, first out), qualifications, or an impression as to dedication and ability from interview (which is inevitably subjective, but which may be the best you can do in such circumstances).

When taking over some businesses, you may inherit a pre-existing management structure and you may be able to rely on these members of management to undertake a more detailed assessment based on their knowledge of individual employees.

If dismissing more than 20 employees, special consultation rules may apply and you will need to seek professional advice.

Step 3: Consider alternative employment   9.20

By now you will have realised that the procedure for dismissing after a takeover is broadly similar to that for redundancy, except that you have to establish an economic, technical or organisational reason rather than a diminution in the need for employees to do work of a particular kind. The third stage, after you have provisionally selected which employees to dismiss, is to consider alternative employment.

It is important to remember that the obligation to consider alternative employment *includes* alternative employment in 'associated companies', i.e. not just the company which has bought out the business, but also any parent or subsidiary companies, or other subsidiaries of the parent company.

The procedure to go through when considering alternative employment is set out at **7.30**.

Step 4: Consultation 9.21

After selecting the employees to dismiss, you should write to them in the following terms:

- following extensive review and consideration, you have provisionally selected Fred as one of the people to be dismissed because of the technical/economic/organisational reasons set out in your last letter;

- you have considered alternative employment (if you have any associated companies, name the companies at which you have considered alternative employment) but there are no suitable jobs available;

- invite each employee to a meeting with you to discuss the process of selection and discuss any suggestions they may have for alternative employment. State a date and time for the meeting – there is no reason why it should not be arranged quickly – but if it is inconvenient for the employees you should re-arrange the meetings. Remind them they can have a representative if they wish;

- state the period of notice to which they are entitled (see **12.11**) and state whether you will want them to work out their notice periods or whether you will pay in lieu of notice;

- if you are offering a termination payment, state what it is. Remember that when dismissing because of a takeover, you are not legally obliged to pay a redundancy payment;

- emphasise that your letter is not a letter of dismissal, and that they remain employed by your company until further notice.

Meetings with employees 9.22

At the meeting with each employee, you should try to have someone available to take notes. Go through your selection criteria and explain to the employees the reasons for selecting them. If they disagree with your use of the criteria (for example, they say that they have been employed for eight years and not two), you will need to take this into account and may need to reconsider your selection. If they disagree with your choice of selection criteria (for example, say that you should have worked on a 'LIFO' not 'FIFO' basis), explain to them that the choice of selection criteria was a business decision and it is too late to change them.

You should also ask each employee whether they have any suggestions as to alternative employment, and whether there are any people whom you could contact on their behalf to try to help with finding a new job. Make a note of every suggestion made.

The letter of dismissal   9.23

You should allow several days to elapse after your meetings with the employees. If any suggestions were made for alternative employment, you should consider these (and ensure, if possible, that there is some record – such as a memo to a colleague in another department, or associated company, asking if a particular vacancy is still available). You can then write to the employees in the following terms:

- thank them for attending the meeting with you (or, if they failed to attend, make reference to this);

- if they agreed with your application of the selection criteria, mention this. If they disagreed, briefly set out the reasons for their challenge and state why these reasons are not valid;

- refer to any suggestions they made for alternative employment. Mention what steps you have taken to look into these suggestions, and explain why it is not possible to offer the alternative employment. If alternative employment is available, set out the terms of the job offer and ask them to confirm their acceptance within, say, seven days. If they did not make any suggestions as to alternative employment during your meeting, mention this. State that you will continue considering them should any suitable job vacancies arise over the next few months;

- offer a right of appeal. See **CHAPTER 11** for more information;

- state what their last day of work will be. If you are paying monies in lieu of notice, set out your calculation of the notice pay in your letter. Set out any termination payment that you are making voluntarily, making sure you state that it is an '*ex gratia*' payment. Enclose a cheque or state when a cheque can be expected;

- enclose a copy of the employee's P45 or state when it can be expected;

- if possible, add a personal paragraph so that the letter does not appear mass produced. State that you will happily provide references. Note that, unlike with dismissals for misconduct (see **3.24**), there is no reason why you should not give good references for employees.

Dismissing employees when taking over a contract
9.24

It can be particularly difficult to tell, when taking over a contract, whether the contract amounts to an 'economic entity' or 'undertaking' so as to make TUPE apply. If TUPE does apply, you are deemed to have taken over the employment of all the employees who worked wholly or mainly in that undertaking.

Theoretically, you should be able to negotiate an indemnity or contribution from the person providing you with the contract in case there is a transfer of employees and you are found to be liable for unfair dismissal. In practice, however, if you have obtained the contract in a competitive tender situation, you will be unlikely to be able to negotiate such an indemnity.

When will a transfer take place?
9.25

A one-off contract, on its own, is unlikely to amount to an economic undertaking. If you take over such a contract, and nothing else, you are probably safe and will not find that you are responsible for taking over the old contractor's employees.

If, however, you take over other aspects associated with the contract, for example equipment, materials or even some members of staff, you are at risk of an employment tribunal finding that TUPE applies.

If there are a number of employees who worked for the old contractor, and you consider yourself to be at risk of a tribunal finding that TUPE applies, you are well advised to seek professional advice.

What if TUPE does apply when taking over a contract?
9.26

If TUPE does apply when taking over a contract, you will need to go through exactly the same procedure as when taking over a business, as set out above.

137

Chapter 10
Dismissals for
Other Reasons

Introduction

10.1

In order for a dismissal (whether actual or constructive) to be fair, you must establish that the reason for the dismissal is either capability, conduct, redundancy, contravention of a statutory provision or 'some other substantial reason' (*section 98* of the *Employment Rights Act 1996*).

The most common 'other substantial reason' will be a business reorganisation or taking over somebody else's business and dismissing employees (see **CHAPTERS 8** and **9** respectively). This chapter deals with dismissals for other common reasons. Theoretically, anything may be capable of amounting to a fair reason for dismissal: however, in practice a number of identifiable categories have arisen over time. These are:

(a) where continued employment would contravene a statutory requirement: this is not strictly an example of 'some other substantial reason', but is a express reason for dismissal in its own right;

(b) where there are personality clashes between Fred and other employees;

(c) where you are put under pressure to dismiss Fred by a customer or supplier;

(d) where Fred reaches retirement age;

(e) where Fred was engaged for a fixed period or for a fixed task;

(f) other, miscellaneous reasons.

When dismissing for any of these reasons, except reason (d), you will have to give Fred his full notice. See **CHAPTER 12** for what you must pay on a fair dismissal.

Consultation procedure

10.2

Note that in the above cases, you will often have to go through a consultation procedure with the employees or consider alternative employment. It is not proposed to set out the detailed requirements for these in this chapter such procedures are set out in full in preceding chapters. Unless stated otherwise, you must always comply with the minimum statutory dismissal procedures set out in **APPENDIX 1**.

(a) Where continued employment would contravene a statutory requirement 10.3

If continuing to employ Fred would place either him or you in breach of a duty or restriction imposed under an enactment, you will be entitled to dismiss Fred (provided you first consider alternative employment, or making adjustments to his duties so that he can continue in employment).

The most common example of this occurs if Fred needs to drive as part of his duties, and he is banned from driving (thus rendering it illegal for him to continue driving for you). Note that if driving is only a small part of Fred's duties, and you could allocate the driving to somebody else and find alternative work for Fred, then a dismissal is likely to be unfair. Likewise if Fred was able to use public transport rather than driving himself, and doing so would not significantly affect his work, you would also be acting unreasonably in dismissing him.

If you wrongly believe that the ongoing employment of Fred would be in breach of an enactment, this will not suffice under this heading. It may, however, be sufficient to justify 'some other substantial reason'.

This is one of the few exceptions where the statutory minimum dismissal procedures do not apply. However, you should still consider the availability of alternative employment, and ensure you invite Fred to a meeting to discuss the situation, otherwise a tribunal will probably rule you have acted unfairly irrespective of the statutory minimum dismissal procedures.

Example

Trust House Forte dismissed an employee after being wrongly told by the Department of Employment that he would not qualify for a work permit. In fact, he did qualify and the Department had misinformed the employers. The Employment Appeal Tribunal held that the employers were not entitled to claim that continued employment would be a breach of an enactment, but that their reasonable and genuine belief that they would be in breach amounted to some other substantial reason justifying the dismissal – *Bouchaala v Trust House Forte Hotels [1980] IRLR 382.*

(b) Personality clashes with other employees 10.4

If other employees do not get on with Fred, and the personality clashes cause significant disharmony in the workplace, this may amount to some other substantial reason enabling dismissal of Fred.

Example

> Ms Treganowan worked in an office with other women who disapproved of her loose morals. She had an illegitimate child, of which the other workers disapproved, and would boast of a relationship with a boy almost half her age. The atmosphere in the office had become extremely tense and hostile and was seriously affecting the company's business. It was held that the dismissal of the employee was fair for 'some other substantial reason' – *Treganowan v Robert Knee & Co Ltd [1975] IRLR 247.*

If the personality clash is between two people only, you may have some difficulty justifying dismissal of one as contrasted with the other, since it may not be easy to establish who is at fault. In such a case, if the personality clashes make it impossible for you to carry on employing them, you may be able to dismiss both. Ensure that you have given both of them formal warnings. Also consider whether either or both staff members can be moved to a different department or given some other form of alternative employment.

When most people can't work with an employee 10.5

If the personality clash is more general, and the majority of your workforce cannot work with Fred, you will need to go through the following steps:

● ask the other employees to put their grievances relating to Fred in writing (this will be extremely helpful evidence at a tribunal hearing);

● give Fred at least one, and preferably two, formal warnings in writing. Ensure you meet him to discuss ways in which he can attempt to improve his relationship with other members of staff;

● discuss the situation with other employees. Satisfy yourself that there is no likelihood of matters improving. Keep notes of these conversations;

● consider whether Fred can be relocated or offered some other alternative employment;

● if there is no alternative, dismiss him.

Personality clashes arising from an employee's sexual orientation 10.6

Until the end of 2003, it was sometimes legitimate to dismiss an employee is his/her sexual orientation caused problems with other employees.

Example

> An audit clerk insisted on wearing various badges proclaiming that she was a lesbian, including badges saying 'Dyke', and 'Lesbians Ignite'. She ignored instructions from her employers to remove the badges and was eventually dismissed. The Employment Appeal Tribunal held that a balance must be struck between the freedom of the employee and the needs of the business (which included avoiding badges which were potentially offensive to customers and other employees). Accordingly the dismissal was fair – *Boychuck v HJ Symons Holdings [1977] IRLR 395.*

Since December 2003, it has been unlawful to dismiss an employee because of his or her sexual orientation. To do so means you would be liable for a potentially unlimited discrimination award.

Industrial action by other employees 10.7

Although it may be legitimate to dismiss Fred if other employees complain about him and cannot get on with him, if matters go further and the other employees begin or threaten industrial action (such as a strike) in order to put pressure on you to dismiss Fred, this industrial pressure must be disregarded in assessing whether or not Fred's dismissal is fair. This is discussed further at **18.14**.

(c) *Pressure by customers or suppliers to dismiss* 10.8

Sometimes a major customer or supplier may be unwilling to work with Fred. Fred may have upset them in some way and they choose to exercise their commercial muscle in order to secure his dismissal.

Example

> An employee of a company, whose biggest client was the US navy, stole a lighter belonging to a naval officer. The navy insisted that the employee

> be dismissed, and it was held that the employer had not acted unreasonably in bowing to the demands of their best customer in a situation such as this – *Scott Packing v Paterson [1978] IRLR 166.*

In order to establish that the dismissal of Fred in these circumstances is fair, you will need to prove that you have balanced the potential injustice to your business if the customer goes elsewhere against the injustice to Fred if you dismiss when there is no fault on his part. Bear in mind that it may be easier to justify dismissing Fred when the pressure comes from a major customer rather than a major supplier. If the customer is only a minor one, you may also have difficulty justifying Fred's dismissal.

Before dismissing Fred you should take the following steps:

- if you feel able to do it, ask the customer/supplier for a letter confirming that they insist Fred be dismissed and setting out their reasons. Unless you feel it wholly inappropriate, write to the customer/supplier and ask them if they would be satisfied if you issue Fred with a final written warning instead of dismissing him. If you prefer to do this orally, keep notes of the relevant conversations;

- consider if there is any alternative employment you can offer Fred, possibly with an associated employer, which would not involve Fred coming into contact with the customer;

- consult Fred while this is going on (and, if appropriate, forbid him from contacting the customer/supplier). Make sure Fred is kept fully informed (and keep notes of your discussions with him). Ensure you have a face-to-face meeting (or, at the least, invite him to one) to comply with the minimum statutory dismissal procedures (see **APPENDIX 1**).

- if the person putting pressure on you is a supplier rather than a customer, consider whether you can go elsewhere to purchase the items you buy from the supplier. This will not be possible if the supplier is a monopoly supplier or considerably cheaper than his competitors; however, it will impress a tribunal if you can show you have considered finding alternative sources for your materials.

If all else fails, you can go ahead and dismiss Fred. Remember to offer him a right of appeal.

(d) Dismissing when retirement age is reached
10.9

At present, the law provides that employees cannot claim unfair dismissal or redundancy once they reach or exceed retirement age. If there is no contractual or 'normal' retirement age, the retirement age is deemed to be 65 for both men and women.

This rule will change or be abolished in December 2006 in order to comply with age discrimination laws which must be introduced by then.

(e) Engaged for a fixed period or task only 10.10

If Fred is engaged for a fixed period or task, and the period expires or the task is completed, you may no longer wish to employ Fred. The expiry of the fixed term (the correct term has recently changed to 'limited term', but most people still use the phrase 'fixed term'), without renewing it, is *deemed* to be a dismissal for unfair dismissal purposes. Often, however, the completion of the task will be a 'substantial reason' for dismissing him.

You also need to bear in mind that it is unlawful to discriminate against fixed-term employees – either by offering them a lower package, or by not renewing their contracts when they come to an end – unless there is 'objective justification' (lawyers' language for 'a good business reason') for not offering them another suitable job or extending their contract.

(f) Other, miscellaneous reasons 10.11

The following is a list of some other cases in which tribunals have decided that the employer has established 'some other substantial reason' for the dismissal. Remember that the fact that other employers have persuaded a tribunal that their dismissal was fair does not mean that you will be able to persuade a tribunal that your dismissal of Fred was fair in similar circumstances. The overriding test is that you have to have acted reasonably in accordance with the merits of the case.

- where Fred is about to go and join a competitor: *Davidson v Comparisons [1980] IRLR 360*;

- dismissal of a spouse where the husband and wife lived together for work and the other spouse had been dismissed: *Kelman v Orman [1983] IRLR 432*;

- where Fred was in prison and thus unable to carry out his duties: *Kingston v British Railways Board [1984] IRLR 146*;

- where an employee said he intended to resign to go and live in Australia. The employers treated him as having ceased working even though he never formally resigned. After he changed his mind he claimed unfair dismissal. The belief that the employee had resigned was some other substantive reason justifying the dismissal: *Ely v YKK Fasteners [1993] IRLR 500*.

- where an employee, who had not been dismissed, kept insisting that he had been dismissed. The employers eventually gave up trying to persuade him that he still had a job: *Brown v Tomlinsons Dairies (unreported, EAT 10/4/02).*

Examples where dismissal is <u>not</u> justified **10.12**

By contrast, the following situations have been held *not* to give rise to 'some other substantial reason' justifying the dismissal:

- a rumour that Fred is about to leave and set up a rival company: *Betts v Beresford [1974] IRLR 271;*

- dismissal of a spouse where his wife, also previously employed by the same employer, is dismissed after stealing from the employer: *Wadley v Eager Electrical [1986] IRLR 93.*

It can be seen that these cases are similar to the respective examples of *Davidson* and *Kelman*, set out in **10.11** above, and thus demonstrate that tribunals vary enormously in their approach (as can circumstances in individual situations).

Chapter 11
Internal Appeals

Introduction

A right to appeal is a fundamental part of the new statutory minimum dismissal procedures, which came into force in October 2004. The failure to offer a right of appeal – no matter how small your company – will almost always make a dismissal automatically unfair and increase compensation.

An appeal can often be of great advantage to an employer. Although it means that a certain amount of management time will have to be written off, the following two benefits come about:

- if there were procedural defects in your original decision to dismiss, a properly held appeal can cure those defects and prevent the dismissal from being held to be unfair;

- Fred may be more inclined to regard himself as having been treated fairly and reasonably. This may, in some cases, actually ward off an application to an employment tribunal.

For all these reasons, the opportunity to appeal should always be offered.

The appeal hearing

11.2

Unless totally impractical to do so, someone senior to the person who took the decision to dismiss should conduct the appeal. However, for the sake of consistency, the word 'you' will continue being used in this chapter to describe the person chosen to handle the appeal procedure.

An appeal hearing can take two forms. In the absence of Fred's contract of employment dictating the form it should take, you can choose whichever form suits you best. The two types of appeal hearings are these:

Rehearing: this involves you having another hearing at which all the evidence is presented from scratch and Fred presents his arguments all over again. It is essentially a second bite at the cherry, but will allow you to remedy any procedural defects that happened first time around.

Review: this is simply giving Fred the opportunity to question the decision-making process by suggesting, for example, that you did not have all relevant information last time, or you took irrelevant information into account, or that you were biased.

Decide whether you prefer a rehearing or a review. A review will normally be more appropriate when the issue that Fred is appealing about is one of selection for redundancy. Further, if there are a substantial number of witnesses, a review will often be easier. However, reviews lack the main advantage of rehearings in that they cannot cure any defects in the original procedure.

Request in writing 11.3

You will have invited Fred to request an appeal in writing in the dismissal letter. Although a written appeal request is preferable, as it enables you to know the basis of Fred's appeal, under the statutory minimum appeal procedures a verbal request for an appeal will suffice. If Fred says to you, verbally, that he wants to appeal, you should write to him, acknowledge that he has asked for an appeal, and ask him to set out his grounds in writing. However, if he fails to do so, you must still hold an appeal meeting and give a decision – or any dismissal will be automatically unfair.

If you have given him a reasonable time limit during which he has to request an appeal, you are justified in refusing to hold an appeal if he fails to appeal within that time. However, you run the risk of a tribunal saying that the period you allowed was too short – and the consequence of that, under the new statutory procedures, is severe – a finding of automatic unfair dismissal and an increase in compensation. A week should normally be sufficient, but until cases have been through the courts subsequent to these new laws (which came into force in October 2004), it is impossible to give clear guidance.

Even if Fred were to present his request for an appeal a few days late, you will often be better off by conducting the appeal in any event. The reason for this is twofold. First, it is risky to assume a tribunal will agree that your timeframe was reasonable *and* that Fred, in presenting his appeal a few days later, had taken an unreasonable amount of time. Second, if you refuse to allow Fred to appeal, he will feel aggrieved and will consider that you are acting unfairly (in a moral, rather than legal, sense). This may encourage him to complain to an employment tribunal in circumstances where he might not otherwise do so.

Who should conduct the appeal? 11.4

If you are a medium or large company, the appeal should always be conducted by somebody senior to the person who conducted the original disciplinary proceedings. Historically, tribunals used to regard it as unfair if there was any discussion about the case between these two people; however, nowadays tribunals realise that discussion is inevitable.

Bear in mind that if the case proceeds to a tribunal, you will probably be cross-examined on the degree of interaction that the original decision-maker had with the appeal decision-maker. An employee's lawyer will be keen to establish that there had been considerable discussion and that the appeal decision-maker, therefore, had not come to the appeal with an open mind. Avoid this by minimising your discussions about the merits of the appeal.

If you are from a small company, and there is nobody else of senior managerial status who can realistically conduct the appeal, you should see if there is somebody of equal level. If not, you should conduct the appeal yourself – which is an artificial but necessary exercise. If conducting the appeal yourself, a rehearing will usually be inappropriate and a review is the better, and easier, approach to adopt.

Conducting a rehearing   11.5

After you receive Fred's request to appeal, you should write to him stating as follows:

- you will arrange an appeal hearing. State a date, time and place. Indicate that the date can be rearranged if inconvenient for him. If known, state the name of the person who will be conducting the appeal hearing;

- the appeal will take the form of a rehearing. This means that he will be allowed to make any submissions he wishes on whether or not he committed the act(s) you dismissed him for, or whether he was not performing his duties properly, and whether dismissal was an appropriate sanction. He will also be allowed to call witnesses or put forward any other documents that are relevant, whether or not he relied on them at the original hearing(s);

- he can have a representative present if he wishes (see **4.13** for more information on representatives);

- (if appropriate) the person conducting the appeal will not discuss the matter with the person who took the original dismissal decision except insofar as is necessary for a basic understanding of the case;

- that, if he prefers, he can simply put submissions in writing (rather than having an oral hearing);

- if Fred elects to put his submissions in writing, you should treat it as a review rather than a rehearing. Consider the submissions and decide whether you think the original decision was reasonable or unreasonable. If you are satisfied that the original decision to dismiss was reasonable, you should write a full letter to Fred setting out your reasons and confirming that the dismissal will stand see **11.13**. It is important to take care over this letter since it will be the only evidence a tribunal will see as to whether or not you conducted the appeal properly or merely treated it as a rubber-stamping exercise.

If, by contrast, you decide that the original decision to dismiss was not reasonable, see **11.14**.

If the employee does not attend 11.6

If Fred does not attend the appeal or present written grounds for you to consider, you should write to him and offer him one further opportunity to attend. If he fails to do so a second time, you should consider any written submissions he has presented and decide, on that information, whether to allow or reject the appeal. Make sure you remember to write to him with your decision and the reasons for it (recording his failure to attend).

Note taking and witnesses 11.7

As ever, it is important that someone take a note of what is said at the appeal meeting. You should open the meeting by introducing everyone (unless to do so would be ridiculous) and, if appropriate, confirm to Fred that you have not discussed the facts surrounding his dismissal with the person who took the original decision. Explain to him that you are going to re-examine the evidence, listen to everything he has to say and then make a completely fresh decision.

If there were witness statements from the original hearing, it is up to you whether you rely on these alone or invite the witnesses to the appeal hearing. If Fred is alleging that they have fabricated their statements, it may be desirable to actually see them so that Fred can put his allegations to them. However, on an appeal hearing you have more latitude than at the original hearing and you should not be criticised for relying on witness statements alone or for refusing to allow Fred to cross-examine the witnesses.

Fred must be allowed to make any other representations that he sees fit. You should examine any documents he puts forward. Do not be afraid to ask him questions or test his evidence as with the original hearing, you should allow him the opportunity to explain any inconsistencies in his evidence (and his failure to do so will strengthen the case for upholding the dismissal).

Ensure that Fred understands that he is entitled to appeal against both the finding of misconduct (or incapability, or selection for redundancy, or whatever the underlying reason for dismissal was) and the decision to dismiss (rather than impose a warning or suspend). If he chooses to make representations on the latter, take a careful note of what he has to say.

Conclude the meeting by saying that you will write to Fred over the next few days with your decision. Do not be pressed into giving a preliminary answer.

Reconsider evidence 11.8

Once the meeting is over, consider the evidence afresh. You should take into account the matters mentioned in paragraphs **4.20** and **4.44**. If you are of the view that Fred probably did commit the acts complained of (or was incompetent), and that dismissal is a reasonable sanction, you should uphold the decision to dismiss. See **11.13** for information as to what your letter to Fred should contain.

On the other hand, you may think that dismissal is not appropriate. If so, you should write to Fred and formally reinstate him. This will involve making up all back pay that he lost between the time of his dismissal and the date of reinstatement (or, if you gave Fred pay in lieu of notice, it may entitle you to demand some of that money back again). See **11.14** for information as to an appropriate letter.

Conducting a review 11.9

If you prefer to conduct a review, rather than a full rehearing, you will be examining the decision-making process and deciding whether the decision to dismiss was a reasonable one. This may involve reconsidering Fred's scores under the selection criteria when he was dismissed due to redundancy. When doing this, you will still need to consider the original evidence, but will be more concerned with whether the original decision-maker took into account irrelevant facts (or failed to take into account relevant ones) or was biased when deciding what to do.

The main danger with this approach is that it can be seen as a simple rubber-stamping procedure. Little can be done about this, so you need to be as open and candid about reviewing the original evidence as you can be.

Notification of review 11.10

Write a letter to Fred, as in **11.5** above, inviting him to an appeal hearing. This letter should refer to an appeal by way of review, and state that Fred will be allowed to challenge the original decision on the grounds that irrelevant matters were wrongly taken into account, or relevant matters omitted. Say in the letter that it is not a rehearing, and that although Fred will be allowed a representative, he should not bring any witnesses unless there is new evidence which was not presented at the original hearing.

Again, if Fred is content for the appeal to take place on paper, you should review the evidence that was seen by the original decision-maker and consider whether the decision to dismiss was reasonable or unreasonable.

Conducting the review hearing 11.11

At the review hearing, you must be careful not to give Fred the impression that you are deciding the matter from scratch. Ensure that a careful note is taken so that you will be able to prove the content of the meeting to a tribunal should matters progress that far.

Explain to Fred that you are concerned solely to review the original decision to dismiss and not to re-determine his guilt or innocence. Do your best to ensure that he understands the distinction: if he feels that you are trying to confuse him with terminology then he is more likely to lodge a claim against you.

Ask Fred to take you through his grounds of complaint. Try to help him focus on discussing the evidence that came out during the original investigative hearing and not, instead, developing new lines of argument. If, however, he does have new evidence which was not considered first time round (for example, a witness has come forward and said that he saw somebody else stealing the money from the till) then you will need to consider this evidence to see if it puts a different complexion on the matter.

Once Fred has made all of the points that he wishes to, you should tell him that you wish to consider your decision. Do not give any indication, at that stage, what your decision is likely to be.

Consider if original decision was reasonable 11.12

When considering your decision, you are not concerned with whether the original decision to dismiss was the right one in the circumstances, but whether it was a *reasonable* one in the circumstances. Consider each of the points raised by Fred and decide whether it indicates bias or inappropriate considerations by the original decision maker. Once you have been through Fred's arguments, and considered each one in turn, decide whether the original decision was a reasonable one.

If you consider it to be reasonable, you will uphold the decision to dismiss. If you consider it to be unreasonable, you will need to reinstate Fred. As discussed above, this will entail making up all back pay that Fred lost between the time of his dismissal and the date of reinstatement. Alternatively, if you gave him pay in lieu of notice, you may be entitled to demand some of that money back again.

You will need to write to Fred in appropriate terms, informing him whether you have upheld or reversed the decision to dismiss.

Upholding the decision to dismiss   11.13

Your letter should state the following:

- that you write further to your meeting on [date]. State who was present at the meeting, and whether it was a rehearing or a review;

- if it was a rehearing, summarise the gist of the evidence and state your conclusions of fact. It is unwise to take more than two or three paragraphs for this the more detail you go into, the more you are opening yourself up to cross-examination at an employment tribunal hearing. State that you have reconsidered the sanction and that you think dismissal is appropriate;

- if it was a review, list Fred's main points of criticism. Answer each one with one sentence; this may be no more than 'we feel that the original decision was reasonable and can be justified on the evidence'. If possible, however, go into a little more detail so that a tribunal can see you have given full consideration to Fred's points;

- state that, in the circumstances, you are upholding the decision to dismiss. You should normally state that this is the end of the dismissal procedure and there is no further appeal – as if Fred believes the dismissal process is continuing, he sometimes receives a longer period in which to lodge a tribunal claim.

The letter should be posted to Fred's home address (since, by this stage, he will already have been dismissed). This will conclude the dismissal process.

Reversing the decision to dismiss   11.14

There are two possibilities. You may have decided that you cannot justify the original decision that Fred was guilty of misconduct or incompetence; alternatively you may be satisfied of his culpability but think that dismissal is too excessive a punishment. If the latter is the situation, you may wish to issue a formal written warning.

Your letter should contain the following points:

- you refer to your meeting on [date];

- after carefully considering what Fred had to say, you are pleased to inform him that you are reversing the original decision to dismiss. As a result he will be reinstated in his old position and should come back into work on [date];

- if you are going to issue a warning, state that you are instead issuing a formal warning in respect of his conduct/capability. Inform him that if he commits the same breach or offence, or any other offence, or fails to improve his work standards (as appropriate) he may face dismissal in the future. State that you take his actions extremely seriously and have only reinstated him because of the matters he raised on this occasion (you may need to change this around to find the right form of words);

- set out the position on pay (subject to the point at **11.15** below). Whether or not you have issued a formal warning, you will need to put Fred back in the financial position that he would have been in if you had not dismissed him;

- if you are reversing your decision on your findings of fact (i.e. you are no longer satisfied that Fred is not up to the job or that his conduct was improper) you may wish to apologise for any inconvenience caused. It is worthwhile being gracious since, if you should have reason to dismiss Fred on a later occasion, you do not wish to be accused of harbouring a grudge against him.

Send the letter to Fred by post. If you do not hear from him, contact him by telephone and ask him whether or not he is returning to work. You should be aware that you can still be found liable for unfair dismissal even when you have offered the job back: your offer of reinstatement may have an effect on the award which Fred receives, but will not prevent a tribunal from regarding him as 'dismissed' unless you have very clearly drafted disciplinary rules enabling you to withdraw a dismissal, or substitute another sanction, during the appeal stage.

Payment on reinstatement 11.15

On reinstatement, you will need to pay a sum of money to Fred which puts him back in the position he would have been in if he had not been dismissed.

You should calculate the number of days' earnings that he has lost and add it to his next paycheque. Alternatively, you may prefer to enter into an agreement with him expressing the payment to be damages for lost earnings during a period of unemployment. If you adopt this approach, you need only pay him his net loss i.e. his loss of earnings after deductions both of income tax and any sums he received by way of income support or unemployment benefit (NB he is unlikely to have received the latter if he was dismissed because of his conduct). This may be financially advantageous to you; however, there is a danger in doing this because, if Fred does not accept reinstatement, the letter can be used against you as an admission of liability. If you wish to adopt this approach, it is best to wait until Fred has agreed to reinstatement.

If you paid Fred pay in lieu of notice, it may be the case that his lieu of notice period takes him beyond the reinstatement date. In that case, there will be monies owing from him to you! It is a commercial decision for you to make as to whether you wish to pursue this sum. You are not entitled to set-off these excesses against Fred's next paycheques (unless he has agreed that you may do this in writing in advance) this would amount to an unlawful deduction of wages. Instead, you should bring proceedings to reclaim the balance in the County Court (almost certainly by way of small claims arbitration, which currently deals with all claims worth under £5,000).

Chapter 12
What You must Pay when Dismissing Someone

Introduction 12.1

When you dismiss Fred properly, you will normally have to make some sort of payment to him. This usually falls into one or more of the following categories:

(a) pay in lieu of notice, if you have not required Fred to work out his notice period;

(b) associated entitlements, such as outstanding holiday pay and accrued bonuses or commissions. This includes any contractual payments that you must pay if you are dismissing him for particular reasons;

(c) a redundancy payment, if you have dismissed Fred due to redundancy.

You may also wish to give Fred an *ex gratia* payment i.e. one which you strictly do not have to pay but you wish to pay voluntarily as additional compensation. This may occur in an ill-health or redundancy dismissal, but is not normally appropriate in misconduct dismissals.

Each of these is discussed below.

Always pay monies owing 12.2

The obligation to pay monies on dismissal is entirely separate from the issue of whether the dismissal is fair or unfair. If you fail to pay monies that are properly owing to Fred, such as pay in lieu of notice, it will have no effect on whether the decision to dismiss was fair or unfair. However, it is unwise not to make these payments, for the following reasons:

● whereas Fred might not have considered an unfair dismissal claim, he will justifiably resent your failure to pay him his entitlements. If he puts in a claim for monies owing in such circumstances, he is far more likely to add a claim for unfair dismissal. He is certainly likely to seek legal advice which, in turn, may increase the chance of an unfair dismissal claim being brought against you;

- if and when he does claim these sums from you, he will succeed. If the claim is brought in the small claims court (which deals with all claims under £5,000), you will have to pay the costs of issuing the claim form, interest, together with Fred's loss of earnings in going to court and travel expenses. There is also a small risk of you having to pay full legal costs if the court decides you have acted unreasonably;

- if a claim for unfair dismissal is brought against you, although your failure to pay these sums will not make the dismissal unfair, a tribunal might consider your conduct unreasonable. This may, in turn, have some bearing on their perception of you in determining whether you have acted reasonably in connection with other matters relating to the dismissal.

Clearly if there is a genuine dispute over whether Fred is entitled to monies, such as commission payments, you would be justified in withholding the monies and either seeking resolution through the courts or settling the matter amicably with him. Nevertheless, where Fred's entitlement is clear you should pay the monies at the time of his dismissal.

Make calculations clear   12.3

It is also important that you make it very clear how you have calculated any payments made to Fred. This is for two reasons. Firstly it is a criminal offence not to specify exactly how certain payments, such as a redundancy payment, are calculated. Secondly, if Fred later challenges your calculation of his payments, there will be a clear record of how those calculations were performed.

Pay in lieu of notice   12.4

This is often considered a simple matter to calculate but can, in fact, be quite complex. There are two questions. Firstly, when is Fred entitled to pay in lieu of notice? Secondly, how much should you pay him?

When is someone entitled to pay in lieu of notice?   12.5

When you dismiss Fred, he will be entitled to a notice period unless the dismissal is for gross misconduct (see **4.25**). If he is dismissed for gross misconduct you should not give him any pay in lieu of notice: to do so would indicate that he was entitled to a notice period, which is inconsistent with your defence that you had to dismiss him immediately without giving notice.

158

When dismissing Fred you have a choice. If his notice period is, say, six weeks, you can adopt any of the following options:

- require Fred to work for you for during the notice period and pay him in the ordinary way (e.g. weekly in arrears);

- tell Fred that his employment ends immediately and pay him the six weeks' pay in lieu of notice as a lump sum;

- tell Fred that he need not come into work, but that you want him to be at home and available for work at your discretion (this is commonly known as 'garden leave'). In this case you should continue paying him in the ordinary way during the notice period;

- a combination of the above, for example requiring Fred to work for a further two weeks and then giving him the final four weeks' pay as a lump sum.

This is an obligation 12.6

The obligation to pay monies in lieu of notice is exactly what it says. If you do not allow Fred to work out his notice period, you should pay him the wages that he would have received if you had allowed him to work out the notice period.

Breach of contract compensation 12.7

If you dismiss Fred without notice, and do not require him to work out the notice period, then you are technically acting in breach of contract (your obligation being to give him a certain number of weeks' notice during which he can work). This will be the case unless Fred has a clause in his contract that states that you are entitled to pay him money in lieu of notice (unless you state in your dismissal letter that you are not exercising the right to pay money in lieu of notice).

If you are technically in breach of contract, as you usually will be, then any pay in lieu you make to him is taken to be as compensation for this breach of contract. There is, however, a curious legal quirk. The law says that when you are in breach of contract, you compensate Fred only for his actual financial losses. If he were to find another job, his income from this job would be set-off against what you should pay him as compensation for your breach of your obligation to give him a working notice period. Thus, if Fred was entitled to six weeks' notice at £270 per week (i.e. £1,620), you breached the contract by not permitting him to work for those six weeks, and after two weeks Fred obtained another job for £275 per week, you would only have to pay him £400 (i.e. the £1,500 less the £1,100 he actually earned during those six weeks).

159

Loophole: compensation awarded for loss of earnings only   12.8

Very few employers take advantage of this loophole, unless Fred is entitled to a particularly long notice period (e.g. six months or more), and it would be very expensive not to take advantage. This is for several reasons: many employers are unaware of the loophole, many regard it as immoral to take advantage of it in this way, and again it may prompt Fred to initiate litigation against you.

There is a potential disadvantage to making use of this loophole: for technical reasons, you will lose the ability to enforce any restrictive covenants (such as non-competition clauses) in Fred's contract of employment. This is a technical and difficult area, and if you wish to rely on restrictive covenants you should seek specialist advice.

If Fred does have a long notice period, and you believe that he is likely to obtain employment during the notice period, you may be better off adopting this route and not paying him any monies in lieu of notice at the time of dismissal. If the amount of notice money at stake is small, you may be best simply paying it up front.

Note that if you dismiss Fred due to long-term illness or similar incapacity, you will have difficulty justifying a belief that Fred is likely to obtain employment elsewhere during his notice period. Adopting this route might be perceived by a tribunal (should Fred claim for unfair dismissal) as an indicator that you are deliberately attempting to avoid paying monies that are lawfully due to Fred. The associated stigma will not assist in defending any unfair dismissal claim.

How much should you pay in lieu of notice?   12.9

This section is based on the assumption that you are not taking advantage of the loophole set out at **12.7**. To do so, whilst legally justifiable, is widely regarded (other than in cases of very long notice periods) as shabby behaviour and poor industrial relations.

Pay net salary, not gross   12.10

When paying Fred in lieu of notice you pay him only his net, not gross, salary. If you paid him his gross salary, he would in fact be recovering more than if he had continued working throughout his notice period (since deductions would have been made for tax and national insurance contributions). You therefore pay him his net salary, plus other usual benefits, for such amount of the notice period during which you do not require him to work.

How much notice should you give? 12.11

If Fred has a written contract, it should stipulate the number of weeks' notice that you are obliged to give him. If there is no written contract, but you have agreed with Fred that he would be entitled to a certain amount of notice, this will be binding on you.

If nothing has been agreed as to the length of the notice period, then you are obliged to give Fred a 'reasonable' notice period. The length of a reasonable notice period will depend largely on the nature of the work he does and his seniority. Thus a reasonable notice period for somebody who has been working as a receptionist for four years may be one month, whereas a reasonable notice period for somebody who has been an executive sales director for a similar period may be, say, three months. Unless there has been express agreement to the contrary, three months is the maximum that the law will usually assess as a reasonable notice period.

Minimum periods of notice 12.12

The above is subject to one exception. The law lays down minimum periods of notice depending on the length of employment. If this minimum is longer than the notice period in Fred's contract of employment (or the period that was agreed between you) then it takes precedence. There is no minimum notice that must be given by you if Fred has been employed for less than one month. After this, the minimum notice periods are as follows:

- One month to two years – one week;
- Two to 12 years – one week for every complete year of employment;
- Over twelve years – 12 weeks.

Thus, for example, if Fred had been working for one day less than eight years and his contract stated that he was entitled to one month's notice, you would have to give him seven weeks' notice. This is because the minimum notice period is one week for each complete year (of which Fred had only completed seven) and this minimum period takes precedence over the shorter notice period in Fred's contract.

Holiday pay, pensions and other benefits 12.13

If you are paying Fred for seven weeks' in lieu of notice, you should work out his net pay during this period. You do not need to give extra for holiday pay which he would have earned during those seven weeks. This is because holiday pay is, in reality, no more than a right not to work on certain days yet be paid

161

normal wages. Since this is exactly what Fred is doing when he is paid in lieu, he is not entitled to be paid twice for the same loss.

If you make pension contributions on behalf of Fred, you should take these into account.

What is the position with overtime and bonuses? If Fred was contractually entitled to overtime then you must pay him the net equivalent of the overtime he would have earned during those seven weeks. If you awarded overtime at your discretion then you do not have to pay Fred for it. Likewise, if Fred would have received a bonus (such as a Christmas bonus) during those seven weeks, you remain obliged to pay it to him if he was contractually entitled to it. Contractual entitlement can be inferred, if there is nothing in writing, from the fact that you had regularly paid such a bonus over the years.

Associated entitlements 12.14

In addition to pay in lieu of notice, you must also pay Fred any monies to which he has already accrued entitlement. Most commonly, this will be untaken holiday pay. Note that you can require Fred to take the holiday during his notice period. If he is entitled to seven weeks' notice and he has one week's holiday accrued, you could state in the letter where you set out his final payments that you are giving him seven weeks' notice, of which you are requiring him to take the last week as accrued holiday and you will pay him normally for the first six weeks. You should not adopt this approach when you are dismissing Fred for gross misconduct, when an immediate dismissal is necessary.

Periodic bonuses 12.15

An area which often causes difficulty is where Fred is given a periodic bonus, but the notice period does not take him to a date which triggers this bonus. Fred may argue that he has worked through some of the period which would have resulted in a bonus, and thus should be entitled to a proportion of the bonus on a *pro rata* basis. The true position will depend on the terms of the contract between you and Fred. If there is a lot of money at stake, seek legal advice. If it is not cost-effective to seek legal advice, either take the risk of Fred taking you to court successfully, or negotiate a settlement with him. Any legitimate dispute over bonus payments will have no bearing on whether a dismissal is fair or unfair.

Shares and investment 12.16

Some contracts of employment provide for certain other events to be triggered on dismissal, unless the dismissal is for a specified reason (such as gross misconduct). This is common where Fred has invested money in the company, or where he has a share option agreement. This falls outside the scope of this book and you should consider seeking specific legal advice if this situation arises.

Redundancy payment 12.17

If you have dismissed Fred due to redundancy, you must pay him a redundancy payment. Remember the definition of redundancy set out at **7.3**: if Fred's dismissal does not fall within this definition, then you do not need to make a redundancy payment. Many employers make the mistake of labelling a dismissal as being due to redundancy when it is not. It is often the case, however, that the incorrect labelling of a dismissal as redundancy coupled with a prompt redundancy payment deflects many employees from bringing unfair dismissal claims.

Entitlement to redundancy pay 12.18

If Fred has been working for less than two years, or if he is under 18 or over 65, he is not entitled to a redundancy payment. If the usual retirement age at your company is less than 65, and Fred is over that age, he will likewise not be entitled to a redundancy payment.

In addition, if Fred is 64 years old (but has not yet reached 65, at which point his right to a redundancy payment ceases) then for each complete month that Fred is over 64, his redundancy award is reduced by one-twelfth. Thus if Fred is made redundancy three months before his 65th birthday, he will only be entitled to one-quarter of the normal redundancy pay (since it would have been reduced by nine-twelfths).

Remember that if Fred has unreasonably refused an offer of suitable alternative employment, he will not be entitled to a redundancy payment: see **7.39**.

Calculation of redundancy pay 12.19

The formula for calculating a redundancy payment is as follows:

Redundancy payment = L x P x F

where 'L' is the length of Fred's employment with you, 'P' is Fred's weekly pay (subject to a weekly maximum, currently £270) and 'F' is a multiplication factor which takes account of Fred's age. Each of these is addressed below.

'L' – length of employment – points to consider
12.20

The first factor is the number of complete years which Fred has been continuously employed by you or any associated employers (i.e. subsidiary or parent companies, or another subsidiary of your parent company). Bear in mind the following points:

- if Fred has been employed under different fixed term contracts then the length of these contracts should be combined to give a total length of employment. Periods whilst Fred is on holiday or temporarily absent will count if he remains employed by you during such periods;

- if Fred was absent through sickness or injury, his period of continuous employment will continue accruing provided he remained employed by you. If you had dismissed him whilst he was ill (whether due to his illness or not) but rehired him when he recovered, then up to 26 weeks can be counted towards continuous employment if he was incapable of doing his usual kind of work during this period. As soon as the absence extends beyond 26 weeks, his continuity of employment will be broken and the counter re-sets to zero when he is rehired by you;

- female employees may also count weeks during which they are absent due to pregnancy or maternity leave the former is limited, however, to 26 weeks;

- you do not count any period during which Fred worked for you when he was under 18 years old;

- if, during any part of a week, Fred was on strike then the entire week will be discounted for the purpose of calculating the total length of employment. The fact that he was on strike will not, however, re-set the counter to zero.

If you have bought your business from another employer and Fred worked for the old employer, then his continuity of employment will transfer and you should take into account his length of service before you bought the business.

Once you have calculated Fred's total length of employment, and made any necessary adjustments as set out above, the figure 'L' will be the number of complete years employment that Fred has achieved. As mentioned above, if Fred has been working for less than two complete years, he is not entitled to any redundancy payment.

'P' – weekly pay
12.21

The rules relating to the date on which you calculate Fred's weekly pay are complicated and depend on the manner of termination and the length of the notice period. In general, if you have not required Fred to work out all of his notice period then you calculate a week's pay as of the date that Fred's employment finished. If you did allow Fred to work out his full notice period (which is common in cases of redundancy) then you calculate Fred's weekly pay as of the date that you would have given Fred notice of dismissal if you had given precisely the minimum amount of notice required by law (see **12.12**).

What is a normal week's pay? You should work out what Fred was earning in a normal week at the above date. This is calculated by reference to the number of hours he was obliged to work. Either this will be stated expressly in his contract, or will have arisen by custom and practice (for example, a normal working week might be 37 hours even if there is no written contract setting this out). Overtime is ignored, even if it is regular, unless you are contractually obliged to provide Fred with overtime and he is contractually obliged to do it.

Example

> An employee's contract provided for a 40 hour week. He regularly worked a 58 hour week which, it was said, was necessary for the employer's business. Nevertheless, the court held that the normal week's work was 40 hours since he was not obliged to work for longer than this under his contract – *Lynch v Dartmouth Auto Casings [1969] 4 ITR 273*.

You should work out what Fred's contractual wage would have been during the week in which the above date falls. This will usually exclude overtime, as stated above, but will include any regular bonuses or commissions which he would have received provided that he was contractually entitled to them. If the bonus is in respect of a longer period, it should be calculated on a *pro rata* basis.

Gross, not net pay   12.22

Unlike pay in lieu of notice, you use Fred's gross, not net, pay. This will yield the figure 'P' for the redundancy payment, subject to one caveat. If his weekly pay, 'P', is greater than a set maximum amount, 'P' is limited to the maximum amount. The maximum is currently £270 per week. This limit changes on 1 February every year, adjusted by (approximately) the rate of inflation. Thus if Fred is earning over £14,040 per annum (on the basis of a normal working week, excluding overtime) he will exceed the maximum figure and you will simply calculate his redundancy payment on the basis of a weekly wage of £270.

'F'– multiplication factor   12.23

For every year of continuous employment (i.e. 'L'), working backwards from the date of dismissal, you adjust Fred's redundancy payment by a factor depending on his age during the year in question. You do this by calculating the factor 'F' as follows:

- for every year during the whole of which Fred was 41 or over, F is 1.5;

- for every year during the whole of which he between 22 and 41, F is 1.0; and,

- for every earlier year, i.e. during the whole of which he is between 18 and 22 (since years under 18 do not count), F is 0.5.

Examples of calculating redundancy payment   12.24

The above formula appears complex when set out on paper. In reality, it is quite simple. The following hypothetical examples demonstrate how a redundancy payment is calculated in practice.

Scenario 1

Fred is 35 years old. He has been working for you, without a break, for seven and a half years. His gross annual salary at the date of dismissal is £7,280, i.e. £140 per week. He usually earns an extra £40 to £50 per week doing overtime, although he has no right to the overtime work.

Redundancy payment = L x P x F.

– L = 7 (Fred has worked for seven complete years you do not include parts of years);

– P = £140 (i.e. Fred's weekly gross wage. You do not include his overtime since he is not entitled to it under his contract);

– F = 1.0 for all of his employment (since, during each of the seven full years he has been working, he has been aged between 22 and 41).

Accordingly his redundancy payment is £980, i.e. 7 x £140 x 1.0.

Scenario 2

Fred is 45 years old. He has worked for ten years and two months, although was absent through illness for four months (during which he remained employed by you and received statutory sick pay). His basic salary at the time of leaving was £18,200. He received commission on top of this.

Redundancy payment = L x P x F.

– L = 10 (since Fred has been working for ten complete years. You count the period of his absence since he remained employed by you)

– P = £270 (although Fred's actual weekly gross wage was £350, and was in fact even higher due to commission payments, 'P' is capped at the weekly maximum of £270);

– F = 1.5 for four years (since he was 41 or over for four complete years) and 1.0 for the remaining six years.

Accordingly his redundancy payment is £3,240. This is calculated on the basis of the four years when Fred was over 41, i.e. 4 x £270 x 1.5 plus six years when Fred was under 41, i.e. 6 x £270 x 1.0.

Ex gratia payments   12.25

Some employers choose to give an extra sum to Fred as gratuitous compensation for being dismissed. You should not do this in cases of gross misconduct. If you do make an *ex gratia* payment, you should make it clear in writing that it is being made on an *ex gratia* basis. This is because, in certain circumstances, an *ex gratia* payment can be used to reduce the amount of any compensation if the dismissal is later found to be unfair: see **13.21**.

Do not write in a letter that the *ex gratia* payment is being made on the basis that Fred does not bring a claim for unfair dismissal. Legally, this is of no effect and will only cause a tribunal to take a dim view of you. If you genuinely want to head off any potential claim, it must be done on the basis of a formal settlement: see **CHAPTER 15**.

Taxation of termination payments   12.26

In general, all payments to employees arising from employment are taxable, and deductions for tax should be made under the normal PAYE system. However, the first £30,000 of most termination payments will be tax-free, and can therefore be paid to Fred without tax being deducted.

Notice pay   12.27

If Fred is working out his notice, his salary will be taxed in the normal way.

If you are not requiring him to work out his notice (but, instead, are paying him a lump sum representing his notice pay), then the obligation to deduct tax will depend on the wording of Fred's contract of employment and the precise way in which your letter of dismissal is phrased:

(a)   if Fred's contract has a clause stating that you are entitled to pay him a lump sum in lieu of notice, then this lump sum will be taxable in the normal way *unless* you make it clear in the dismissal letter that you are not exercising your rights under that clause, but are instead choosing to dismiss him without notice and pay him compensation for breach of notice provisions. For technical reasons, the first £30,000 of any sum paid to him will then be tax-free *but* (also for technical reasons) you will not be allowed to enforce any restrictive covenants that appear in Fred's contract;

(b)   if there is no such clause in Fred's contract, any lump sum you pay in lieu of notice will be tax free (up to the first £30,000).

Redundancy pay   12.28

Redundancy payments are regarded by the Revenue as falling into the £30,000 tax-free band. This is a legal provision for the statutory redundancy payment (i.e. that set out at **12.17** above), and an Inland Revenue concession for any additional redundancy payment contained in Fred's contract. There is a (small) risk that the Inland Revenue might withdraw this concession at any time.

Ex gratia payments   12.29

Ex gratia payments made on termination of employment will always fall within the £30,000 tax-free band, unless the contract of employment states that an *ex gratia* payment 'will' be made on termination of employment. In that case, it would not truly by an *ex gratia* payment, but would instead be a contractual termination payment (which is taxable in full).

Chapter 13
What do You Pay if You get it Wrong?

Introduction

What happens if you get it wrong: if you dismiss Fred without going through the proper procedures, or if another manager at your company dismisses Fred when he was not authorised to do so?

Even if you think that you have dismissed Fred fairly, you may want to know how much you may be liable to pay so that you can make a sensible attempt at settling any claim.

There are three separate elements in what you have to pay Fred, namely:

(a)   contractual monies notice period, or pay in lieu of notice;

(b)   a 'basic award': this is a fixed sum depending on Fred's age and length of service. It is calculated according to a precise formula;

(c)   a 'compensatory award': this is usually the biggest section of any award. It reflects the loss of earnings that Fred has suffered due to being dismissed.

A tribunal might also order that Fred be reinstated or re-engaged (see **13.34**). If this happens, and you refuse to comply with the order, you may also have to pay an 'additional award'. This is a discretionary sum, and will be between 26 and 52 weeks' pay depending on the circumstances of the dismissal. If you can persuade a tribunal that it was not practicable to comply with an order for reinstatement or re-engagement then you will not have to pay the additional award. This will not be an easy task, since before making the order the tribunal would have considered that it was practicable for you to comply.

Contractual monies

If you dismissed Fred for gross misconduct, you do not have to pay him any contractual sums reflecting a notice period. In all other cases, you do. If you did not do so at the time of dismissal, the tribunal may order you to do so. It can only do so, however, if Fred has specifically claimed notice money or

169

breach of contract in his Originating Application. If he has not done so, the tribunal is not normally permitted to make a separate award reflecting the monies that Fred would have earned during his notice period.

If the tribunal does not make an award for contractual notice pay, it will usually include the same sum in the compensatory award, and thus Fred gets the benefit of notice monies in any event. The one exception is if Fred received more than £55,000 to reflect his loss of earnings as the compensatory award. As set out below, this sum is (normally) the maximum that the tribunal can award as a compensatory award, but it can award damages for a contractual notice period on top of this.

Calculating contractual monies 13.3

The method of calculation for contractual monies is set out in **CHAPTER 12**. If you paid notice monies to Fred at the time you dismissed him, you will not have to pay the same sums again.

Basic award 13.4

The basic award is a lump sum theoretically intended to compensate for loss of a job. It depends on pre-dismissal salary, length of service and age. The maximum that can be awarded is £8,100. The basic award is calculated according to a standard formula which is almost identical to calculation of a redundancy payment the difference being that, unlike for a redundancy payment, Fred is entitled to half a week's wage for each year he worked whilst he was under 18. See **12.19** for the method of calculating this.

Redundancy and contributory fault 13.5

If you dismissed Fred for redundancy, and paid him a redundancy payment, then any redundancy sum paid will be set-off against any unfair dismissal compensation. In other words, if you paid a redundancy payment (calculated according to the formula set out at **12.17**) then you will not have to pay a basic award if you are found to have unfairly dismissed Fred.

Sometimes a tribunal might find that Fred had contributed to, or caused, his own dismissal. Say, for example, Fred had been stealing from your company but you dismissed him without going through a proper procedure. The tribunal might find that the dismissal was technically unfair, but reduce any theoretical compensation by up to 100%. If it does this, it will usually reduce the basic award by this percentage as well as the compensatory award. Contributory fault is addressed in more detail at paragraph **13.24**.

Minimum basic award 13.6

If the dismissal is automatically unfair on the grounds that you have failed to comply with the new statutory minimum disciplinary procedures introduced in October 2004, there will be a minimum basic award of four weeks' pay (again, with a maximum of £270 per week).

Retirement 13.7

If Fred is within one year of the normal retirement age for his job (or, if there is no normal retirement age, within one year of 65 years old), the basic award is reduced by one-twelfth for each month of that year. If, therefore, Fred was dismissed two months before his 65th birthday, he would only be entitled to two-twelfths of his basic award.

Compensatory award 13.8

The compensatory award can be difficult to estimate, and this chapter gives only an overview as to how tribunals calculate compensatory awards. As stated above, the purpose of the compensatory award is to compensate Fred for being out of a job, and it broadly reflects the earnings he has lost (or is expected to lose), with various adjustments made to that starting figure. The overall test is that the award should be 'just and equitable': however, tribunals now calculate the award according to clearly laid down guidelines.

If, immediately after his dismissal, Fred obtained a better paid job, then he would have suffered no financial loss and will usually receive no compensatory award (except for a small award discussed at paragraphs **13.17** and **13.18**). If Fred is at fault and is found to have contributed to his dismissal, an award will be reduced (or extinguished) to reflect this fault. If you gave Fred an *ex gratia* payment when dismissing him, you will usually get credit for this when the award is calculated. If the dismissal was unfair on technical grounds only, and Fred's dismissal was inevitable, he will receive little or nothing as a compensatory award. However, in cases where you failed to follow the minimum dismissal procedures (set out in **APPENDIX 1**), and where you are unable to prove that dismissal was an inevitability or that he deserves to have no award on the basis of his conduct, the basic starting point of the loss of earnings will be subject to an uplift – normally of 10%, although it can be as high as 50%.

When calculating the compensatory award, a tribunal will go through, in order, the following stages:

(1) calculate the financial loss that Fred has suffered;

(2) give credit for any payments made by you;

(3)   make an appropriate deduction for contributory fault;

(4)   apply an uplift if you failed to comply with the statutory minimum dismissal procedures, or a reduction if Fred failed to comply; and,

(5)   impose a total limit on the compensatory award. At the time of writing, this limit is £55,000.

It is important to follow the above steps in the correct order since this may make a significant difference to the end result.

Step 1: Calculate the financial loss the employee has suffered   13.9

There is a standard method followed by courts when assessing the financial loss flowing from a dismissal. Essentially, a tribunal looks at what Fred would have earned if he had remained in employment, and deducts what he actually did earn (or, if he could have earned money by making reasonable efforts, what he should have earned).

A tribunal will usually consider the following items when calculating Fred's financial loss.

Loss of earnings up to date of tribunal hearing   13.10

The tribunal will calculate Fred's loss of wages up until the date of the hearing. This calculation is based on his net, not gross, wage. The starting point will be from the date up to which you paid him i.e. the later of the date of dismissal or the expiry of his notice period.

If Fred would have received a wage rise during the period between dismissal and the hearing, his net wage will be based, for the appropriate period, on the theoretical increased wage.

If he has obtained a new job, the loss of earnings will be the difference between his old net earnings and his new net earnings. If he earns more in the new job, he would have suffered no loss of earnings. If he has been dismissed from a subsequent job, the loss of earnings will usually (but not always) be calculated on the assumption that he had not been dismissed a second time, since the second dismissal would not be attributable to your dismissal of him.

Hypothetical calculation

Fred earns £200 per week net at the date of his dismissal. He finds a new job after ten weeks, paying £150 per week net. The tribunal hearing is five weeks later. Fred's loss of earnings up to the tribunal hearing is £2,250, namely: 10 weeks x £200 = £2,000, plus 5 weeks x £50 (i.e. £200 – £150) = £250.

Value of benefits   13.11

When calculating Fred's net loss of earnings, you should also take into account the value of any benefits that he received. These might include:

- *Tips*: tribunals will take tips into account when calculating the compensatory award, but not when calculating the basic award. It is usual to work out Fred's total tips over a period of 12 weeks prior to dismissal and then take the average weekly figure.

- *Bonuses*: if Fred would have received a bonus (such as a Christmas bonus or a performance related bonus), the tribunal will usually compensate him for this loss. The question is one of fact: had he remained employed, would he have received the bonus? If he was entitled to the bonus under his contract, or if all other employees received a bonus, you will have great difficulty persuading a tribunal that Fred would not have received it.

- *BUPA or PPP benefits*: this will normally be valued on the basis of the cost to Fred if he were to take out the same medical cover himself.

- *Use of a company car*: although if the car was provided for business purposes only, there is no personal loss to Fred if he no longer has use of the car. It is conventional for tribunals to use tables provided by the AA to calculate the value of the loss of a car.

- *Loss of pension rights*: if your company makes pension contributions on Fred's behalf, and he is unfairly dismissed, he will lose out on pension contributions and the tribunal will attempt to assess this loss. Pension losses are difficult to calculate and, usually, a tribunal will adopt a very rough-and-ready approach rather than attempting complex actuarial calculations.

  (1) *Money Purchase Scheme*: With a money-purchase scheme (i.e. where contributions are placed in a 'pot' reserved for Fred, and the money in the pot is used to buy an annuity when Fred retires) the loss is simply the value of the contributions that you would have made. This will be calculated for pension contributions both up until the date of the hearing and for a period into the future – see **13.16**. Note that Fred's contributions are not included, since he will receive the money into his own pocket and is free to continue to make contributions should he so wish.

  (2) *Final Salary Scheme*: A final salary scheme is one where Fred is entitled to a pension of up to two-thirds of his final salary on

retirement, depending on the number of years for which contributions have been made on his behalf. His loss is therefore the difference between his final pension (given he has been dismissed and you are no longer making contributions) and what his final pension would have been if you had continued making contributions. The loss of enhancement of accrued rights then has to be calculated this is because the pension that Fred will eventually receive will be based on a lower salary (i.e. his leaving salary) than that which he would have had if he had remained employed by you (since he probably would have received a salary increase every year). This sum then has to be adjusted to take account of the fact that Fred is receiving the money now rather than in, say, 20 years' time. The method of calculating final salary pension losses is outside the scope of this book. Traditionally, these calculations (which can involve large sums of money) have not been taken as seriously as they might, due to the historical limit on a compensatory award of £12,000. However, now that the maximum is £55,000, the pension loss can become a very substantial sum of money. If pension losses are significant in your case, seek professional advice from a specialist employment lawyer. Check that the lawyer is experienced in calculating pension losses, since pension loss cases are one of the most misunderstood areas of law.

Unemployment benefit   13.12

You are not able to set-off unemployment benefit or income support against Fred's earnings. Thus you cannot try to argue that, because Fred is in receipt of £50 per week income support, his net loss is not the £200 per week that he was earning before the dismissal, but is only £150 per week. This is because you are responsible for paying the DSS back any social security benefits received by Fred and then deducting them from his total award after the award has been assessed. This is explained further at **15.1**.

Retirement   13.13

If Fred was close to retirement then, in addition to facing a reduction in his basic award (see **13.7**), his loss of earnings would only be calculated up until the date that he would have retired. This is on the basis that if he had not been unfairly dismissed, he would have ceased earning a wage at that point in any event.

Incorrect procedures   13.14

Sometimes the tribunal might find that your dismissal of Fred was unfair because you did not follow appropriate procedures. It might consider, however, that if you *had* followed an appropriate procedure, you would still have dismissed Fred. This happens most often in redundancy and gross misconduct cases. In such a case, the tribunal might decide that if you had followed a proper procedure, Fred would have been employed for a further, say, two weeks. Accordingly the tribunal would award only two weeks' loss of earnings and there would be no further compensatory award given. If you failed to follow the minimum statutory dismissal procedure, then that (say) two weeks' loss of earnings would be subject to an uplift of (normally) 10% – see **13.22** below.

Failure to mitigate loss   13.15

If Fred is offered a job and refuses it, or if he fails to look for new employment, the tribunal may say that he has failed to 'mitigate his loss'. This means, in practical terms, that his ongoing loss of earnings will be attributable to his failure to take reasonable steps to minimise his financial loss, and not to your unfair dismissal of him. Since you are not required to pay for his failure to look after his own interests, any loss of earnings claim will stop at the point where a tribunal believes Fred could or should have obtained new employment.

Hint

It is open to you, in a compensation hearing, to suggest that Fred has failed to mitigate his loss. It may therefore be a sensible option, if Fred was dismissed for redundancy or some other similar reason, to offer him his job back. If he refuses to accept his old job back, there is often a chance that a tribunal will find that he failed to mitigate his loss – see *Wilding v British Telecom* (below). This will prevent a large loss of earnings claim from accruing.

Example

Mr Wilding worked for British Telecom for 29 years. He developed back problems and, from 1997, was no longer able to work. He was dismissed on grounds of capability in early 1998. For various reasons, the employment tribunal held it to be an unfair dismissal. After that decision, but before the tribunal re-met to decide how much money they would award Mr Wilding, British Telecom offered to re-engage him. Mr Wilding refused, because he no longer trusted BT. The Court of Appeal decided that he had acted unreasonably in refusing the offer of re-engagement, and limited compensation to the amount he would have lost if he *had* gone back to work for BT – *Wilding v British Telecom plc [2002] IRLR 524.*

Future loss of earnings 13.16

If, by the date of the tribunal hearing, Fred remains unemployed or on a lower wage than before, the tribunal will usually award an element of future earnings to compensate him for the ongoing loss of earnings.

The weekly loss of earnings is calculated the same way, i.e. if Fred has no job, it will be his net earnings (plus benefits) before dismissal, whereas if he has a new job but on a lower wage, his loss of earnings will be the difference between the two.

How far into the future will a tribunal look? There is no set rule; however, the majority of tribunals follow a similar practice. When Fred remains out of employment at the date of the hearing, most tribunals award about six months' future loss of earnings. If Fred is employed, but on a lower wage, a tribunal will often award between six and twelve months' loss of salary. The exception is if Fred is within two or three years of retirement age, when a tribunal will often award loss of earnings to take him all the way up to his expected retirement age.

There is no logical reason for these figures: it is merely a question of practice that has arisen over time.

Loss of statutory protection 13.17

Employees are not entitled to certain rights, such as unfair dismissal or redundancy rights, until they have been working for a new employer for one or two years (respectively). Accordingly, when you dismiss Fred, he will have a one- to two-year period in his new employment during which he will lack employment rights. This is reflected in an unfair dismissal award by giving a small sum for loss of statutory protection. Conventionally, this figure is around £250.

Expenses in finding new employment 13.18

The compensatory award will also include a sum to compensate or reimburse Fred for any out of pocket expenses to which he has been put because of having been dismissed. This may include the cost of looking for new employment, for example the cost of buying newspapers (for job adverts), cost of postage, stationery and telephone calls, and the cost of transport to and from job interviews.

In exceptional cases, tribunals have awarded substantial sums for expenses associated with changing jobs. This has even gone as far as, in one case, ordering the ex-employer to pay Fred's costs of moving house to change jobs. In practice, however, the value of an award for these expenses is usually modest – often £50 or £100.

Step 2: give credit for any payments made by you
13.19

It would be unfair if you voluntarily paid Fred a leaving bonus and then were not given credit for having given this payment. Likewise, it would be wholly lacking in common sense if you paid Fred a month's pay in lieu of notice, but a tribunal did not give you credit for such payment.

Pay in lieu of notice
13.20

Theoretically there are two methods of factoring in sums paid by you in lieu of notice:

- work out Fred's loss, and then give credit for the sums that you paid in lieu of notice; or,

- calculate Fred's loss from the time that the pay in lieu of notice expired.

On first glance, there would not seem to be any practical difference between the two. However, the effect of taxation means that the first method is more favourable to employers. Indeed, it is this method that tribunals adopt. The difference between the two approaches is shown in the following example:

Example

An employee was given three months' pay in lieu of notice (although, in fact, he was only entitled to one month). The tribunal assessed his loss of earnings as seven months. It followed method (ii) and awarded him four months' net loss of earnings (i.e. seven months, less the three months paid). The Employment Appeal Tribunal held that this was wrong. It said that the correct approach was to calculate the full loss of earnings, which would be calculated as seven months' net earnings, and then deduct the sum actually paid (i.e. method (i)). Since the three months' salary paid by the employer had been gross, not net, a greater sum was deducted and the employer ended up paying less to the employee than he would otherwise have done – *MBS v Calo [1983] IRLR 189.*

Other sums paid   13.21

Sometimes employers will pay a voluntary sum upon dismissal. This might occur if you were dismissing Fred due to ill health after many years of service, or if you were paying him an enhanced redundancy payment.

The general rule is this: if you pay a voluntary, or *ex gratia*, sum to Fred at the time of his dismissal, the tribunal will try to decide whether or not you would have paid it in any event if Fred had been dismissed fairly at a later date. If you would have made the *ex gratia* payment in any event, then you will not be given credit for it when the compensatory award is calculated. This might happen if you are paying a leaving bonus to employees selected for redundancy, but get the redundancy selection procedure wrong. If a tribunal decides that you would have paid a £1,000 bonus to each employee if you had got the procedure correct, it will not allow you to have a windfall of that £1,000 (by deducting from the unfair dismissal compensation) simply because you got the procedure wrong.

Usually, however, tribunals will readily accept that *ex gratia* payments made by you can be deducted from any compensatory award.

Note that, when giving credit for *ex gratia* payments, if the reason for dismissal is redundancy then the *ex gratia* payment will first be set-off against the basic award, and the excess (if any) set-off against the compensatory award. In all other cases, i.e. where the reason for dismissal is not redundancy, the entire *ex gratia* award will be set-off against the compensatory award. This will make a difference where further reductions are made to the compensatory award because of fault by Fred (see **13.24**) or because of the effect of the cap on the compensatory award (see **13.30**).

Do not be misled into thinking that, because credit is usually given for *ex gratia* payments, you will be guaranteed the full benefit of the *ex gratia* payment if Fred is found to be unfairly dismissed. There are two crucial factors which can significantly diminish, or extinguish, the benefit to you of an *ex gratia* payment. In particular:

(a)   where the compensatory award is reduced because Fred contributed to his own dismissal through his own fault. This percentage reduction, which is discussed at **13.24** below, is applied to the compensatory award aftercredit has been given for your *ex gratia* payment. The effect of the *ex gratia* payment is therefore reduced. This is best demonstrated by way of a hypothetical example:

Hypothetical example

A tribunal assesses Fred's loss of earnings at £6,000. You gave him an *ex gratia* payment of £1,500. The tribunal also finds that he was 50% to blame for his own dismissal, and thus reduces his compensatory award by 50%. If the reduction by 50% occurred first, you would have to pay £1,500 only, i.e. £3,000 (being £6,000 x 50%) less the £1,500 *ex gratia* payment. However, the correct method is for the *ex gratia* payment to be deducted first. When this is done, Fred's award is £2,250, i.e. £4,500 (being £6,000 – £1,500) x 50%. Thus you would, in practice, only get credit for 50% of your *ex gratia* payment. Ironically, the greater the reduction for Fred's contributory fault, the less credit you get from your *ex gratia* payment. Thus if Fred's award were reduced by 80% because of his fault, you would only get credit for 20% of your *ex gratia* payment.

(b)　where the statutory cap on the compensatory award is reached (currently £55,000). This cap is imposed as the very last stage of calculating the unfair dismissal award. Therefore if Fred's loss of earnings is £75,000 and you paid him £15,000 as an *ex gratia* payment, the fact that you are credited with £15,000 (so as to make the loss of earnings only £60,000) is irrelevant since you will not have to pay more than the £55,000 statutory cap in any event. The statutory cap is discussed further at **13.30**.

Step 3: Apply an uplift if you failed to comply with the statutory minimum dismissal procedures, or a reduction if Fred failed to comply 13.22

If the dismissal is automatically unfair because you have failed to comply with the statutory minimum dismissal procedures which were introduced in October 2004 (see **APPENDIX 1**), Fred's compensatory award will be subject to a percentage uplift. (Note that this uplift does *not* apply if the dismissal is automatically unfair for *other* reasons, such as a dismissal for whistleblowing.)

The standard uplift is 10%. Thus a compensatory award of £15,000 will normally be increased to £16,500 if you have failed to comply with the minimum statutory dismissal procedures.

However, tribunals have a discretion to apply an uplift of up to 10%. At the time of writing, before these new laws have come into force, there is no guidance as to the circumstances when a tribunal will go above the 'normal' 10%. It is likely, though, that a higher percentage uplift will only be applied in cases where the employer has deliberately decided to flout the statutory dismissal procedures, rather than a case where the employer has simply got it wrong inadvertently.

In exceptional circumstances, a tribunal can decline to apply any uplift. Again, there is no guidance, at the time of writing, on what 'exceptional circumstances' means. It is likely that this will only apply to very minor, technical breaches where the tribunal believes the employer was doing his best to comply, and where the failure to comply made no difference to the end result.

Note that any uplifted award will still be subject to the £55,000 statutory cap, discussed below.

Reducing the award if Fred failed to comply   13.23

If it was Fred who failed to comply with the statutory dismissal procedures (as set out in **APPENDIX 1**), then his award will be reduced unless he can bring himself within one of the exceptions, for example that it was not practicable to comply within a reasonable period, or he was in fear of physical violence or harassment.

The most common way in which he can fail to comply is to fail to take reasonable steps to attend the disciplinary meeting, or to fail to appeal (although the minimum procedures seem to indicate that an appeal is *optional*, a reduction *will* be made if Fred chooses not to appeal) – see **13.28**.

As with uplifts, the standard reduction will be 10%, although the tribunal can reduce by up to 50% and in 'exceptional circumstances' can decline to make any reduction.

Step 4: Make an appropriate deduction for contributory fault   13.24

The importance of procedural correctness when dismissing Fred cannot be overstated. Dismissals are frequently held to be unfair, even in cases where Fred's conduct warranted immediate dismissal, simply because the employer had not engaged in sufficient investigation or consultation to satisfy the tribunal. Since October 2004, many dismissals will be *automatically* unfair if you have failed to follow the minimum dismissal procedure at **APPENDIX 1**.

However, the tribunal is entitled to reduce the compensatory award in circumstances where Fred has been guilty of improper and blameworthy conduct which caused or contributed to his dismissal. This reduction is usually applied on a percentage basis: thus where the tribunal thinks that Fred is 75% responsible for the dismissal, the award will be reduced by 75%. The reduction should be applied against both the basic and the compensatory award, although the tribunal can reduce the compensatory award only, or reduce the two awards by different percentages. Although there would seem to be no logical reason for treating the two awards differently, the courts have made it clear that it is not improper to do so.

Hypothetical example

Somebody is stealing tyres from your factory. Circumstantial evidence points to Fred, and you dismiss him without inviting him to a disciplinary meeting. After the dismissal, Fred is investigated by the police and convicted by the criminal courts of theft. Although the tribunal would find that the dismissal was automatically unfair, because you failed to comply with the statutory minimum dismissal procedure by not inviting him to a meeting, it would significantly reduce Fred's award (quite possibly by 100%). Note that an alternative approach would be for the tribunal to say that although the dismissal was unfair, if a proper investigation had taken place a fair dismissal would have occurred, say, two weeks later thus Fred is entitled to his basic award and two weeks' salary as the compensatory award. An employer would prefer the former approach since, if Fred was a longstanding employee, the basic award could be quite substantial. Both approaches are equally viable.

What amounts to blameworthy conduct?   13.25

An inability to do the job properly will rarely amount to blameworthy conduct. The fact that somebody does not measure up to the job cannot be something that disentitles them from receiving compensation when you dismiss them unfairly. If you appointed an inappropriate person or failed to train them properly, the fault is yours and not theirs.

The harshness of this rule is mitigated to some extent, in cases of procedural unfairness, by the fact that you will often be able to demonstrate that if you had operated the correct procedures, you would have dismissed Fred anyway within a few weeks/months: thus his compensatory award would be limited to these few weeks'/months' pay. This is discussed further at **13.14**.

The one exception to this rule is where a tribunal is satisfied that Fred's inabilities are due to his own fault in the sense of indifference or idleness (rather than simply lacking the intelligence or experience for the job). In this case, his conduct will be blameworthy and a reduction for contributory fault will be made. However, such reductions tend to be at the lower end of the scale, and rarely exceed 50%.

Need to demonstrate blameworthiness   13.26

Blameworthy conduct will usually exist where Fred commits an act which is morally or legally wrong. The mere fact that he refuses to obey your instructions will not necessarily amount to blameworthy conduct.

Example

> An employee was dismissed because he refused to obey an instruction which would have involved illegally falsifying records. The employer argued that any compensation should be reduced because he contributed to his own dismissal by refusing to obey instructions. The National Industrial Relations Court (the predecessor of employment tribunals) held that there should be no reduction in his award because his conduct was not blameworthy – *Morrish v Henleys (Folkestone) Ltd [1973] 2 All ER 137.*

The need for blameworthiness is important. If Fred is in breach of an express term of his contract of employment, this will usually be sufficient to amount to contributory fault. It has even been said by the Court of Appeal in one case that if Fred is merely 'bloodyminded' this may be sufficient to amount to blameworthy conduct (*Nelson v British Broadcasting Corporation (No 2) [1979] IRLR 346*). However, a morally or legally culpable act, such as theft, violence or provocative conduct is usually required before a reduction can be made for contributory fault.

Three things which cannot be blameworthy   13.27

There are three things which legally cannot amount to blameworthy conduct:

- when Fred joins, or refuses to join, a trade union. The law gives trade union membership (or non-membership) certain privileges, and one of these is immunity from being found to have been contributorily at fault in a dismissal. This is to prevent an employer from arguing that Fred caused his own dismissal by refusing to join a trade union in a closed-shop situation (closed-shops are, in any event, no longer lawful);

- when Fred is involved in industrial action (such as a strike or a work-to-rule), the fact that he is involved in the industrial action cannot amount to contributory fault. If, whilst participating in the industrial action, he engages in conduct which goes beyond mere participation (such as throwing stones), then this may amount to contributory fault;

- when the blameworthy conduct is discovered after the dismissal. This is because the blameworthy conduct must cause or contribute to the dismissal and, if it was not known about, it could not have caused or contributed to it. This is different from the hypothetical example set out at **13.24** above because, in that example, the employer dismissed Fred because of the theft of tyres, even if he lacked sufficient proof at the time, and thus the dismissal was caused because of Fred's conduct.

Not exercising the right to appeal   13.28

What if Fred fails to exercise his right to an internal appeal against your decision to dismiss?

Unless he can bring himself within one of the exceptions (such as being in fear of physical violence if he exercises his right to appeal), Fred's failure to appeal will mean that *he* is in breach of the minimum dismissal procedures. As a result, a tribunal will reduce his award. The normal reduction is by 10%, although the tribunal has discretion to reduce the award by up to 50% (or, in exceptional circumstances, to make no reduction at all).

Likewise, if the employer prevents Fred from appealing against his dismissal, the employer will be in breach of the statutory minimum procedure and the dismissal will be automatically unfair. In addition, Fred's compensation will be subject to an uplift (see **13.22**).

What percentage reduction should be applied?   13.29

Guidance from the Employment Appeal Tribunal indicates that a finding of 100% contributory fault (so that Fred receives no compensation whatsoever) should be rare. This is because, by the very fact that dismissal is unfair, it follows that the employer is at fault in some way (even if only through failing to follow proper procedures). Accordingly Fred cannot be said to be the sole cause of his dismissal, since some fault lies with the employer thus a finding of 100% fault is inappropriate.

However, the Employment Appeal Tribunal has shown a marked reluctance to reverse the decisions of employment tribunals when they do find Fred to be 100% responsible. In practice, such a finding is not as rare the appellate courts might wish. Situations when a finding of 100% contributory fault is made will usually be situations involving substantial violence (i.e. something more than throwing a few punches in a fight), theft involving large sums of money or long-term dishonesty.

A common scenario is where dismissal was not a reasonable response to Fred's actions, i.e. where Fred was technically at fault but you have gone over the top in dismissing him. Examples include peripheral involvement in a minor fracas by a long-standing employee, the use of postage stamps for personal mail or intoxication at work (without aggravating factors). In such a scenario, Fred will usually be found to be contributorily at fault; however, the percentage reduction will be small: perhaps around 25%. Tribunals can vary enormously in the reductions they apply, and there are no real guidelines so as to enable a prediction of the likely degree of contributory fault found in any given case.

Step 5: Imposing the statutory cap   13.30

It is important to go through the above three stages in the correct order since, as demonstrated, the order of applying the reductions can make a difference as to the final sum arrived at.

Amount of the statutory cap   13.31

Once the above three steps have been gone through by the employment tribunal, it will apply the statutory cap to the total compensatory award. At the time of writing, this cap is £55,000. This sum is the top limit that a tribunal can award as the compensatory award. This does not include the basic award (which has a current maximum of £8,100 – see **13.4**). The very large awards, in the tens or hundreds of thousands of pounds that are sometimes seen reported by journalists, are in discrimination cases where no upper limit for the award exists.

Applying the statutory cap   13.32

Thus if Fred's net salary is £4,000 per month, the hearing is nine months after the dismissal and the tribunal decides to award him a further twelve months' future loss of salary, his loss of earnings would be £84,000. Even if you had given him a £5,000 *ex gratia* payment (bringing the award down to £79,000) and he was found to be 25% responsible for the dismissal (bringing the award down to £59,250), the tribunal could only award a maximum of £55,000 for the compensatory award.

Exceptions where there is no limit to compensatory award   13.33

There are several exceptions to the £55,000 statutory cap. In the following situations, there is *no* limit to the compensatory award:

(a)   when the dismissal is found to be unfair under the whistleblowing legislation (i.e. where Fred has disclosed confidential company informa-tion and it is in the public interest that it be disclosed);

(b)   where Fred was dismissed for a reason connected with health & safety;

(c)   where the tribunal has ordered the reinstatement or re-engagement of Fred (see **13.34**), this will usually include an Order for back pay. There is no limit of £55,000 on the Order for back pay. If you do not comply with the Order for reinstatement/re-engagement, the tribunal will order compensation in the ordinary way and order you to pay an additional sum (known as the 'additional award' – see **13.42**). Therefore where the compensatory award comes about because of the employer's failure to comply with an Order for reinstatement/re-engagement, the limit of £55,000 does not apply (because otherwise the employer might be in a better position financially by refusing to comply with a tribunal Order to reinstate than by complying with it).

Reinstatement and re-engagement   13.34

The tribunal can order that you reinstate or re-engage Fred and pay him back-pay to put him back in the position he would have been in had he never been dismissed. There is a box on the Originating Application (the form that he fills in to start his claim) in which Fred can tick a box stating whether he is seeking reinstatement, re-engagement or just compensation.

If Fred has ticked either of the first two boxes, or if he has told you that he wishes to be reinstated or re-engaged at least seven days before the hearing, you must come to the tribunal prepared to give evidence on whether reinstatement/re-engagement is practicable. If you fail to do so, the tribunal will adjourn and must order you to pay Fred's legal costs unless you can establish a 'special reason' (which is undefined) for your failure to bring evidence on the practicability of reinstatement/re-engagement first time around.

What is the difference between reinstatement and re-engagement?   13.35

Reinstatement involves replacing Fred into the job he had before you dismissed him. Re-engagement involves the tribunal specifying the nature of the employment that Fred is suited for, the amount payable to him (including benefits) and any other rights and privileges (including seniority). It is then up to you, or an associated employer, to re-engage him before a specified date in a job of your choice provided it complies with the specifications laid down by the tribunal.

When the tribunal order reinstatement or re-engagement, it will always make an order requiring that Fred receives all back-pay between the date of dismissal and the date of reinstatement or re-engagement.

When will the tribunal order reinstatement or re-engagement?   13.36

A tribunal will never order reinstatement or re-engagement unless Fred asks for it. If he does ask to be reinstated or re-engaged, he can indicate a preference (although the tribunal will not be bound by it).

Two tests of practicability   13.37

The crucial question for the tribunal to decide when determining whether to order reinstatement or re-engagement is the practicability of such an Order. This will involve you providing evidence on, and the tribunal considering, the nature of the jobs that are available for Fred (including his old job). If there is a job that is fairly suitable for Fred, even if it is dissimilar to his old job, the tribunal may consider re-engagement in this post. The tribunal will not, however, expect you to create a job for Fred or dismiss existing employees in order to make room for Fred.

There is one exception: if you have replaced Fred, the tribunal may expect you to engage Fred in addition to the replacement (or dismiss the replacement) unless you can satisfy the tribunal that:

- it was not practicable for you to arrange for Fred's work to be done without engaging a permanent replacement (i.e. it was not practicable to engage a temp pending the outcome of the employment tribunal hearing); or

- you hired the permanent replacement after a reasonable time had elapsed and Fred had not told you that he wished to be reinstated or re-engaged, and that when you engaged the permanent replacement, it was no longer reasonable for you to expect Fred's work to be done except by a permanent replacement.

Unless you can satisfy one of these two tests, the tribunal will consider reinstatement/re-engagement as if you had not hired the permanent replacement and Fred's job was still being done by a temp.

How can you resist an Order for reinstatement/re-engagement?   13.38

An important factor in whether it is practicable to order reinstatement or re-engagement is whether such an Order will cause disharmony amongst other members of staff. If Fred is no longer trusted by other members of staff, the tribunal is unlikely to order you to re-employ him (unless he can be moved to a different department or an associated employer). If his job involves contact with the public and his conduct, whilst not warranting dismissal, makes his continuing contact with the public undesirable, then the tribunal is unlikely to order reinstatement. Likewise, if yours is a small business and you would be in day-to-day contact with Fred, and there has been a breakdown in your personal relationship caused by the litigation, the tribunal is unlikely to order that you continue working together.

A mere assertion by you that one of the above reasons applies is unlikely to satisfy a tribunal. You should obtain written evidence that employees are unhappy about continuing to work with Fred, or get Fred to admit when he gives evidence that he would be uncomfortable returning to work. If, as suggested at **13.15**, you offered Fred his job back and he refused, this might be a good reason for arguing against reinstatement (since it shows that he no longer has confidence in working for you).

What if you do not comply with an Order for reinstatement or re-engagement? 13.39

If you do not comply with an Order for reinstatement or re-engagement, Fred can take you back to the tribunal. Likewise if you offer Fred a job, purporting to comply with an Order for re-engagement, but the new job is not suitable, he can take you back to the tribunal. The tribunal will consider the same question as before, namely whether it was practicable for you to comply with the Order. This time, however, you have the benefit of hindsight (so that you can say why it was not practicable) rather than providing speculative forecasts.

Again, in considering practicability, the tribunal will not take into account the fact that you have hired a replacement for Fred unless you can bring yourself within one of the two limbs of the test set out at **13.37**.

Tribunal reconsiders 13.40

If the tribunal agrees, second time around, that it was not practicable for you to reinstate or re-engage Fred, then it will assess the basic and compensatory award as if the Order for reinstatement/re-engagement had never been made.

Penalty for not complying 13.41

If, however, the tribunal considers that it would have been practicable to comply with its Order, it will:

- calculate the basic and compensatory award as if the Order for reinstatement/re-engagement had never been made, with the exception that the £55,000 cap on the compensatory award will not be applied: see **13.32**; and

- it will order you to pay an 'additional award' as punishment.

How is the 'additional award' calculated? 13.42

The additional award is calculated on the basis of between 13 and 26 weeks' pay, unless the reason for the original dismissal was also discriminatory on grounds of sex or race, in which case it will be calculated on the basis of between 26 and 52 weeks' pay.

For the purpose of calculating a week's pay, the tribunal will take Fred's gross weekly wage but apply a maximum of £270 per week; thus the calculation is similar to that performed when calculating the basic award (see **13.4**). Therefore the maximum payable is £14,040 (i.e. 52 weeks x £270 pw).

How will the tribunal decide where to place the award within the scale (i.e. should it award at the bottom of the scale, being 13 weeks' pay, or towards the top of the scale, being either 26 or 52 weeks' pay)? This is very much a matter for the tribunal's discretion: however, an employer who deliberately flouts the tribunal's order will generally have to pay at the higher end of the scale, whereas an employer who genuinely believes that reinstatement is not practicable (even if the tribunal disagrees) is more likely to pay at the lower end of the scale.

Chapter 14
Tactics before the Tribunal Hearing

Introduction 14.1

This chapter is concerned with procedural steps you can take once you discover that Fred is contemplating a claim for unfair dismissal. There are two purposes to taking these procedural steps:

- you will often be able to obtain additional information about his case, which will enable you to be better prepared at a hearing; and

- you can place pressure on him and force him to undertake additional work, which may expose weaknesses in his case and may make him inclined to accept a lower settlement offer than he would otherwise do.

Not all of the following steps will be appropriate in any given case. However, you should familiarise yourself with the procedural applications available which can be used to place pressure on Fred.

Basic outline of procedure 14.2

The first you will hear about a claim of unfair dismissal, unless Fred has informed you in advance of his claim, will be the Claim Form arriving on your doorstep. This used to be called an 'Originating Application', and is often referred to as an 'IT1' or 'ET1' (being the HMSO reference number for the Claim Form).

In order to claim, Fred will have sent a Claim Form to his local employment tribunal. At the time of writing, the Claim Forms and Response Forms are being fundamentally redesigned; it is believed that, from April 2005, the new forms will become compulsory and any claim (or response) *not* on the standard form will be rejected.

The tribunal will also reject the Claim Form if, from the information given, the tribunal thinks that the employee has failed to use your internal grievance procedure in cases where it is obligatory to do so (basically, any case other than unfair dismissal *but* in constructive dismissal cases, the employee must try to use your internal grievance procedure before he is allowed to bring a tribunal claim).

Assuming the employee has used the correct form, and (if necessary) has lodged an internal grievance and waited the requisite 28 days, the tribunal will forward a copy of the Claim Form to you, with your Response Form enclosed for you to complete and return. This is often referred to as an 'IT3' or 'ET3' and used to be known as a 'Notice of Appearance'.

You should complete the Response Form, which contains space for you to set out the reasons why you dispute Fred's claim. You have 28 days in which to complete and return the form. Until recently it used to be the case that the tribunal would always allow an extension of time, but a recent change in the rules provides that they will not allow extra time unless you have a good reason for the delay. Do not ignore this form: if you do not return it you may not be allowed to defend the proceedings and the tribunal can enter 'default judgment' against you (which means you will be deemed to have unfairly dismissed Fred, who automatically wins his claim).

If you think you may not be able to comply with the 28-day limit, write to the tribunal as early as possible, explaining your reasons for seeking further time and asking for an additional, say, 14 days.

Claim is against the wrong company   14.3

Employees sometimes get the name of the employer wrong on their IT1 forms. If Fred is employed by a small company, it is not uncommon for him to state the name of the managing director (rather than the name of the limited company) as his employer. Provided you are not misled by this (for example, if you operate several similarly named companies and Fred has named the wrong one as his employer) a tribunal is likely to allow Fred to amend his claim form: accordingly there is little point in making an issue out of this.

If, however, Fred really has claimed against the wrong company, you may wish to include this as one of your grounds of defence on the Response Form. If the tribunal does not allow Fred to amend his IT1, and it is found that he has claimed unfair dismissal against the wrong person or company, his claim will fail. Further, by the time of the hearing the three months (sometimes six months) for presenting a claim will have elapsed, and thus it will be too late for Fred to start a new claim against the right employer.

Notice of hearing   14.4

Unless you or Fred make any of the applications set out below, the next document you will receive will be the Notice of Hearing. This is simply a form that tells you where and when the hearing will take place. If you cannot attend on the date stated, or if you do not think enough time has been allocated to the hearing, you must write to the tribunal immediately stating your reasons for seeking an adjournment. If you wait until a few days before the actual hearing date to request an adjournment, it is likely that your request will be refused. See **16.3** for a more detailed discussion of adjournments.

Procedure at the hearing itself is addressed in **CHAPTER 16**. However, before the hearing there are various steps that are often taken, known as 'interim' steps. These include exchanging documents and witness statements with the other side, and procedures for formally requesting documents or answers to questions. Methods of doing these, and the tactical advantages and disadvantages of doing so, are addressed below.

Using a lawyer 14.5

Using a lawyer may mean you have a better chance of winning your claim: a lawyer will (or should!) have experience of similar cases, and will be able to distinguish arguments which are likely to impress a tribunal from those which will not. You will also receive objective advice from somebody who is not emotionally bound up in the dismissal.

Lawyers also encourage settlement. It may be galling to have to pay Fred a few thousand pounds as a nuisance settlement. However, the alternative is losing several days' productivity for yourself and, possibly, a number of other employees who would be called as witnesses at a tribunal hearing. In addition, you would be saving the cost of spending more on lawyers (if you were planning to do so). This is a commercial decision for you to make, but when balancing these factors against the additional risk of having to pay Fred thousands of pounds in compensation should you lose your case, the commercial arguments usually support paying Fred a token sum in order to be rid of his claim.

Using an employment consultant 14.6

The obvious disadvantage of using a lawyer is cost. At the end of the day, if you are willing to spend a few thousand pounds on a lawyer, you should also be willing to offer that sum to Fred in order to make his claim go away.

You may choose, instead, to engage an employment consultant. These are people who are (usually) not legally qualified but who have set themselves up in business representing companies at employment tribunals. Some employment consultants are very good and will do an excellent job. Others may not be so good. Employment consultants are not regulated by any professional body and may not be insured if they are negligent in the preparation of your case. As with a lawyer, it is unwise to use an employment consultant unless you have seen him in action or have a personal recommendation from someone whose judgment you trust.

There are two disadvantages in using an employment consultant. First, any correspondence between you and a solicitor is regarded as 'privileged'. This means that it is confidential and the tribunal cannot order you to produce it. There is some doubt concerning whether correspondence with an employment consultant is privileged, or whether the tribunal is entitled to demand copies of letters from and to the consultant. This could be dangerous since your letters may contain damaging admissions, or the consultant's letters could contain unfavourable advice. The Employment Appeal Tribunal has decided (*New Victoria Hospital v Ryan [1993] IRLR 202*) that tribunals should be allowed to look at correspondence between an employer and an employment consultant, on the basis that litigants were only entitled to protection from disclosure of advice given by qualified lawyers. After the end of the case, it gave permission to the employer to appeal, but the employer did not do so. Take this risk into account when deciding whether to engage a lawyer, an employment consultant or, indeed, nobody at all. Second, and perhaps more importantly, you *cannot recover any costs paid to an employment consultant*. In certain circumstances, a successful employer can recover his legal costs back from the employee (see **16.40**). However, you cannot recover the fees that you have paid to an employment consultant.

What will a lawyer cost? 14.7

How long is a piece of string? Some lawyers will agree to represent you for a fixed fee (although this is not common). Others will be willing to represent you for a percentage of money that they may save you (although you are at their mercy when they tell you what Fred's claim might have been worth and thus how much you have saved). Most frequently, however, you will be charged at an hourly rate.

Do ensure that your solicitor has experience of employment matters. Employment law and procedure can be complex, and there is little purpose in paying large fees to someone who is simply working out of a book like this one!

A broad average for engaging a high street solicitor to manage a basic one-day unfair dismissal claim would be around £3,000 to £5,000. Many solicitors will recommend that you engage a barrister for the tribunal appearance. If you engage a relatively junior barrister, who has been practising for two or three years, he is likely to charge up to £750 for one day's hearing (this includes all necessary preparation before the hearing) and perhaps £500 for a second day. For a more senior barrister you will be looking at higher figures – perhaps around £1,250 to £1,500 for a one-day hearing.

Remember you will probably be unable to recover these fees from Fred even if you win the hearing. Having your 'day in court' can cost much more than settling.

If you are unable to find a lawyer through personal knowledge or recommendation, send an email to solrecommend@danielbarnett.co.uk stating (a) where you are based; and (b) giving a one-paragraph outline of your problem. I (or someone on my behalf) should normally be able to give you one or two names to approach.

Was the claim lodged in time? 14.8

An unfair dismissal claim must normally be lodged with the tribunal within three months of a dismissal. Extensions of time are only granted in limited circumstances: see **18.9**. The three exceptions are:

(a) in normal dismissal cases, where Fred reasonably believes that your disciplinary process is ongoing on the day the three months expires; and

(b) in constructive dismissal cases, where Fred *either* lodged a Claim Form within three months (but it was rejected because he had not tried to use your internal grievance procedure and waited 28 days), *or* he sent you a formal grievance letter within the three months.

In either of those cases, Fred is given an extra three months (i.e. six months in total from the date of dismissal) to bring a claim.

(c) Where it is 'not reasonably practicable' for Fred to lodge his claim within three months. This means 'not reasonably feasible' and tribunals interpret it fairly strictly. In general, an extension will only be granted if Fred was incapable of lodging his claim within the prescribed period (through illness or other incapacity) or if he was unaware of the facts which would give rise to his claim. If he has received erroneous legal advice he will not normally be entitled to an extension of time (his remedy being to sue his advisers).

Subject to these exceptions, if Fred fails to lodge his application within three months, his claim will be dismissed.

The onus is very firmly on Fred to present his claim within the time limit. There is no obligation on you to assist him in doing this.

Leaving it to the last minute 14.9

If Fred posted his claim to the tribunal at least two clear days before the expiry of the three- (or six-) month period, and it is delayed because of postal delays, a tribunal will normally say that it was not reasonably practicable for the claim to have been presented in time.

Pre-hearing review 14.10

If Fred does present his claim outside the three- (or six-) month limit, the tribunal will send both of you a notice stating that it appears that Fred is out of time for presenting his claim and that you are required to attend a pre-hearing review (which, until October 2004, was known as a 'preliminary hearing') to determine whether or not the tribunal has jurisdiction to hear the matter. In order to be allowed to continue with his claim, Fred will have to show both that it was not reasonably practicable for him to present his claim within the three months, and that he has presented it within a reasonable time of it becoming practicable.

If Fred's Claim Form states (in a constructive dismissal case) that he has used the internal grievance procedure, but you do not agree, you must make this clear in your Response Form and ask for a pre-hearing review.

Likewise, in a normal dismissal scenario, if Fred has presented his Claim Form outside the three-month period but within six months, you may wish to challenge his belief that you were still engaging in a disciplinary procedure on the day the three-month period expired. If there is correspondence showing the disciplinary process concluded within three months (and Fred *knew* that to be the case), you should write to the tribunal and ask for a pre-hearing review to decide whether Fred presented his claim within time.

Offering a job back 14.11

As you have seen in CHAPTER 13, the bulk of any award Fred receives for unfair dismissal will be the salary that he has lost as the result of being unemployed. He is under a duty to mitigate this loss by accepting any reasonable job that is offered to him. If you are prepared to have him back (which might be the case if you dismissed him for redundancy or because of a business relocation), and you are not confident about your chances of success at the hearing, you should offer him his old (or an alternative) job.

Although he is not obliged to take the job, there is a chance that you will be able to persuade a tribunal that Fred should not be entitled to any compensation for loss of salary from the date that you offered the job to him. A tribunal will reject this argument if it decides that your job offer was not realistic, in that Fred's dismissal took place in such circumstances that he could not reasonably be expected to re-start work (due to the acrimony of dismissal or the nature of the allegations made against him indicating that your new job offer is a sham).

However, if you would consider taking Fred on again, you cannot lose anything by offering him a job. If he accepts, he may well agree to drop his claim (although you should not insist on this, or, indeed, suggest it prior to him recommencing work). In any event, his claim for loss of earnings will be frozen at the date that he re-started work, and will not continue on into the future.

What you must not do is make an offer to Fred and then, if he accepts it, dismiss him again. He would be entitled to claim unfair dismissal for the second dismissal as well as the first one, and, in those circumstances, the second dismissal would undoubtedly be unfair. You would not be able to argue that Fred lacked one year's employment in respect of the second dismissal (assuming he had it for the first). This is because the 'one year employment' rule has an exception, namely if Fred had been working previously and there had been a 'temporary cessation of work' (which would be the case if you had dismissed and then re-hired him), his continuity of employment would continue running.

Pre-hearing review – establishing 'little reasonable prospect of success'   14.12

This is one of the best ways of putting pressure on Fred if his claim is weak. In essence, you can ask the chairman to look at the Claim Form and decide whether Fred's case has little reasonable prospect of success (until October 2004, the test was '*no* reasonable prospect of success'). If he decides that Fred's case, based on the Claim Form, does not have a reasonable prospect of success, he can order Fred to pay a small deposit as a condition of continuing to bring his claim. Sometimes a chairman will call for a pre-hearing review on his/her own initiative.

The test that a chairman applies, i.e. 'little reasonable prospect of success', is not an easy one to satisfy. The chairman holds a hearing, looks at both the Claim Form and Response Form, and reads (or listens to) any written (or oral) submissions made by yourself and Fred.

It is important to note, however, that evidence is not permitted at a pre-hearing review. It is not a mini-trial: rather it is an attempt to weed out cases which appear hopeless simply on reading the claim form. If you and Fred are in dispute over the circumstances leading up to his dismissal, a pre-hearing review will not be appropriate. If, however, Fred states in his claim form that 'I was drunk on duty when operating dangerous machinery and, just because I hit somebody after having received three warnings for violence, I was sacked' then a pre-hearing review would be a wise tactical move since, on the face of his application, he would have no reasonable prospect of success at a full tribunal hearing.

Employee ordered to pay a deposit   14.13

If a chairman accepts that Fred's claim has little reasonable prospect of success, he can order Fred to pay a deposit before he is allowed to continue with his claim. This deposit is small, usually being £500 (which is the maximum) but sometimes being reduced if Fred is of limited means.

The tribunal which actually hears the full case will not be told, and is not permitted to know, about the requirement that Fred pay a deposit. If Fred is particularly belligerent about his claim, and is able to risk a £500 deposit, winning a pre-hearing review may be a pyrrhic victory. However, sometimes it can do a remarkable job of focusing Fred's mind on the weaknesses of his case statistically, about two-thirds of claims where the employee has been ordered to pay a deposit are struck out because he fails to come up with the money.

Only use this tactic if his case is very weak   14.14

If a chairman is not persuaded that Fred's claim has little reasonable prospect of success, he will permit Fred to continue with his claim unfettered by the need to put down a deposit. This is a result which should be avoided. First, it means that you have wasted your own time, particularly if you attended the hearing rather than making written representations. Secondly, and more fundamentally, it will boost Fred's opinion of the merits of his claim and increase his determination to proceed. He may misunderstand the nature of the pre-hearing review, and believe that a chairman has told him he is likely to succeed at the full hearing. This makes him less likely to accept a nuisance value settlement of his claim at a later date.

It follows that this tactic, although potentially rewarding, should not be used unless Fred's case comes across as lacking in merit on paper. Do not be tempted by the thought that you can persuade the chairman that Fred is lying or mistaken: the chairman will not be interested in hearing evidence or testing the relative strengths of each side's claims. It is only if Fred appears to have little reasonable prospect of success on a plain reading of his Originating Application that this procedure should be utilised.

Obtaining further details of the employee's case   14.15

Sometimes Fred's claim form will be a bare assertion that you dismissed him unfairly. Sometimes he will give a long, rambling account of every perceived discourtesy to him which occurred over the last five years. Sometimes Fred will set out the details of his complaint on the form in reasonable detail. It is often the case, however, that you will want to know more about exactly what he is alleging, in order to enable you to prepare a defence properly.

You can write to Fred and ask him for further details of his case. This letter should take the form of short questions. For example, if Fred asserts that 'I was told that I could use the machine without engaging the guard', you might ask

'Who told you you could use the machine without engaging the guard?', 'On how many occasions were you told this?' and 'Please state the date and location of each occasion and the gist of the words used.'

Send a copy of this letter to the tribunal at the same time. This is so that, if Fred later denies having received the letter, you can prove that you had written it on the date you claim.

If Fred fails to provide a reply (or satisfactory answers) within 14 days, you should write to the tribunal and ask them to make an Order requiring Fred to answer the questions. Enclose another copy of the original letter, state the date it was first sent and either that you have not received a reply, or that the reply was unsatisfactory (and enclose a copy of the unsatisfactory reply). The tribunal will then make an Order, if it considers it appropriate, that Fred should answer the questions (usually within a further 14 days).

What questions will a tribunal consider appropriate?   14.16

A tribunal will not allow you to ask a long list of questions which are of marginal relevance only, oppressive (in that they require unreasonable time or expense to provide answers) or that ask for evidence.

Whether or not your questions are asking for evidence is not always obvious. If you ask Fred for the grounds on which he says, for example, he was not fairly selected for redundancy, then this is asking for further details of his claim. If, by contrast, you ask Fred which witnesses he is going to call in support of his claim, or how a particular document assists his case, then this is asking for evidence. If in doubt, ask the question! The worst that can happen is that the tribunal will decline to make an Order forcing Fred to answer.

A common ground for ordering further details is when an employee states that the points supporting his case 'include' certain matters. In such a situation you should ask whether there are any other points on which he relies. A tribunal should support you and make an Order if Fred fails to respond.

Example

An employee, who was dismissed for making fraudulent expense claims, alleged that he was only doing what had been done by other employees over a long period of time and that it had been condoned by management. The Employment Appeal Tribunal ordered that the employee should give more details concerning the allegation that other employees had been permitted to steal – *International Computers Ltd v*

197

Whitley [1978] IRLR 318.

Example

An employee claimed he had been dismissed for 'redundancy/ victimisation'. The tribunal ordered him to give further details about the redundancy and victimisation, and state the name of the person who he said had been victimising him – *Colonial Mutual Life Assurance Society v Clinch [1981] ICR 752.*

What if the employee does not comply with a tribunal's Order to answer questions?   14.17

If Fred fails to comply with an Order of the tribunal within the time allowed, you should immediately write to the tribunal and tell it. You can suggest an appropriate penalty, although the tribunal is entirely free to do as it chooses.

There are two possible penalties for non-compliance with a tribunal's Order to answer questions. First, a tribunal can make a costs order against Fred for unreasonable conduct (see below). However, the costs attributable to the request for answers are unlikely to be large.

The second penalty is that the tribunal can strike out all, or some, of Fred's claim. In other words, the tribunal can either throw out the entire claim, or the part of it which he has failed to give further details of. This is, needless to say, a particularly satisfying way for an employer to avoid having to go to a full tribunal hearing and risk paying large sums of money. However, before a tribunal is allowed to strike out any, or all, of Fred's claim, it must first write to him asking him why he has failed to comply with the Order. This requirement takes much of the sting out of the striking out provisions because, in reality, if Fred offers an explanation and provides the answers a tribunal will always give him the benefit of the doubt and not strike out his claim.

Asking for further details   14.18

Asking for further details is a useful tactic to adopt whilst waiting for a hearing date. Unless your requests are irrelevant, at the very least you will get a clearer idea of the case Fred intends to bring against you. This is beneficial for three reasons:

- you are better able to investigate his complaints, obtain all relevant documents and evidence, and ensure that yourself and other witnesses are prepared to be cross-examined on the points he raises;

- you can often tell as much about Fred's case from what he does not say as from what he does say. If there is a particularly damaging fact, of which you do not know if he is aware, the fact that he does not mention it when supplying further details will be a strong indicator that he is not aware of it;

- the more information Fred provides in writing, the more scope you have for discovering an inconsistency when cross-examining him at the tribunal hearing.

There is a chance that Fred will decide he simply cannot be bothered to answer the questions and continue his claim, thus giving you the opportunity to have his claim struck out.

Obtaining copies of the employee's documents   14.19

Tribunals tend to be tolerant of litigants who turn up clutching reams of documents that you have never seen before. Sometimes, you may be permitted an adjournment: however, it is obviously preferable to know what documents he has well in advance of the hearing.

It is now standard practice in most tribunals for the tribunal to send out standard directions which include a requirement for each party to send each copies of all documents which they intend to rely upon.

Asking for disclosure   14.20

There may be situations when you believe Fred has documents, which you have not seen, which might help your case. An example would be if you have dismissed Fred for breaking (or preparing to break) confidentiality clauses or restraint of trade clauses in his contract of employment. Another example would be if you dismissed Fred for theft of large sums of money you may wish to see his bank account to see whether large deposits, which cannot be his salary, have been made.

You should first write to Fred asking for voluntary disclosure of the documents. Be specific in what you want. If you simply ask for 'all relevant documents' you are unlikely to receive any sympathy from a tribunal when seeking an Order to enforce the request. Your request should state precisely which documents you seek.

If Fred fails to produce the documents within 14 days of your request, you should write to the tribunal asking for an Order that Fred produce copies. Enclose a copy of your earlier letter to Fred and confirm that he has not responded (or, if he has responded inadequately, enclose a copy of his reply).

You then need to set out the reasons why the tribunal should order Fred to supply the documents. This is not always straightforward. You must justify your request by proving that production of the documents is necessary for disposing fairly of the proceedings. To do this, you will need to show that you are doing more than simply fishing for evidence. Set out your reasons for suspecting that Fred has relevant documents in his possession.

The tribunal will either decide upon your application or, if it wants to hear Fred's argument as to why he should not have to supply the documents, it may call both sides for a 'directions' hearing. This is a hearing where the chairman, who is legally qualified, listens to submissions from both sides and decides whether or not to order Fred to produce the documents.

Unless the point being argued is complex, and lawyers are involved, these hearings will usually be fairly short (no more than 30 minutes). Nevertheless, before attending such a hearing you should weigh up the advantages of getting copies of the documents you have requested against the cost involved (and time wasted) in attending the tribunal hearing. If you decide not to proceed with the application, you should write as soon as possible to both the tribunal and to Fred stating that you are withdrawing your application and asking that the directions hearing be 'vacated' (this means cancelled!). It is, however, up to the tribunal whether they cancel the hearing it may be that the chairman thinks it would be unjust not to consider whether you are entitled to the documents, and thus insists on having the hearing anyway.

Penalty for non-compliance 14.21

The penalties for non-compliance with an Order are as set out in 14.18 above and, again, the tribunal must write to Fred seeking an explanation for failure to comply with an Order before it is allowed to strike out his claim (or part of it). Alternatively, the tribunal (when hearing the actual case) can refuse to allow Fred to rely on any documents that he has failed to supply in advance in breach of an Order.

What if the employee tries to obtain your documents? 14.22

Fred will frequently ask to see a copy of his personnel file or of any notes you made during the dismissal process. He is entitled to these documents (unless documents in his personnel file are so old they cannot conceivably be of any use) and it is sensible to release these on request without the additional burden of a directions hearing.

However, sometimes Fred will ask to see documents that you do not want him to have access to. Your reluctance to provide copies can be for several reasons. He may be asking for an oppressive amount of documentation, so that the time and cost involved in collating the documents is unreasonable. He may want to see confidential information. Sometimes you may wish to stop him seeing documents because they harm your case!

If the tribunal has ordered you to disclose relevant documents, you must do so (subject to appealing the order – and if you want to do that, seek legal advice without delay). If there is no such order, there is no legal obligation to disclose documents. Tribunal's attitudes differ if the employer has refused to comply with a request from the employee for documents. Some tribunals will adopt the approach that, if Fred had not applied for an Order from the tribunal requiring disclosure, it is his problem and you have not acted improperly. Other tribunals will think you are engaging in undesirable tactical manoeuvring, and will be unimpressed.

When will a chairman order disclosure? 14.23

In order to persuade the chairman that he is entitled to see the documents, Fred must show that production is necessary to dispose fairly of the proceedings. Once he has overcome this hurdle (and, if you can show that the documents are not relevant, that is the end of the matter), it is for you to show that it would be oppressive for you to be ordered to produce them. This will frequently depend on the attitude of the individual chairman: some consider it to be oppressive to produce anything other than the most vital documents, whereas others will allow Fred to have copies of a whole range of company documents.

You should note that the fact that a document is confidential will not be a defence if it is necessary to produce it to dispose fairly of the proceedings (although confidentiality may be a factor in deciding whether production would be oppressive). Some chairmen will ask to look at the document themselves, without showing it to Fred, so that they can weigh up the relevance against the confidentiality factor.

Remember that any correspondence with your legal advisers, or with witnesses in connection with Fred's claim, will be 'privileged' and the tribunal cannot order you to produce copies see **14.6**.

Forcing witnesses to the hearing   14.24

You can ask the tribunal to issue a witness summons (better known by its name in the criminal courts as a subpoena), which compels a named individual to come to the tribunal hearing and bring any specified documents.

This is more usually done by an employee (if, for example, Fred is alleging that you treated another employee less severely, he may wish to compel that employee to give evidence). If you wish to rely on another employee's evidence, you can simply tell them to attend. However, the need for you to issue a witness summons may arise if persons other than your own employees are relevant witnesses. Examples would include a customer against whom Fred used violence, or a competitor whom you suspect Fred has approached with an offer to pass on confidential information.

If you compel a witness to attend against his will this can, obviously, end up being counterproductive. The witness will resent being forced to spend a day at the tribunal, and may not co-operate in the witness box. If you call a witness yourself (rather than if he is called by Fred), you are deemed to be putting him forward as an honest and credible witness and thus are not usually allowed to cross-examine him. Accordingly you may end up in a worse position than if you had not called him at all.

Note that the power to compel a witness to attend a tribunal hearing is limited to people in the United Kingdom. If the potential witness lives overseas, the tribunal is not permitted to issue a witness summons against him.

The witness summons   14.25

You need to know the name and address of any witness you want to summon to the tribunal hearing. If you do not have their name and address, a witness summons cannot be issued. Sometimes you may be able to ask Fred for a potential witness's details: see **14.15** above.

Before applying to the tribunal for a witness summons, you must ask the witness if he will attend voluntarily. If he agrees to do so, you will not be entitled to a witness summons (unless you can show that there is a good reason why his agreement should not be taken at face value).

If he fails to answer your letters, if his agreement is ambivalent (such as, 'I'll try to turn up, but I might have to be away on business') or if his own employer will not release him for the day without a witness summons, you should write to the tribunal, asking for a witness summons. The letter must include the following points:

- the witness's name and address;

- the gist of the evidence that you expect the witness will give. If you do not explain the reason why you think his evidence is relevant, the tribunal will not issue a summons;

- the reason why it is necessary to issue a summons (i.e. why the witness will not attend voluntarily). Attach any reply from the witness, or the letters which you wrote to him to which he failed to reply;

- identify any documents that you want the witness to bring with him.

How the tribunal responds to a request for a witness summons
14.26

On receipt of your letter, a chairman will consider it. He has three options:

- your request can be refused. This will usually be on the basis that the chairman thinks that the witness will not be of much help, or that he is willing to attend voluntarily (i.e. without an order). You are able to re-apply if additional evidence turns up;

- your request can be granted. The tribunal will send a witness summons directly to the witness by recorded delivery and will send a copy to you. It will not inform Fred of the witness summons;

- a copy of your application can be sent to Fred, and his comments invited on whether a witness summons should be issued. The tribunal will give Fred a set number of days within which to respond, after which the chairman will reconsider the matter.

What if the witness does not want to attend?
14.27

If a witness does not want to attend the hearing, he can write to the tribunal and ask to have the witness summons discharged. The chairman will send you a copy of his letter and allow you to comment on it before making a decision. Usually the witness will seek to have a summons discharged on one of the following three grounds:

- he is not able to offer any useful evidence (since, for example, he did not actually see Fred stealing the company's property);

- the evidence that he can give is not disputed by Fred, and thus his evidence can be presented in writing rather than by personal attendance; or

- he is unable to attend the hearing. Unless he gives a good reason, the chairman is unlikely to discharge a witness summons on this ground. Mere inconvenience is not sufficient, and since the Department of

Education and Employment will reimburse any travel expenses or loss of earnings (up to a set maximum), cost of travel or loss of earnings will not be valid reasons either. If he does have a good reason for not being able to attend the hearing, the chairman will consider whether to adjourn the hearing and fix a new date or whether to release the witness completely. You should indicate your preference, and the reasons for it, in any letter you write to the tribunal commenting on the witness's application.

Chapter 15
Settling Claims

Introduction

Settlement should be encouraged. If you are going to pay money to a lawyer to represent you, you should ordinarily be willing to pay that amount directly to Fred as a nuisance settlement. Many employees, if not properly advised, have little idea of how tribunals assess compensation. Accordingly, if Fred is prepared to accept £1,000 plus an apology or a reference (irrespective of whether you feel an apology is deserved) it would be commercially unwise to, instead, pay £5,000 to lawyers and still risk having to pay Fred considerably more should he win the tribunal hearing.

There are other advantages to settling a claim. These include:

- you will not lose the time entailed in preparing for a hearing and your employees will not have to lose a day's work attending the tribunal;

- when you settle a claim, you can do so on any terms you think appropriate. These can include agreeing to provide a carefully worded reference for Fred. Often this can be a vital incentive to Fred to settle at a sum considerably lower than he might achieve if he went to a tribunal, since tribunals are not allowed to order you to provide a reference;

- the DSS does not claw back from a settlement any benefits, such as income support, received by Fred whilst he was unemployed (as happens when the tribunal makes an award). Thus, if Fred's claim was worth £10,000 and he won this amount in a tribunal, but he had received £2,000 in social security benefits whilst waiting for the tribunal hearing, you would have to pay Fred £8,000 and pay the DSS £2,000. If Fred's claim is settled before a hearing, the DSS does not get to recoup benefits. It is common practice to split the recoupment between the parties: thus you might pay £9,000 to Fred which means you save £1,000 and Fred gets an extra £1,000.

How to settle

With most legal disputes, such as disputes between you and a supplier, you can settle a claim at any time simply by agreeing the terms of settlement (whether by word of mouth or in writing). With employment disputes, you cannot do this. Parliament has provided two specific mechanisms for settling unfair dismissal claims. If you do not adopt one of these two mechanisms, the settlement will not be binding and Fred can continue with his claim even if he has taken the settlement monies.

The two methods of settling unfair dismissal claims are by going through a conciliation officer at ACAS, or entering into a formal compromise agreement (which is a written contract of settlement, containing certain formalities, in connection with which Fred needs to obtain specific independent advice for it to be binding).

Settlement through ACAS   15.3

You can settle a claim through ACAS both before or after Fred's claim has been issued. Copies of the IT1 and IT3 will automatically be sent to an ACAS conciliation officer, who will contact you and Fred at some point before the hearing to see whether he can help you come to a settlement. In most unfair dismissal cases, from October 2004 there will be a 13-week 'conciliation period' during which the case will not be heard. This is intended to give the parties time to try to settle their case.

Fred may also invoke the assistance of a conciliation officer, before he issues the claim, simply by contacting ACAS. Although, technically, you can do the same, there is little advantage for employers in taking steps that will focus Fred's attention on a claim before he has issued it. Further, an ACAS officer might remind Fred of the time limits for presenting a claim which, if he is unaware of them, he might otherwise miss (and thus be prevented from claiming unfair dismissal, subject to an extension of time – see **18.9**).

An ACAS officer will not try to force settlement on you. He will encourage you and Fred to discuss your case, through him, and will act as a conduit for any offers. He will take offers back and forth until agreement is reached (or it becomes clear that no settlement is possible). Not only is this service of great assistance where there is animosity between you and Fred (which might escalate if you negotiated with each other directly), but you are given 'thinking' time when an offer is made in either direction.

When negotiating through ACAS, you are able to settle a claim on any terms that you want, including a reference or confidentiality clauses. The conciliation officer will offer both sides general advice, but will not give specific advice to either of you. They are meant to be neutral and should not favour either employer or employee. Although they are not meant to disclose to Fred any information you reveal to them without your permission (or vice versa), mistakes sometimes happen: thus it is prudent not to mention anything to the conciliation officer which may be damaging to your case and of which Fred is unaware. Anything said to the conciliation officer, even if you have given him permission to pass the information onto Fred, is regarded as 'without prejudice' (i.e. confidential) and should not be revealed to a tribunal by Fred without your consent.

The settlement form 15.4

Usually, once a settlement is reached, the conciliation officer will produce a standard form (known as a 'COT3'). He will help you ensure that the agreement is clearly worded and covers all the terms you want included in the agreement. Technically, however, it is not necessary for the settlement to be set out in writing if both sides have agreed the terms through the conciliation officer, it will be binding.

Example

An employee and employer agreed a settlement through the ACAS conciliation officer. The officer then sent a COT3 form to the employee for signature. He refused to sign it and tried to continue with his claim in the tribunal. Both the employment tribunal and, on appeal, the Employment Appeal Tribunal, held that the oral agreement through the conciliation officer was binding and that the tribunal claim was not allowed to proceed – *Gilbert v Kembridge Fibres Ltd [1984] ICR 188.*

Wording of the settlement document 15.5

The wording on the COT3 is important. You want to make sure that you limit Fred from bringing as many claims as you possibly can. It is no good settling an unfair dismissal claim if he can issue a claim the following day for breach of contract or sex discrimination. It used to be traditional to use the following wording in a COT3 agreement:

'in full and final settlement of all claims which Fred might have against us arising out of his employment or out of its termination.'

This was fairly bland wording and many employees did not realise that it precluded them from bringing any further claims against their employers of any nature (unless unrelated to employment).

Recently the courts have stated that such wording, although effective to prevent an unfair dismissal claim continuing (or other linked claims, such as a claim for unpaid wages or redundancy pay), will not be effective to exclude all claims. In order to do that, more stringent wording will be needed. You should discuss the wording to be used with the conciliation officer.

If a claim has already been issued, a sensible alternative form of words might be:

> 'In full and final settlement of all claims which arise under the Originating Application number _____ or such claims as may be brought on the basis of the facts alleged therein.'

Limitations of ACAS 15.6

One limitation on the use of ACAS is that the conciliation officer must be actively involved in bringing about the settlement. ACAS will not 'rubber-stamp' an agreement that you and Fred have come to without its assistance. The alternative method, therefore, of making a settlement binding on Fred is to enter into a formal compromise agreement.

Compromise agreements 15.7

In order for a settlement to be binding, unless it is done through ACAS, the following requirements must be met:

- the agreement must be in writing;

- it must relate to the particular complaint, or claim, that Fred is bringing (or proposes to bring) against you. Accordingly the written agreement must specifically mention each claim that is being settled, for example an unfair dismissal claim together with claims for unpaid pay in lieu of notice and holiday pay;

- Fred must have received advice from an independent adviser, who is covered by a policy of insurance, as to the terms and effects of the agreement and, in particular, on its effect on his ability to pursue his rights before an employment tribunal;

- the written agreement must identify the adviser and state that all the relevant conditions required for compromise agreements are satisfied.

A sample compromise agreement is set out at **APPENDIX 5**.

Employee has to get independent advice 15.8

Until recently, it was necessary for Fred to seek independent advice from a qualified solicitor or barrister. This requirement has now been relaxed, so that a compromise agreement is binding if Fred has received advice from a 'relevant independent adviser' who is covered by an insurance policy. This covers lawyers, certain trade union officials and certain Citizens' Advice Bureau workers.

Before entering into a compromise contract, therefore, you should ensure that Fred has consulted a Citizens' Advice Bureau or a solicitor. It used to be common practice for employers to pay for Fred to obtain independent legal advice (up to a limit of, say, £250). Now that Citizens' Advice Bureaux advisers are capable of ratifying an agreement, this is no longer so necessary.

Chapter 16
Preparing for and Conducting the Hearing

Introduction   16.1

This chapter is concerned with the presentation of your case, should you decide not to have legal representation for the tribunal hearing. It contains general advice about how to prepare for the hearing and the procedure that will be followed in tribunals.

Preparation for the hearing

Hearing date   16.2

In unfair dismissal claims, there is normally a 13-week 'conciliation period' during which no hearing (other than pre-hearing reviews or case management conferences) will take place. This 13-week period starts running from when the tribunal sends you a copy of Fred's Claim Form (and the Response Form, which you must complete within 28 days). However, where Fred is also claiming some specific other matters – the most important being non-payment of past wages, the conciliation period is only seven weeks.

You should be given at least 14 days' notice of the hearing date (although, in practice, considerably more notice will be given). Many tribunals now contact the parties before fixing a hearing and set out a range of possible hearing dates. They then invite both sides to respond with their dates to avoid, after receipt of which a mutually convenient date will be allocated.

Most tribunal cases are allocated one day for the hearing. This is enough time for the majority of standard unfair dismissal cases that involve two or three witnesses. If your case is complex, or there are a large number of witnesses and the case is likely to take longer than one day, you must write to the tribunal as soon as possible: ideally, before the hearing date is fixed. If a case is not concluded on the day of the hearing, it will not continue the following day but will be adjourned, part-heard, to a day which may be several months away. This inevitably means that the parties' and, more importantly, the tribunal members' recollections of the evidence dims. Since you, as the employer, usually give your evidence first (see **16.21**) it means that the tribunal may have forgotten much of what you had to say. Avoid this by ensuring that you have told the tribunal that your case might take longer than the allocated day.

Adjournments of the hearing date   16.3

If you need to apply for an adjournment (for example, because a witness is unavailable), you must do this as soon as possible in advance of the hearing. Some tribunals now refuse any requests for an adjournment made less than 14 days before the hearing and require both parties to attend and explain to the full tribunal why the adjournment is needed. Clearly this wastes both time and money: thus if an application to adjourn can be made earlier, it should be.

You can make an application in writing. Address your letter to the Clerk to the Employment Tribunal, and ask him to place your letter in front of the duty chairman. State the case reference number, the hearing date and set out your reasons for an adjournment. If a witness is out of the country on the date set for the hearing, try to obtain a short letter addressed to you from the witness and enclose a copy with your letter to the tribunal.

If the application is on the grounds of ill-health of a witness, ask the witness for a certificate from his doctor. Many tribunals have had experience of employers who seek repeated adjournments with the intention of delaying the date that they may be ordered to pay compensation thus unsupported applications for adjournments are sometimes viewed with scepticism.

Applying for a stay due to simultaneous
legal action   16.4

An occasional ground for an adjournment is that there are proceedings being taken simultaneously in the County Court or High Court. This will usually occur if Fred is claiming large sums for breach of contract (rather than unfair dismissal) which exceed the employment tribunal limit of £25,000. It may also occur if you are seeking to rely on a restraint-of-trade clause and are seeking an injunction in the courts. It is neither cost effective nor desirable to have the same issues tried in both an employment tribunal and in other courts. Since cases in the courts invariably take longer to bring to trial than cases in the employment tribunal, it is usual to apply for the employment tribunal proceedings to be adjourned, or 'stayed', pending a decision in the courts.

A tribunal is likely to grant a stay if the issues before the High Court or County Court are similar to those which the tribunal will have to decide. In particular, if the issues are complex or there is a large amount of money at stake, a tribunal will be reluctant to hear the case before the other court (since it might bind the other court by its decision). Sometimes, employees will be able to obtain legal aid to bring or defend proceedings in the ordinary courts, and the availability of legal representation is a factor which disposes tribunals to allow a trial to take place elsewhere.

If, however, the issues for the courts and tribunal are very different, the tribunal is unlikely to grant a stay. This might happen if Fred claimed compensation, or 'damages', for a long notice period in the High Court (where the only issue might be whether he had failed to seek employment elsewhere so as to minimise his financial losses) and unfair dismissal in the employment tribunal (where the issue might be whether he had been fairly selected for redundancy).

Likewise you might want to apply for a stay if you have dismissed Fred for misconduct and he is being prosecuted in the Crown or Magistrates' Court for the relevant offence. If Fred is convicted, it will clearly assist your case in the employment tribunal proceedings (note: an acquittal will not necessarily damage your case since the issue for the employment tribunal is not whether Fred was guilty, but whether you had reasonable grounds to believe he was guilty). In this scenario you would again write to the tribunal, as set out above, and ask for a stay pending resolution of the criminal proceedings.

Costs of adjournment   16.5

Tribunals are free to award legal costs (or, since October 2004, compensation for your preparation time) against any party in the event of an adjournment. They are not fettered by the rules which apply at the conclusion of a case, when they can only award costs in certain circumstances. If Fred applies for an adjournment on the day of a hearing, in circumstances where he could have applied earlier in writing and saved you the cost of attending, you may wish to ask the tribunal for the costs wasted by the hearing. The costs that can be awarded are governed by strict rules: see **16.40**.

Witness statements   16.6

If a case goes as far as the tribunal, you should always make attempts to settle it (unless you are wary of setting a precedent which might encourage others to claim). The advantages, and formalities, of settlement are set out at in **CHAPTER 15**. If, however, settlement does not appear likely then you will need to commence detailed preparation for the hearing itself.

Prepare witness statements for every witness you intend to call. The statements should be carefully drafted and must include everything that you would want your witnesses (yourself included) to say if they were giving evidence in the witness box. This is because the tribunal will often expect the statements to stand as your entire evidence (subject to other matters which may come to light during and after cross-examination).

The witness statements should state at the beginning whose witness statement it is. It should be set out in short, numbered paragraphs, and each paragraph should deal with one point only. This makes it easy to cite a particular section of the statement when referring to a specific item of evidence. The statement should start in a standard way by describing yourself, the company, and then move on to the specifics of the claim.

Hypothetical statement

Statement of Nikolas Jacob

1. I am the managing director of Special Clothing Limited, and I make this statement in connection with the unfair dismissal claim brought against the company by Fred. The contents of this statement are true to the best of my knowledge, information and belief.

2. The company is a small company which has been trading for seven years. It deals in distributing 'seconds', i.e. clothes carrying brand-names which do not meet the manufacturers' standards, to whole-sale outlets. We employ 15 people in total.

3. Fred has been employed by us since 12 September 1992. He was employed as a telephone negotiator. He was dismissed on 17 December 1997 for misconduct …

You should ensure that your statement (or statements, if more than one witness is to be called) deals with the procedural steps you have taken as well as the substantive reasons for Fred's dismissal. The statement should be signed and dated at the end.

Exchanging statements   16.7

The tribunal's standard directions usually require you to exchange your statements with Fred seven or fourteen days before the hearing. If no such direction is issued, you should try to agree with Fred to exchange statements in advance. If this does not occur, you should exchange them on the morning of the hearing, before you enter the tribunal room.

214

Documents   16.8

You should arrange a bundle of documents for the tribunal's use. This bundle should contain all relevant documents which might be referred to during the proceedings. You should ask Fred, a week or two before the hearing, if there are any additional documents that he wants in the bundle. Any documents he supplies should be incorporated into the bundle or, if he does not cooperate, the bundle should be clearly labelled with the words 'Respondent's Bundle' to indicate that it contains your documents only.

The bundle should be paginated and arranged in a sensible order. Although this sounds obvious, make sure that all the bundles have the pages in identical order with the same numbering: it is remarkable how frequently bundles have pages in different orders. This causes confusion and is frustrating for the tribunal.

It is often convenient to divide the bundle into sections as follows:

- the Claim Form and Response Form, together with any formal further information provided. Although the tribunal will already have copies of these, their inclusion in the bundle makes it easier to refer to them;

- all documents which are relevant to the decision to dismiss, such as written warnings, complaints by customers, notes of investigative and disciplinary meetings, details of how you selected Fred for redundancy, any statements produced at the time of the dismissal (rather than for the tribunal hearing itself after the unfair dismissal claim was lodged), the letter of dismissal and any documents relating to appeals. Arrange these, as far as possible, in chronological order;

- other relevant sections from Fred's personnel file, including his contract of employment (if one exists) and job appraisals;

- correspondence arising in connection with the unfair dismissal claim, again arranged in chronological order;

- witness statements: both your witnesses and Fred's.

Documents not to include   16.9

Note that certain documents must not be included in the bundle or produced to the tribunal. These are letters between you and Fred (or his advisers) in which you or he try to settle the claim. These letters are known as 'without prejudice' and cannot be shown to the tribunal unless both sides agree. Note that a letter does not have to be marked 'without prejudice' in order to attract this immunity from production: if it is part of a series of correspondence that is a genuine attempt to settle any issues in the claim, it automatically attracts that immunity. Conversely, any letters labelled 'without prejudice' do not automatically attract immunity from production unless they are part of a series of correspondence which is genuinely intended to settle the claim thus they can be produced to the tribunal.

Indexing the bundle   16.10

You should ensure that the front page of the bundle contains a proper index of the documents. Describe the documents in as short and neutral a form as possible thus the index should state 'p 7 Letter from Fred dated 15 January 1998' rather than 'p 7 Letter from Fred in which he lies about his reasons for not attending work'.

You should prepare six copies of the bundle for the tribunal: one for each of the three members of the tribunal, one for you, one for Fred and one for the witness box. If you are able to, you should send a copy to Fred a week before the hearing.

Trial preparation – before the hearing   16.11

Ensure that the trial bundles are in good order. Contact each of your witnesses and remind them of the time and place of the hearing.

As employer, you will usually present your case to the tribunal first (see **16.21**). Tribunals no longer require opening speeches (except in the most complicated of cases), and they ask you to launch straight into presenting the evidence.

You then need to decide exactly what evidence each of your witnesses will give (including yourself). If you have already prepared witness statements, you should already have done this. If not, prepare a list of the main points which each witness must give evidence on. Although hearsay evidence is allowed in an employment tribunal, it is best to limit each witness to giving evidence on matters which they personally saw or heard. This list, if no witnesses' statements are available, will form the basis of your examination of your witnesses.

You must also consider what documents you want the tribunal to see. It is your responsibility to check that the tribunal is shown all relevant documentation. If you do not introduce the documents yourself, the tribunal may not see them. The mere fact a document is in the bundle does not mean that it will be read. The documents should be identified by one of your witnesses during their evidence.

Consider what the employee's evidence will be   16.12

Next, consider the evidence that Fred is likely to call. Think about how he is likely to try to establish that you have unfairly dismissed him. You will have his Claim Form, and possibly other documents, which set out his case. Anticipate the ways in which he might try to cross-examine you, and think about your responses.

You will also need to prepare your cross-examination of Fred's witnesses. The content of an effective cross-examination is considered at **16.29**. Whilst preparing, try to make a list of any inconsistencies within Fred's case (for example, where his account is inconsistent with a document) so that you can challenge him on these points.

You will have seen on the Claim Form that there is a box which Fred would have ticked requesting reinstatement, re-engagement or compensation only. If he has ticked either of the first two, or told you at least seven days before the hearing that he wishes the tribunal to consider ordering that he be reinstated or re-engaged by you, then you must be prepared to give evidence to the tribunal on the practicability of reinstatement or re-engagement (or you will probably be required to pay Fred's legal costs, or compensation for wasted preparation time, caused by an adjournment). This is discussed further at **13.34**.

Preparation time   16.13

An experienced advocate, working efficiently, can prepare a straightforward employment tribunal claim in several hours if all the materials (witness statements, bundles) are in good order. A difficult case can take several days or even weeks to prepare. Do not underestimate the amount of work it takes to prepare a case thoroughly: it is wise to allow a full day without interruptions even if the case is straightforward.

Last minute settlement offer   16.14

You may wish to make one last attempt to settle the claim. Fred's feelings of resentment at being dismissed have probably been replaced with nerves by the day before the hearing. He may be seeking a way to avoid the hearing without being seen to surrender. A sensible offer, possibly even coupled with an apology (thereby allowing Fred to save face), may encourage him to withdraw his claim.

Any settlement at this stage will have to go through ACAS (see **CHAPTER 15** on settlement): there will be insufficient time for Fred to obtain independent advice so as to render any non-ACAS settlement binding. If your case is weak, there may be very sound commercial reasons for settling the case at this stage.

The hearing   16.15

Take a book with you. This may sound absurd, but there can sometimes be long waits (for example, if your case is 'floating' or if the tribunal takes a long time to make up its mind).

Procedure on arrival   16.16

Get to the tribunal early. Most tribunal cases start at 10.00am, and the doors open at 9.00am. There are often last-minute things to do, and it is important to be around to deal with them. Check in at reception and tell the receptionist that you will be representing yourself. You will be asked for the names of your witnesses (and their job titles) so that the tribunal has a list of the evidence you are calling.

There will be a list, somewhere in reception, of all the cases that the tribunal is hearing that day. Check that your case is on the list and make a note of the name of the chairman and the clerk (in case there are any queries afterwards). Your case may be 'floating', which means that you have not been allocated to a particular tribunal. This happens because tribunals know that many cases settle shortly before the hearing, and therefore they list too many cases on the assumption that some of them will settle. If you are floating, you may have a long wait (and, indeed, you may not get called on at all: if this happens, it is extremely frustrating but there is nothing that can be done about it).

You will be directed to the Respondents' (meaning employers') waiting room: the tribunals have separate waiting rooms for employees and employers. At some point, the clerk will come and introduce himself to you. He will ask you for four copies of your bundles (one for each of the three tribunal members and one for the witness box). He will also ask you whether each of your witnesses prefers to swear on the Bible or affirm. If you have any questions about procedure, ask the clerk before you go into the hearing.

The Department of Trade and Industry will repay your witnesses' expenses. Ask the clerk before you go in for witness expense repayment forms: you will not be told about the witness expense procedure and you must ask for the forms. Your witnesses will be entitled to reclaim their travel expenses and loss of earnings, up to a certain limit, irrespective of whether you win or lose.

You should also, about 20 minutes before the hearing, go into the Applicant's (employee's) waiting room and speak to Fred. You do not need permission to go in there: simply knock and walk in. Give Fred a copy of the bundle (assuming you have not sent it to him earlier) and check whether he will be relying on any other documents. If he tells you that he has no other documents, and then produces some during the hearing, you are quite entitled to complain to the chairman that Fred has misled you. Although the chairman is unlikely to do anything about it, it may affect Fred's credibility.

Dealing with the press 16.17

Occasionally, litigants may be approached by the press whilst waiting to go into the tribunal (although – unlike five years ago – press rarely attend tribunal hearings 'on spec', but only if they have been tipped off that an interesting case is being heard). They will ask you what your case is about. There is no obligation to talk to the press and you are quite entitled to decline to comment. Publicity tends to be a bad thing for employers, since reporters tend to be interested in the more salacious details of a case. The press are also likely to approach Fred and ask him what the case is about. Even if you both decline to comment, they are usually entitled to sit in the tribunal to find (and report) any interesting cases.

If the employee does not turn up 16.18

If Fred does not attend, the clerk will try to contact him by telephone. If he appears to have a genuine reason for not attending, the tribunal will usually adjourn the case. If he does not have a good reason, or cannot be contacted, the tribunal is likely to dismiss his claim. If the claim is dismissed and it transpires that Fred has a good reason for not attending (for example, he was stuck on a broken down train), he can apply for a 'review' (which, in practice, means a rehearing) – see **16.47**.

Going in 16.19

The clerk will come and collect you when the tribunal is ready to start the hearing. They will normally have read the Claim and Response forms, and occasionally (if the bundle is short) they may have skimmed through the bundle of documents. Sometimes they will want to discuss the case in private before starting the hearing, in which case you may not start promptly at 10.00am.

Your witnesses will go into the tribunal at the same time as you: they are entitled to watch the entire hearing and are not required to wait outside until it is their turn to give evidence. You can ask the chairman for particular witnesses to wait outside. To do so is unusual, however, and it is unwise unless you have a good reason.

It is natural to be nervous whilst waiting for the hearing to start. Indeed, barristers often feel nerves, even after years of training, in their first few years of practice. But most people find their nerves disappear very quickly once the proceedings start.

Wait outside the tribunal door until the clerk tells you to go in. When you go in, you will see the three tribunal members sitting at a long desk (often on a slightly raised platform). You will also see a long table facing the tribunal (at which the parties sit), a chair and table for the witness and rows of chairs at the back of the room for observers (which includes witnesses when they are not giving evidence). The public and press are usually allowed into tribunals to watch. The employer always sits on the tribunal's right-hand side (i.e. on the left-hand side of the long table as you face them). Walk straight to your chair and sit down: you do not need to wait to be invited to sit. Do not speak until spoken to (other than a brief 'good morning' if you wish).

The chairman, who sits in the middle, will be a lawyer specialising in employment law. The two wing members provide a balanced view of employment relations from a practical perspective: one will have been appointed by a trade union, and the other by an employer's association. You will not be told which is which. They will all be accustomed to employees and employers representing themselves and will always do their best to ease nerves and explain the procedures to you.

Addressing the tribunal   16.20

All questions and remarks are addressed to the chairman. Unless being asked a question by one of the wing members, do not speak directly to them. You address the chairman as 'Sir' or 'Madam'. Unlike an ordinary court, you do not stand to address the tribunal, but remain seated.

Order of proceedings   16.21

As employer, you will usually present your case first (since it is up to you to establish the reason for Fred's dismissal). If, however, you deny dismissing Fred (for example, if he resigned and is claiming constructive dismissal) then he will present his case first. Occasionally, if Fred is claiming discrimination (on grounds of sex, race, disability, sexual orientation, religion or belief) as well as unfair dismissal, the tribunal may ask him to present his claim first. In such a case, the procedural order in the following sections will be reversed.

Opening speech   16.22

If you are unrepresented, the chairman will usually introduce himself and explain the order of proceedings. He will also tell you what he thinks the important issues are, and give you the chance to comment.

Although it used to be common for the employer to make an opening speech, this no longer happens (except in the most complicated of cases, when each side will usually be asked to prepare written opening submissions in advance).

Presenting your case 16.23

It is for you, and only you, to decide what evidence you wish to call and the order in which you wish to call it. If there is a person whose evidence will be central, such as a person with whom Fred was fighting, it is customary to call him first. Likewise, it is customary to call the person who actually took the decision to dismiss as early on as possible.

If you are the witness, you will not have anybody asking you questions but will have to rely on your memory (or a witness statement).

To call a witness to the stand, simply say 'I call [*name*] to give evidence' or 'my next witness will be [*name*]'. One of the tribunal members will then administer the oath.

Witness statements 16.24

If the witness has provided a statement that you wish to rely on, your opening questions will follow a standard format. This is set out in the following example:

Q. Please state your name and address.

A. Justin Donn, 8 Landsdown Court, Hendon NW4.

Q. What is your job title and for whom do you work, Mr Donn?

A. Assistant manager at Special Clothing Ltd.

Q. Please turn to page 22 of the bundle.Is that document your witness statement?

A. Yes.

Q. If you turn over the page, you will see a signature. Is that your signature?

A. Yes.

Q. Have you recently read the contents of your witness statement?

A. Yes.

> Q. Are its contents true?
>
> A. Yes.

You then ask the witness to read his statement aloud. This can be a slow process, but most tribunals prefer to have the evidence read out (rather than reading it to themselves) as they like to assess the witness whilst he is reading. As he reads, refer him to relevant documents in the bundle and ask the tribunal to read them (unlike the witness statements, documents do *not* need to be read aloud). If you have any additional questions concerning matters which are not covered in the witness statement, you can ask them at this stage.

No witness statement? 16.25

If the witness does not have a witness statement, or if you do not want to rely on it, you will need to take him through the events in question carefully (so as not to miss anything out). However, nowadays the vast majority of chairmen will not allow a witness to give evidence if you have failed to provide a witness statement in advance, in accordance with tribunal directions.

Start, as above, by asking for the witness's name, address and job details. You should already have prepared a list, for each witness, of the points which you wish them to give evidence on. Go through this list, asking them as many questions as are necessary in order to bring out the necessary points.

When asking questions of your own witnesses, you are not normally allowed to ask 'leading questions'. A leading question is not, as is commonly believed, a question where the person answering does not like the answer. Rather, it is a question where the answer you are seeking appears within the question, such as 'did you then see Fred take some money out of the till?' or 'did you then tell Fred to go home for the rest of the day'. Instead, you should ask questions such as 'what happened next?' or 'what did you then say?' This method of questioning has the advantage that the tribunal is less likely to think that you, as employer, are influencing the testimony of your witnesses by the way you phrase your questions.

There are two main exceptions to the prohibition on asking leading questions, namely:

- where the answer is not contentious, for example 'are you Fred's line manager?' or 'were you in the office at about 4.00pm on Monday, 21 September 1998?';

- where you are seeking to elicit a negative response, such as 'Q. Was Peter acting at all aggressively before Fred punched him?' A. 'No.' This is an exception because if you had to ask the question in a non-leading way, i.e. 'what was Peter not doing before Fred hit him?', it would be almost impossible to elicit the answer you are looking for.

The cross-examination 16.26

When you have finished your examination, the witness will be cross-examined by Fred. To formally conclude the examination, say 'no further questions' or 'please wait there – Fred may want to ask you some questions'.

Fred is then given an opportunity to cross-examine the witness. Normally the chairman will stop him (as he would stop you) if Fred asks inappropriate or irrelevant questions. Do not object to Fred's questions unless there is a very good reason (such as Fred is referring to 'without prejudice' offers). Tribunals are not like television courtroom dramas, where objections are common, and parties are usually entitled to cross-examine on any relevant matters. Frequent objections can give the impression – whether rightly or wrongly – that you are trying to prevent the truth coming out.

After Fred has finished cross-examining, the chairman will ask the two wing members if they have any questions. Next, the chairman may ask some questions. Finally, you will be offered a chance to clarify any matters which have arisen during cross-examination. Do not use this opportunity to procure a complete rehash of the evidence. Limit it to one or two central points which require further questioning. If you do not ask any questions in re-examination, it can give the favourable impression that the evidence completely supports your case.

Witnesses who are not attending 16.27

Go through this routine with each witness you want to call. Remember that each of the documents in the bundle has to be identified by a witness; if you forget to do this, the tribunal will almost certainly not read the document and not take it into account.

After your last witness, you can show the tribunal statements from any witnesses who were unable to attend. Although this evidence is hearsay, because the witness is not available to confirm the truth of what is being said, it is admissible in tribunal hearings. If you rely on a hearsay witness statement, the chairman will probably tell you that the tribunal will consider it, but will not be able to give as much weight to it as to the evidence of 'live' witnesses because the witness was not available to be cross-examined.

Closing your case 16.28

When you have finished presenting your evidence, you must formally close your case. This is done simply by saying 'that is the Respondent's case' or 'I have no further evidence'.

Challenging the employee's case 16.29

It will then be Fred's turn to give evidence. Although there is no reason why Fred should not have witnesses to support his case, in practice it is common for an employee to be the only person giving evidence on his own behalf.

Fred (and his witnesses, in turn) will go into the witness box and give their version of events. As they give evidence, you should make a careful note of what they are saying (so that you have a record of their evidence when you cross-examine them).

Sometimes Fred will agree with the gist of your evidence, but go further than your evidence or simply challenge your decision to dismiss. This might occur, for example, when you have dismissed Fred due to persistent absence through illness. He may agree that he was ill for 12 weeks prior to the dismissal, but say that you failed to investigate whether he was likely to be able to return to work and, therefore, the dismissal was unfair.

More commonly, particularly in cases relating to his conduct, Fred's evidence may be wholly different from yours. You may have called witnesses who said that Fred was asleep on duty. Fred denies it. You may have called witnesses who said that Fred attacked a customer without provocation. Fred says that the customer hit him and he was acting in self-defence. The tribunal will be faced with making a decision as to whose evidence is the more reliable.

The purposes of cross-examination are two-fold:

(i)   to elicit additional information from Fred which assists your case; and,

(ii) to attack Fred's credibility, so as to make the tribunal more inclined to prefer your evidence to that of Fred.

(i) Eliciting additional information 16.30

If you feel that there is additional information which Fred has not revealed to the tribunal, or additional information which can be used to make Fred look bad, use cross-examination as the opportunity to elicit this evidence. This method of cross-examination is useful where both sides agree the basic facts, but put a different interpretation on them. An example may assist in understanding how effective this type of cross-examination can be:

Scenario

Fred works in a music shop. He has been dismissed for selling CDs to friends, but not charging for all of them. He agreed in his evidence that he had sold CDs to friends, but said that he had rung all the transactions into the till properly.

Q. The store has a rule against employees serving its friends, doesn't it?

A. Yes but everyone does it.

Q. Were you aware of the rule?

A. Yes.

Q. Had you ever been told by your manager that the rule had been revoked?

A. No.

Q. Had you ever been told by your manager that the rule was not to be taken seriously?

A. No.

Q. What do you think the purpose of the rule is?

A. Well, I suppose to stop fiddling going on.

Q. Do you accept that, when you served your friends, you were in breach of the rule?

A. I suppose so.

Q. And you knew that what you were doing wasn't allowed.

A. I suppose so.

Q. Why did you breach the rule?

A. I didn't think it mattered.

Q. Knowing it was wrong, presumably you didn't advertise what you were doing to Mr Smith [the manager]?

A. What do you mean?

Q. You didn't call out a greeting to your friends when they approached you, or introduce them to any of the other staff.

A. No.

Q. So your manner at the till was designed to conceal the fact that they were your friends.

A. Not really; I just didn't say anything to anyone.

Q. If you met your friends on the street, would you greet them?

A. Of course.

Q. Would you introduce them to whoever you were with?

A. Normally yes.

Q. So the fact you didn't greet them on this occasion, or introduce them to your colleagues, indicates that you didn't want anybody to know they were your friends.

A. It wasn't like that.

It is important to keep questions short and simple. Also, remember to ask questions and not make statements. Long rambling sentences can confuse the tribunal and the witness.

(ii) Attacking the employee's credibility   16.31

If Fred has given a very different account of events, it will be necessary for you to persuade the tribunal that your evidence is more believable than that of Fred.

There are two main ways of attacking credibility, as follows.   **16.32**

Firstly, you can put inconsistent statements to Fred. These may be statements in writing or something he has said earlier in the witness box. Inconsistent statements are most effective when Fred produced the statements himself, as the following example shows:

Scenario

Fred is dismissed for incapability. He complains that the allegations have been made up, and that he is extremely good at his job. He also says that he had never been warned that his job performance was unsatisfactory.

Q. Do you remember complaining in February 2004 that you were being given too much work?

A. Yes.

Q. And, as you were asked to do, you put your grievance in writing to Annabelle Nabarro [the managing director].

A. Yes.

Q. Please turn to page 12 of the bundle – is that your letter?

A. Yes.

Q. Is it in your handwriting?

A. Yes.

Q. And it has your signature at the bottom?

A. Yes.

Q. Please read out the letter.

A. [Reads out letter, which includes the sentence 'It's not fair when I get told off for not working fast enough. Peter [the line manager] expects too much from everyone'.]

Q. Do you accept that you were regularly told off for poor job performance during early 2004?

A. All right.

Q. Why did you tell the tribunal that you had never been told off?

A. Don't know.

Q. Did you take the warnings seriously?

A. Yes *[note: an answer of 'no' would be even better from the employer's point of view!]*

Q. You didn't just forget about them?

A. No.

> Q. If you didn't forget about them, why did you tell the tribunal that
> you had never been warned about job performance?
>
> A. I didn't think they counted!

Inconsistent statements by others   16.33

This approach can also be effective when the inconsistent documents are
prepared by other people. Thus, in the same scenario as above, Fred might
allege that he was not given the opportunity to argue against dismissal. You can
show notes made during the disciplinary interview to Fred and ask him
questions such as 'has the person who made these notes got anything against
you? Then why would he make it up?'.

Challenging the employee's past behaviour   16.34

Secondly, you can attack Fred's credibility by questioning him on why he did
or did not do any particular act. This, again, is best demonstrated using an
example:

Scenario

> Fred is made redundant. He says that, as an alternative to dismissal, he
> should have been offered a transfer to another part of the company. You
> say that he was offered the job, but he turned it down. There is nothing
> in writing (which, ordinarily, would cause you difficulties since a
> tribunal would expect a job offer to be in writing).
>
> Q. How did you know about the other job?
>
> A. I heard about it from a colleague.
>
> Q. Who?
>
> A. I can't remember now: it was ages ago.
>
> Q. When did you hear about it?
>
> A. The week I was sacked.
>
> Q. Was this before or after our meeting?
>
> A. Before, so you must have known about it.

Q. None of that is true, is it? You heard about the other job because I told you about it when we met.

A. It is true. You never mentioned it.

Q. What exactly did you hear?

A. I heard the job was going and that it had not been filled.

Q. Did you approach anybody and ask if you could be considered for the job?

A. No.

Q. Did you not think you were capable of doing it?

A. No, I was quite capable of doing it.

Q. Then why did you not approach anyone and ask to be considered for the job?

A. Well, I assumed that I'd be offered it.

Q. You say I didn't offer it to you during our meeting?

A. That's right.

Q. Then, if you knew about the existence of the job and I didn't raise it during the meeting, why didn't you?

A. I don't know.

Don't argue and don't repeat yourself 16.35

When cross-examining, do not get into an argument with Fred. Exchanges such as 'oh yes you did' 'oh no I didn't' are of very little assistance to the tribunal. If you do not score with a particular line of questioning, move on. Repetition gets tedious very quickly, and if the tribunal gets bored with your cross-examination they may miss important points that you make later.

Questions by the tribunal 16.36

After you finish cross-examining, the tribunal will ask questions and, as with your witnesses, Fred will be given the opportunity to clarify any matters he thinks fit. This procedure is gone through with all of Fred's witnesses.

Closing speeches 16.37

After all the evidence has been heard, both sides are given the opportunity to make a closing speech. The purpose of the closing speech is to allow each side to highlight their best two or three points and submit why their evidence should be preferred to the other side. It is also the opportunity each party has to make submissions on any relevant law.

Fred will make his speech first, and you are then given the final word (again, this is reversed in the circumstances set out at paragraph **16.21**). This places you at two very distinct advantages, namely:

- you get the last word and are able to comment on anything Fred has said during his closing; and,

- whilst Fred is closing, you have a little time to make notes on what you want to say during your speech, or to update what you have already prepared.

What to say 16.38

What should you say when closing? There is no golden rule, although you should avoid repeating the evidence that the tribunal has just heard. Remember that, in cases of misconduct, the tribunal is not concerned with whether Fred actually committed the act in question, but is concerned with whether you undertook reasonable investigations and whether your decision that he committed the act was reasonable. In all cases, the tribunal will also want to be satisfied that you complied with the statutory minimum dismissal procedures.

Often the best closing argument will be a short list of bullet-points indicating why your evidence should be preferred. This can be done by listing inconsistencies in Fred's evidence and identifying places where, if what he said was true, one would have expected him to act differently.

The decision and afterwards 16.39

After your closing speech, both sides will usually be asked to leave the room whilst the tribunal comes to a decision. Sometimes, if it is late in the afternoon, the tribunal might decide to 'reserve' its decision: this means that everyone goes home, and the tribunal will put its decision in writing and send it to both sides. If any further hearing is then necessary (such as to determine compensation for Fred), the parties will be required to return on another day.

Once the tribunal has made its decision, you will be called back into the room. The chairman will give a brief speech and announce whether the dismissal is fair or unfair. He will also tell you whether their decision was unanimous or by a majority (i.e. two to one).

If the dismissal was fair: application for costs   16.40

If the tribunal has decided that the dismissal was fair, you are theoretically entitled to make an application for your legal costs or preparation time. Tribunals will only award costs up to a maximum of £10,000 (unless the parties wish to go through a complicated, and expensive, assessment process in the county court, or agree a higher figure to be awarded).

More significantly, however, tribunals only award you costs if they consider that Fred (or, if he has one, his representative) has acted unreasonably, vexatiously, abusively or disruptively in bringing or conducting the proceedings, or if he has brought a claim which is misconceived. In practice, it is quite unusual for an employment tribunal to award costs. The main exception to this is where either side has asked for an adjournment: in such a case, the tribunal will consider whether any additional costs are caused by the adjournment, and if so, may order the party responsible to pay them (irrespective of whether their conduct was unreasonable etc.). The only other exception is where the employer is aware that Fred is seeking reinstatement or re-engagement, but fails to have evidence ready in such a case, costs will almost always be awarded see **13.34**.

Legal costs (i.e. solicitors' or barristers' fees) can only be recovered if you have been represented by lawyers on the day of the hearing (or, if there is no hearing, when the proceedings ended). So if you start your case using lawyers and then choose to represent yourself at the hearing, you cannot recover those legal costs. Note that fees paid to employment consultants are never recoverable (see **14.6**).

If you do not qualify for a legal costs order, the tribunal can make a 'preparation time order'. This is an award in respect of your preparation time for the case (and, if you used lawyers at any point, *their* preparation time), but not including any time spent at the hearing. An hourly rate of £25 is used (increasing annually, from 6 April 2006, by £1 per year).

Written reasons for the decision   16.41

If the tribunal gave reasons for their decision at the hearing, you will not receive written reasons unless you ask. This should be done at the end of the hearing (if possible) or within 14 days of the decision.

If the tribunal did not give reasons for its decision at the hearing, it will automatically send you written reasons without you needing to make a request.

Bear in mind it can often takes several weeks for the reasons to be dictated, typed, checked, sent to the wing members for comments, amended, signed off by the chairman and then sent out to the parties. It is legitimate to write to the tribunal to chase up written reasons, but you should wait at least two months before doing so. Guidelines from the Employment Appeal Tribunal state that written reasons should always be produced within 3½ months of the hearing: however, this is not always achieved and (in the absence of the delay somehow making the decision unsafe – which is unusual) little can be done about additional delay.

If the dismissal was unfair   16.42

If the tribunal has decided that the dismissal was unfair, they will proceed immediately to a remedies hearing. This is to determine whether they are going to order that Fred be reinstated or re-engaged, and to decide how much compensation Fred will get. Sometimes, if you ask the tribunal or if it is close to 4.00 pm (when the tribunal normally stops sitting for the day), the tribunal will adjourn the remedies hearing so as to enable negotiation to take place.

The remedies hearing   16.43

In the Claim Form, Fred would have ticked a box saying whether he wanted reinstatement (going back in his old job on the same terms, as if he had never been dismissed), re-engagement (coming back to work for you on different terms, i.e. in another job) or compensation only. The majority of employees seek compensation only.

Even if Fred seeks reinstatement or re-engagement, it is uncommon for tribunals to order it unless you are a large organisation or there is little animosity. In circumstances where there is bad feeling between you and Fred, or between Fred and other employees, it is rare for tribunals to make an order that you re-employ him. Reinstatement and re-engagement are discussed in more detail at **13.34**.

Compensation   16.44

The method of calculation of Fred's compensation is discussed in **CHAP-TER 13**. The remedies hearing is a (normally) short hearing when Fred gives evidence as to his earnings pre- and post- dismissal, so as to enable the tribunal to calculate what his compensatory award should be.

If you have evidence that Fred has been working since his dismissal, but he tells the tribunal that he has been unemployed throughout (so as to increase his compensation), you should call evidence showing that he has another job. This is not always easy: the best evidence is a statement from the company for whom he is now working. There are a number of ways to try to obtain this; an effective method is to ask the managing director (or human resources director) to provide a statement voluntarily and – when they refuse – obtain a witness summons requiring them to attend the tribunal hearing to give evidence. This usually results in a remarkably co-operative managing director/HR director who suddenly becomes quite willing to provide a statement if he can be released from having to spend a day at the tribunal.

Deciding the amount 16.45

After having heard the evidence, you and Fred will then be given the chance to make any submissions on the calculation of an award. The tribunal will afterwards ask you again to withdraw whilst they decide the amount of compensation. Once you are called back in, they will explain to both sides how they have calculated the compensation. You will receive an order setting out the total amount payable through the post, but will *not* receive reasons explaining the way it has been calculated *unless* you ask for written reasons at the hearing (or within 14 days of the hearing).

Appeals and reviews

Appeals 16.46

You are only allowed to appeal from an employment tribunal decision if the tribunal has made a legal, rather than a factual, mistake. You cannot appeal simply because you disagree with their decision: they, not you, are the judges. You need to obtain written reasons for the decision before an appeal can be considered, so you *must* ask for them at the hearing (or within 14 days of the hearing) if you are considering an appeal.

Whether the tribunal has gone wrong on a question of law is outside the scope of this book: you should consult an employment lawyer (see **14.7**) if you wish to consider appealing against a tribunal decision. Note that any appeal must be received by the Employment Appeal Tribunal within 42 days of the employment tribunal's written decision being sent out.

Reviews 16.47

A review, which is very different from an appeal, is a much underused procedure. An unsuccessful party has the right, either at the hearing or within 14 days of the written decision being sent to the parties, to ask the tribunal for a review of its decision. Equally, the tribunal can review a decision of its own volition (this may happen if there is a change in the law between the oral hearing and sending out the decision).

A review will normally involve a re-examination of part of the decision and, if granted, can result in an entire rehearing.

A review may be granted in the following circumstances (each of which is similarly applicable to Fred):

• the decision was wrongly made as the result of an administrative error;

• you did not receive notice of the proceedings, i.e. you did not receive notice of the hearing date and so did not turn up to the hearing. This is difficult to establish because there is a presumption that you would have received anything properly posted (and it is rare to find that the Notice was improperly addressed). Tribunals often have great difficulty accepting somebody's assertion that they did not receive a properly addressed and posted document;

• if the decision was made in your absence, you may be entitled to a review if you can show a good and genuine reason for failing to attend. Examples of this might be a car accident on the way to the tribunal, a death in your close family or sudden illness. Tribunals are unlikely to be forgiving of a failure to attend if they think it would have been possible for you to telephone on the morning of the hearing to explain your absence, but you failed to do so;

• if new evidence has become available. Note that tribunals do not like re-opening cases on the basis of new evidence: ordinarily you are entitled to one bite at the cherry only, and you cannot continue litigating cases indefinitely. In order to persuade the tribunal to re-open the case, you will have to show that the new evidence was not available at the time of the earlier hearing and that there were no reasonable grounds for knowing of or foreseeing the existence of the new evidence. If the evidence could have been obtained for the original hearing, a review will not be granted;

• if a review is necessary in the interests of justice. This may occur if there have been substantial procedural irregularities, such as bias by a tribunal member or if one side was not given a proper opportunity to examine witnesses or address the tribunal on a relevant point. The other occasion on which this might happen is where, after the decision, events have occurred which show an assumption of the tribunal to have been wholly wrong. For example, if compensation for a long period of future loss is awarded, but Fred obtains new employment shortly after the hearing, an application for a review might succeed (although, if only a small amount of money is involved, the tribunal will be reluctant to re-open proceedings). Similarly if Fred is convicted by the criminal courts of an offence for which he was dismissed, and of which the tribunal thought him not guilty, the case might be re-opened to reassess the fairness of the decision on the level of contributory fault.

Chapter 17
Common Pitfalls 1 – Situations Deemed to be Dismissals

Introduction

17.1

Before Fred can show he was unfairly dismissed, he needs to establish that he was dismissed in the first place. The law recognises that employers are often in an advantageous position over employees when it comes to the circumstances of terminating employment. Accordingly certain circumstances are regarded as dismissals by tribunals even if you have not actually uttered words such as 'you are dismissed'.

The following circumstances, each of which is addressed below, are situations where the law may regard Fred as having been dismissed – thus allowing him to claim unfair dismissal:

(a)   where you are in breach of Fred's contract of employment (which includes acting in a way likely to seriously damage the employment relationship) and Fred resigns as a result – this is known as 'constructive dismissal';

(b)   where Fred resigns in the heat of the moment but reconsiders and asks for his job back within a short period;

(c)   pressuring Fred to resign ('resign or be sacked') or agreeing a termination payment if he resigns;

(d)   where Fred is on a fixed-term contract and you do not renew the contract at the end of the term;

(e)   where Fred is on short-time or where he has been temporarily laid off for a certain number of weeks;

(f)   where you refuse to allow a female employee to return to work after her maternity period.

Constructive dismissal   17.2

Constructive dismissal is merely a legal phrase meaning that Fred has resigned in circumstances where he is legally entitled to resign because of your breach of his employment contract. The phrase is often incorrectly used to suggest that the dismissal was unfair. Constructive dismissals can be fair or unfair, depending on the circumstances surrounding them.

Fred is entitled to claim constructive dismissal when you are in 'repudiatory' breach of his contract of employment and he resigns because of it.

When will you be in 'repudiatory' breach of contract?   17.3

Not every breach of contract by you will amount to a repudiatory breach which allows Fred to claim constructive dismissal. It must either be a significant breach of an important term, or the last straw following a series of minor breaches.

It is not necessary for there to be a written contract of employment in order for Fred to claim constructive dismissal. A contract can be oral, and certain terms are deemed to be included even if they are not written down (such as a term that you have to pay Fred his wages).

Some examples of breaches of important terms which would entitle Fred to resign and claim constructive dismissal are:

- reducing his wages – *Industrial Rubber Products v Gillon [1977] IRLR 389*;

- failing to pay wages when they fall due – *Hanlon v Allied Breweries [1975] IRLR 321*;

- suspending him without pay (unless Fred's contract of employment specifically states that you can do this) – *Warburton v Taff Vale Rly Co (1902) 18 TLR 420*;

- changes to his working hours – this can be a major change, such as from a day-shift to a night-shift (*Simmonds v Dowty Seals [1978] IRLR 211*), or lesser changes such as requiring Fred to work from 9.00am to 6.00pm when he previously worked from 8.00am till 5.00pm (*Muggridge v East Anglia Plastics [1973] IRLR 163*);

- changing Fred's place of work and expecting him to travel further each day. Unless there is a 'mobility clause' in Fred's contract of employment stating that you can require him to work anywhere (or, say, anywhere within 60 miles of Birmingham), then he cannot be obliged to travel anything more than a 'reasonable distance' to work each day. There is no definition of what amounts to a 'reasonable distance': however, if you require him to work somewhere that entails a significant increase in journey time or cost, then he will probably be entitled to resign and claim constructive dismissal;

- changing Fred's duties so as to involve a loss of prestige (*Coleman v Baldwins [1977] IRLR 342*) or changing his status within the company (*Stephenson v Austin [1990] ICR 609*).

Constructive dismissal not necessarily unfair   17.4

It must be emphasised that the fact you may be in repudiatory breach of contract, meaning that Fred is entitled to resign and claim he has been constructively dismissed, does not mean that the dismissal will be unfair. Sometimes such a dismissal can be justified on the basis of a business reorganisation, provided you have acted reasonably. For example, you may reorganise your business so that employees are expected to work eight hour, rather than seven hour, days. This would be a breach of contract and entitle Fred to resign and claim that he has been constructively dismissed. However, if you gave all employees reasonable notice of the change and offered them a *pro rata* pay rise then the dismissal is likely to be found fair. But be careful – most of the time a fundamental breach of contract (and thus a constructive dismissal) *will* lead to a finding of unfair dismissal.

Reasonable instructions are fair   17.5

Asking Fred to do something which he does not usually do is not necessarily a breach of contract – you are entitled to issue Fred with any reasonable instructions (provided they are lawful). This is addressed in **CHAPTER 6**.

Example

A Health Authority introduced a no-smoking rule for employees. An employee who smoked, and could not obey the rule, resigned and claimed constructive dismissal. The Employment Appeal Tribunal held that the employer was entitled to introduce such a rule and was not in breach of contract in so doing, since there was no contract term that the employees should be allowed to smoke – *Dryden v Greater Glasgow Health Board [1992] IRLR 469*.

Can being 'horrible' to the employee be a repudiatory breach of contract? 17.6

Yes. The law assumes a relationship of trust and confidence between employees and employers, and if you act in a way which is intended (or likely) to damage or destroy this relationship, you will be in breach of contract. Although this is not quite the same as saying you have to act nicely or reasonably towards Fred, if you persistently act unreasonably and Fred resigns as a result a tribunal is likely to decide you were in breach of the duty of mutual trust and confidence.

Although occasional acts of questionable behaviour will not be enough to entitle Fred to resign and claim constructive dismissal, many such breaches can be added together so that the final breach can be viewed as the 'last straw'.

The following are examples of cases where an employer has been found to be in breach of the term of mutual trust and confidence:

- failure to investigate staff's complaints or grievances properly (*Goolds v McConnell [1995] IRLR 516*);

- verbal abuse of employees. In one case a nightclub manager called an employee 'a big bastard, a big cunt, you are pigheaded' (*Palmanor v Cedron [1978] IRLR 303*). In another case, an assistant manager told an employee who had been in the job 18 years, 'You can't do the bloody job anyway'. It was held that this was in breach of the term of trust and confidence – *Cortaulds v Andrew [1979] IRLR 85*. Likewise, constructive dismissals occurred when a female assistant was called 'a bloody fat cow and stupid stuck-up bitch' (*MacNeilage v Arthur Roye [1976] IRLR 88*) or referred to as 'an intolerable bitch on a Monday morning' (*Isle of Wight Tourist Board v Coombes [1976] IRLR 413*);

- arbitrarily refusing to give pay rises to a particular employee when giving pay rises to others (*Gardner v Beresford [1978] IRLR 63*);

- unjustifiably criticising a manager in front of her subordinates, thereby undermining her position (*Hilton Hotels v Protopapa [1990] IRLR 316*);

- failing to provide proper support for staff (e.g. a hairdresser who was given no assistance when her junior resigned, despite complaints and requests for help – *Seligman v McHugh [1979] IRLR 130*). In order for this to amount to a breach of trust and confidence, the overworking of staff would have to be significant and inappropriate – employers are entitled to expect their staff to work reasonably hard.

Resignation by the employee 17.7

In order to establish constructive dismissal, Fred must prove that he resigned *because* of your repudiatory breach of contract. If he had been intending to resign anyway, there will be no constructive dismissal.

His resignation must be reasonably prompt 17.8

It is also important that Fred resigns reasonably promptly after your breach of contract. If he waits, say, three months after you change his working hours, and then resigns, he can be said to have waived his right to resign. Unfortunately, tribunals are not always consistent in determining what a reasonable period is. Some tribunals will expect Fred to resign within a week or two of becoming aware of the breach of contract, whereas some will allow far longer to elapse – particularly if Fred makes it clear he is reserving his position whilst searching for another job.

'Heat of the moment' resignations 17.9

If Fred resigns, using clear words of resignation, one would think that you were entitled to rely on the resignation and that he could not retract it (in the same way that you cannot retract a dismissal, once the words of dismissal are uttered or the letter sent).

However, in the last 20 years the law has introduced an exception to this for 'heat of the moment' resignations. Although you are normally entitled to take a resignation at face-value, if 'special circumstances' exist that alert the reasonable employer that a resignation might not be genuinely intended, then Fred is entitled to a short cooling-off period during which he can ask for his job back. If you refuse to give him the job back during this cooling-off period, you are deemed to have dismissed him.

Example

A mentally handicapped employee resigned after an argument with his managers. He appeared for work the next day, indicating that he had changed his mind, but the employers made him sign a blank payslip (which indicated his employment had terminated). The Employment Appeal Tribunal held that, in all the circumstances, the employers ought

> to have known the resignation might not have been genuine. Their
> refusal to have him back amounted to a dismissal – *Barclay v City of*
> *Glasgow District Council [1983] IRLR 313.*

What amounts to 'special circumstances'?   17.10

The few cases dealing with this point have generally dealt with resignations
uttered in the heat of the moment whilst arguing with the employer. They
have involved shouting, losses of temper and acting in an uncontrolled and
emotional manner.

Example

> Mr Lineham was the manager of a Kwik-Fit depot. In breach of
> company rules, he entered the premises one night to use the toilet. This
> was discovered by security staff and he was given a written warning.
> Whilst being given the warning, an argument ensued and Mr Lineham
> threw his keys down on the table and walked out. The Employment
> Appeal Tribunal treated this as a 'heat of the moment' resignation and
> stated that the employers ought to have allowed a cooling-off period
> before taking the resignation at face value – *Kwik-Fit v Lineham [1992]*
> *IRLR 156.*

In addition, the Barclay case (above) dealt with a mentally handicapped
employee where the employers ought to have known he did not understand
the significance or effect of a resignation. If Fred is calm and rational, a
resignation can safely be accepted at face value and no cooling-off period need
be allowed.

What is a reasonable cooling-off period?   17.11

The courts have given little guidance over what amounts to a reasonable
cooling-off period. It seems, however, that a cooling-off period need only be
very short – perhaps a day or a weekend. Certainly if Fred returns after a week
and asks for his job, you are quite entitled to refuse.

Do you need to offer the job back, or can you sit back and wait for the employee to approach you?   17.12

At present, the courts have said that you are entitled to sit back and wait to see
if Fred approaches you to ask for his job back. Nevertheless, in order to be safe,

240

if Fred has resigned in the heat of the moment (and you are prepared to have him back), you should write to him immediately and ask him to contact you within 24 hours if he wishes to withdraw his resignation. If you do this, you will be protected before any tribunal if Fred then claims dismissal (subject to him bringing a claim for constructive dismissal, and alleging that you were in breach of contract in getting into an argument with him in the first place).

Remember that if Fred does ask for his job back, you are quite entitled to adopt disciplinary sanctions (such as a written warning, or such sanction as you consider appropriate) for both the loss of temper and the conduct which led to the argument (and loss of temper) in the first place.

Pressuring an employee to resign, or offering a 'resignation' package 17.13

Subject to the three exceptions below, never deliver an ultimatum to Fred to resign or be dismissed. Such an ultimatum, should Fred resign in response, is always regarded by the courts as a dismissal. This is because, in reality, it is your action and not Fred's which has caused the employment to terminate.

Many employers consider that the mere fact of Fred agreeing to resign will pre-empt him from bringing an unfair dismissal claim. That is incorrect.

It may be that any such dismissal is fair. If you said, 'if you don't resign, I'll sack you' after Fred has admitted stealing company property, the dismissal will probably be fair. However, in a borderline case, the use of such tactics will predispose a tribunal against you.

The exceptions to this rule 17.14

There are three exceptions to the rule that an ultimatum will amount to a dismissal:

- where the dismissal is not absolutely guaranteed. If Fred commits an act of gross misconduct, and you tell him that he will have to go through the disciplinary procedure and 'there is a good chance you will be dismissed', but you offer him the opportunity to resign, this will not be a deemed dismissal;

- where the ultimatum is not 'resign or be dismissed', but is 'perform or resign or be dismissed', i.e. an ultimatum to do the job properly. This is perfectly proper because you are quite entitled to demand that Fred carries out his duties properly even when his failures to perform do not justify immediate dismissal;

241

- where there is a genuine inducement to resign. If you say to Fred, 'I'll give you £5,000 if you resign – if you don't accept it, you're dismissed without a penny', this may amount to a genuine resignation (and not dismissal) if Fred accepts the money. The issue the tribunal have to decide is precisely what caused Fred's decision to resign. If it was the money, and he would have resigned without the threat, then it will be a genuine resignation. If the principal reason for his resignation was the threat, and he would not have taken the money if he had not been threatened with dismissal, then the tribunal will treat his resignation as a dismissal by you. Common sense suggests that the more money you offer in this scenario, the more chance you have of persuading a tribunal that it was the offer of money that triggered Fred's resignation.

Failing to renew a fixed-term contract 17.15

One of the more surprising situations in which the law deems there to be a dismissal (and thus the potential for an unfair dismissal) is if Fred is on a fixed-term contract and you fail to renew it at the end of the term.

There is a very good reason for this: if employers could avoid unfair dismissal claims by placing employees on fixed-term contracts, then unscrupulous employers could insist that all employees be employed only on short fixed-term contracts, which they might renew (or not renew) at their pleasure.

One year's continuous employment 17.16

Accordingly, if Fred is on a fixed-term contract which you do not renew, the law treats it in the same way as if he had been on a normal ongoing contract and you dismissed him on the date that the fixed term expired. Remember that, at present, employees need one year's continuous employment before they can claim unfair dismissal – thus, at present, if you fail to renew a fixed-term contract after any period of less than one year, Fred cannot claim for unfair dismissal in any event.

Placing the employee on short-time or laying him off 17.17

Sometimes laying Fred off, or placing him on short-time, will amount to a dismissal even if you are contractually entitled to do so. This occurs when specific criteria are fulfilled. In such a scenario, the reason for dismissal is deemed to be redundancy and Fred will be entitled to claim a redundancy payment from you.

In order for this to occur, Fred has to bring himself within some fairly complex rules. In practice, unless Fred is being advised by a trade union, he is unlikely to be familiar with this procedure and will not claim under it.

What do 'lay-off' and 'short-time' mean? 17.18

The terms 'lay-off' and 'short-time' have very specific legal meanings. In order to qualify, Fred must work for you on terms that his right to be paid depends on being provided with work, i.e. he has no fixed wage. This situation is often found with temporary workers or workers in the building trade. He is laid-off in any given week if, during that week, he is provided with no work (and thus entitled to no remuneration). He is on short-time in any given week if, during that week, he is provided with a reduced amount of work so that his remuneration falls below half a normal weeks' pay.

If Fred works in a normal job for a fixed salary (e.g. £250 per week plus overtime) then you are not permitted to place him on short-time or lay him off unless there is a specific provision in his contract of employment entitling you to do so. If there is no such provision, and you lay him off for a week, he is entitled to resign and claim constructive dismissal on the grounds that you have not paid him the salary to which he is entitled.

When is the employee deemed to be redundant? 17.19

This procedure only applies if Fred has been employed by you for two years or more (note: not one year, unlike normal unfair dismissal claims). When calculating whether he has been working for two years or more, you do not count any period during which Fred was under 18 years old. However, weeks in which Fred has been laid-off, or placed on short-time, do count towards the two-year period.

Fred is deemed to be made redundant if the following criteria are satisfied:

(a) he must have been laid-off, or kept on short-time, for either four consecutive weeks or six non-consecutive weeks within a period of 13 weeks;

(b) within four weeks of fulfilling the above four-week or six-week period, he must have told you in writing that he intends to claim a redundancy payment;

(c) within seven days of Fred telling you in writing that he intends to claim a redundancy payment, you do not tell him in writing that you will challenge his right to claim a redundancy payment; and,

(d) he resigns within three weeks of the seven-day period in (c) expiring, giving you a proper notice period (either that which is set out in his contract of employment or, if there is nothing set out, one week).

When can you challenge the employee's right to a redundancy payment? 17.20

If Fred has been laid-off, or placed on short-time, for the requisite periods (as set out above), he is entitled as of right to a redundancy payment unless:

(a) on the date he wrote to you stating his intention to claim, it was reasonably to be expected that, within four weeks of his letter to you, he would start on a period of employment with you of at least 13 weeks during which period he would not be laid-off or kept on short-time for any week; and,

(b) you give Fred notice of that in writing within seven days of his letter to you – see (c) above.

Claiming before resigning 17.21

If you do challenge Fred's right to claim a redundancy payment on the grounds that work can soon be expected, he does not have to resign but is entitled to send in a claim to the employment tribunal without resigning, so that the tribunal can determine whether at the date of Fred's letter, the defence set out in (a) applied. If a tribunal rules in Fred's favour, and considers that as of the date of his letter it could not reasonably be expected that he would soon be provided with at least 13 weeks' work, then he has a further three weeks from the date of the tribunal's decision in which to resign and claim his redundancy payment.

Failing to allow a female employee to return to work after maternity leave

Basic right to return 17.22

All female employees, irrespective of how long they have worked, are entitled to a maternity period of 26 weeks. During this period, a woman has a right to return to work with her seniority, pension rights and similar rights intact. All other terms and conditions must be 'not less favourable' than those which would have applied if she had not been absent.

If you refuse to allow an employee to return to work after her maternity period, you are deemed to have dismissed her. If the reason for the refusal is maternity-related (as it almost always will be, unless you can persuade a tribunal that she would have been dismissed anyway – for example, because of redundancies) then the dismissal will be automatically unfair. In such circumstances, the employee does not need one year's continuity of employment to qualify for an unfair dismissal claim, and she is entitled to bring a claim as of right.

Extended right to return   17.23

If, at the beginning of the 14th week before her expected week of confinement, the employee has been employed for 26 weeks or more (which basically means she will have been working for at least 40 weeks by the expected week of confinement), she has the right to take one year's maternity leave, rather than just six months.

She does not need to tell you that she is exercising this additional right – she is deemed to be doing so, and is automatically entitled to return to work at the end of that period.

Offers of alternative work   17.24

The right to return to work during this additional period, however, is not a right to return to the same job that she was doing at the time she went on maternity leave. If you can establish that it is not reasonably practicable to allow her to return to the same job, she must be offered a job which is both suitable for her and appropriate for her to do in the circumstances. In particular, she has to be offered terms and conditions which are not less favourable than those she worked under before, and her seniority and pension rights must remain intact.

If you fail to offer her similar (or better) employment, then you are deemed to have dismissed her.

Returning early   17.25

Can an employee return to work before the end of her maternity leave period? Yes – but only if she gives you three weeks' notice.

Redundancy   17.26

Even if you have genuinely made the woman's position redundant during her maternity absence, she is entitled to return to any available similar job when her maternity leave expires – and 'trump' other employees or job applicants in connection with that post (see **7.31**).

Chapter 18
Common Pitfalls II

Introduction 18.1

A number of situations amount to specific exceptions from the general rules set out in this book. For example, dismissals for certain reasons will always be unfair, no matter how good your justifications or how much consultation and discussion you went through. Likewise, although an unfair dismissal claim must ordinarily be started within three months of the dismissal, this time limit can sometimes be extended. Unless you are aware of these pitfalls, you may find yourself at the end of a claim that you might otherwise have avoided.

The following matters are discussed in this chapter:

(a)   when the dismissal will automatically be unfair (irrespective of the number of years for which Fred has been employed or the procedure you follow);

(b)   opening yourself up to discrimination claims;

(c)   bringing an unfair dismissal claim more than three months after dismissal;

(d)   dismissing because of pressure by other employees;

(e)   dismissing after less than one year's continuous service;

(f)   the 'without prejudice' dismissal.

Automatically unfair dismissals 18.2

Certain dismissals will always be automatically unfair, irrespective of the business justification or the procedures which you adopt when carrying out the dismissal. Essentially, these dismissals are connected with trade union functions, health and safety matters, pregnancy or asserting a statutory right.

Dismissal for any of these reasons is always unfair 18.3

If a tribunal decides that the reason, or principal reason, for Fred's dismissal is one of the reasons set out below, it will find the dismissal to be unfair. It should be noted that these reasons are summarised and do not follow the exact wording set out in the relevant legislation.

Dismissals for the following reasons will always be unfair.

Trade union related dismissals

- If Fred is, or proposes to become, a member of a trade union.
- If Fred is not, or refuses to become, a member of a trade union.
- If Fred takes part in, or proposes to take part in, trade union activities.

Health and safety related dismissals

- Carrying out activities in connection with preventing or reducing risks to health and safety at work, if Fred been designated by you to carry out such activities.

- Carrying out duties as a workers' representative (or committee member) on matters of health and safety at work, if Fred has been legally appointed or elected as a representative or committee member, or if you have recognised him as such.

- If Fred leaves (or refuses to return to) his place of work in circumstances where he believes there to be serious and imminent danger which he cannot reasonably avert, or if he takes steps to protect himself or others from that danger.

- If there is no health and safety representative or committee at work, or if Fred cannot practicably go through the representative/committee, bringing health and safety matters to your attention.

Pregnancy related dismissals

- Any reason connected with pregnancy.

Asserting a statutory right

- If Fred asserts you breached certain statutory (legal) employment rights, or brings a claim against you alleging such a breach, and you dismiss him as a result, the dismissal will be automatically unfair. The rights protected include claims to a minimum notice period, claims for itemised payslips or written terms and conditions of employment and rights connected with trade union membership or time off for trade union duties.

Other reasons

- If you dismiss Fred because of a transfer of undertakings – which may occur if you take over a business or a major contract – and you cannot establish an economic, technical or organisational reason entailing changes in the workforce, then the dismissal will be automatically unfair. This is considered further in **CHAPTER 9**.

- If you dismissed Fred because he failed to disclose a 'spent' conviction – see **5.4**.

- If you dismiss Fred because he has told you or any other person (subject to certain conditions, such as he has told the other person in good faith, not for personal gain and when it was reasonable to tell that person) anything which suggests or proves:

  (a) a criminal offence has, or is likely to be, committed;

  (b) you or any other person has failed to comply with a legal obligation (which, in some circumstances, includes a breach of his employment contract);

  (c) there is a significant risk to any person's health and safety;

  (d) there is a risk of damage to the environment; or

  (e) you are trying to conceal any of the above.

- If you dismiss Fred because he refuses to work more than a 48-hour week, averaged out over a 17-week rolling period, or if he refuses to sign an opt-out from the 48-hour week. The main exceptions are policemen, some medical (and support) staff, family workers, or employees who set their own hours (such as senior managers). This is a complex area of law, and you should seek legal advice before considering dismissal on this ground.

- If you dismiss Fred because he insists on four weeks' paid holiday.

Selection for redundancy on these grounds is also automatically unfair 18.4

It is also important to bear in mind that if you select Fred for redundancy on one of the above grounds, the dismissal for redundancy will also automatically be unfair. It is crucial to ensure that the above reasons do not form any of your redundancy selection criteria.

Exception to the one year's employment rule 18.5

Ordinarily, Fred requires at least one year's employment with you in order to qualify to bring an unfair dismissal claim.

However, if the reason for the dismissal was one of the above reasons, other than being due to a transfer of undertakings (first reason under 'other reasons' in the above list), it is not necessary for Fred to have worked for one year. Thus he will be entitled to claim for dismissal (and will succeed) if he has only worked for one month but you dismiss him because he wants to join a trade union.

More commonly, if a new employee announces that she is pregnant when she first arrives for work (not having told you at interview), and you dismiss her as a result, you will automatically be found to have unfairly dismissed her even though she has not been working for one year. She would also have a claim for sex discrimination (in which there is no upper limit for compensation), as she would have had if you refused her the job because she told you she was pregnant at interview.

Opening yourself up for discrimination claims
18.6

Employees are entitled to claim sex or race discrimination in addition to unfair dismissal. Since 1995 employees have also been able to claim that they have been discriminated against on grounds of physical or mental disabilities and, more recently, on grounds of sexual orientation, religion or belief.

The advantages to Fred of claiming sex, race or disability discrimination as well as unfair dismissal are threefold:

- the mere allegation of discrimination, as contrasted with unfair dismissal, can place greater pressure on an employer to settle because of the fear of adverse publicity;

- Fred does not need one year's continuous employment to claim discrimination. Thus discrimination is often used as a way of claiming unfair dismissal by the back door when an employee lacks the requisite one year's employment. This is wholly improper, and such discrimination claims are often without merit (even if an unfair dismissal claim might have merit) – nevertheless you should be careful when dismissing to avoid allowing any opening for the employee to allege discrimination;

- at present, most unfair dismissal awards are limited to £63,100 (i.e. a maximum of £8,100 for the basic award and £55,000 for the compensatory award). There is no limit on discrimination claims, and thus employees sometimes claim discrimination in the hope of getting a higher award.

When to be particularly cautious 18.7

Resisting a claim for sex, race or disability discrimination is outside the scope of this book. As with an unfair dismissal claim, if Fred wishes, or is advised, to claim discrimination then you will be forced to fight the claim. Fred's ability to claim discrimination is something you should be aware of and have at the back of your mind so as to avoid saying or doing anything foolish. There are a few elementary steps you can take to show that your dismissal of Fred (or selection of him for redundancy) is not on grounds of sex or race. These steps include:

- be very cautious when dismissing any pregnant employee – unless your justification for dismissal is extremely clear, you may have difficulties persuading an employment tribunal that pregnancy was not the principal reason for dismissal;

- ensure that all the steps you take in connection with the dismissal, including notes of meetings, interviews and consideration of alternative employment are fully documented;

- if you are selecting a large number of people for redundancy, ask a colleague to draw up a list showing peoples' sex and race after you have made your initial selection. Work out, as a percentage, whether the sex and ethnicity of the people you have selected for redundancy broadly matches the spread of sexes and races in your workforce. If there is a significant disparity, for example 20% of the people you employ are black, but 80% of those selected for redundancy are black, you will have difficulty persuading a tribunal that your selection was not affected by racial overtones and you may wish to reconsider your selection criteria. By contrast, if you can show that you monitored the race and sex of employees you selected for redundancy after the initial selection (not during), this will go some way to persuading a tribunal that you are not inadvertently discriminating;

- when dismissing Fred on grounds of ill-health, make sure you have considered whether you can avoid dismissing him by making reasonable adjustments to the workplace – see **2.30**.

Effective presentation at the hearing is crucial 18.8

If Fred does claim sex, race or disability discrimination, it is important to bear in mind that frequently the only way in which a tribunal can judge whether you were guilty of discrimination is by drawing inferences from your manner of giving evidence. Effective presentation at the hearing is particularly important, and if you end up facing an allegation of discrimination you may wish to give particular thought to engaging a lawyer.

Bringing a claim more than three months after the dismissal
18.9

Claims for unfair dismissal must ordinarily be brought within three months of the dismissal (six months for an unpaid redundancy payment).

The three-month period starts running on the date of the dismissal, if it is a summary dismissal, or the date that the notice period expires if you dismiss with notice. Sometimes it is not always straightforward as to when the three-month period starts running: for example if you have paid Fred monies in lieu of notice, a tribunal will often have to construe the letter of dismissal to determine whether the employment ended on the date of the letter or the date that the notice period expired.

Ordinarily, if Fred fails to present his claim within three months, he will be prohibited from claiming. There are two things to note:

- the three-month period includes the day of dismissal. Thus if Fred is dismissed on the 15 February 2004, his claim must be presented by 14 May 2004. If it is presented on the 15 May, it is a day too late and the claim will be dismissed (subject to the exceptions below);

- the claim must be presented *at the tribunal* within three months. This means that it must have been delivered to the tribunal – proof of posting within the time period is insufficient.

What are the exceptions to the three-month limit?
18.10

There are two exceptions to the rule that a Claim Form must be presented at the tribunal within three months of dismissal:

(a) if Fred reasonably believed, on the day the three-month time limit expired, that a disciplinary procedure was ongoing, then the three-month time limit is automatically extended to six months; and

(b) if it was not reasonably practicable for Fred to present his claim within the three-month period, he will be permitted a 'reasonable' extension of time.

Reasonable belief disciplinary process continuing
18.11

Since October 2004, if an employee reasonably believes that the disciplinary process is continuing on the day the three-month period expires, an extension of three months is automatically triggered (meaning that Fred then has six months from the date of dismissal to lodge his Claim Form).

At the time of writing, no caselaw has developed on what amounts to a reasonable belief. Certainly if an appeal process is ongoing, the three-month extension would be triggered.

It is therefore important to ensure that you make it quite clear, when writing to Fred with the result of an appeal (should he bring one), that – assuming the appeal is dismissed – he has reached the end of the disciplinary process.

Not reasonably practicable to bring a claim within three months   18.12

If Fred can establish that it was 'not reasonably practicable' to present his claim within three months, then he will be permitted an extension of time. Tribunals tend to be fairly strict when applying this rule, and it is not easy for employees to satisfy a tribunal that it was not reasonably practicable to bring a claim within three months. Essentially Fred will have to prove that it was not reasonably feasible for him to present his claim within the expected time period.

A tribunal would find that it was 'not reasonably practicable' to bring a claim within three months (and thus allow an extension of time) in the following circumstances:

- if there was a physical problem impeding Fred from claiming, for example he was in hospital with two broken wrists and incapable of writing for three months after dismissal. It is not easy to satisfy a tribunal that physical infirmities rendered it not reasonably practicable to claim;

- if Fred posted his application form by first class post at least two clear days (i.e. excluding weekends and bank holidays) before the three months expires, but it encounters delays in the post, a tribunal will normally say it was not reasonably practicable for it to arrive in time;

- if Fred was actively misled by you as to his rights: this is a loose interpretation as to the meaning of practicability – however, if you have acted fraudulently and misled Fred as to the period in which he has to claim, a tribunal is likely to allow him an extension of time;

- if Fred is unaware of the right to claim unfair dismissal at all – although very few tribunals will accept Fred's word on this since very few employees have not heard of unfair dismissal claims;

- if Fred is unaware of the facts giving rise to the claim during the three-month period, but becomes aware of new facts which give rise to a claim subsequently, he will usually be granted an extension of time if it was reasonable for him to be unaware of those facts previously and the acquisition of the new facts is crucial in the decision to bring the claim. A classic example of this is where you have said Fred's job was redundant, but he discovers outside the three-month time limit that you hired somebody to replace him (thus indicating that no redundancy situation actually existed).

By contrast, a tribunal would *not* find that it was 'not reasonably practicable' to bring a claim within three months (and thus would not allow an extension of time) in the following circumstances:

- ignorance of the three-month time limit for bringing the claim. If Fred has engaged lawyers or advisers, and they do not tell him of the three-month limit, he is able to sue them for negligence but will be unable to proceed with a claim against you;

- failure by his solicitors or other advisers to present the claim in time;

- failures of the postal service when Fred leaves it to the last moment to present a claim. If Fred leaves it till the day before the time limit expires and thereby takes the risk of the claim not arriving in time, he will probably not be permitted an extension of time. If, however, he has posted the claim in good time and unexpected delays occur which could not ordinarily be anticipated then, subject to satisfying the tribunal that the claim form was posted on the date claimed (which may not be easy), Fred is likely to obtain an extension;

- waiting for the outcome of other proceedings – if Fred was waiting for the outcome of criminal or other civil proceedings before presenting his unfair dismissal claim, this will not mean that it was not reasonably practicable to bring the unfair dismissal claim within three months of dismissal.

If it was not reasonably practicable for Fred to present his claim within three months, what extension of time will be given? 18.13

If Fred can persuade the tribunal that it was not reasonably practicable to present his claim within three months, he will be entitled to proceed with the claim provided he can satisfy the tribunal that the claim was presented within a 'reasonable time' after the three-months expired. Accordingly Fred does not become entitled to bring his claim irrespective of how late the application was lodged.

There is no firm rule as to how long is allowed to elapse between Fred becoming aware of his right to bring a claim and actually presenting it once he has gone past the three-month limit. If he presents it within a week of becoming aware of all relevant facts, this is likely to be a reasonable period. A month may well be too long, depending on his reasons for taking a full four to five weeks to fill in a form. Anything over two months is likely to be regarded as going beyond a 'reasonable period' and thus Fred will not be permitted to proceed with the claim.

Dismissing because of pressure by employees   18.14

Sometimes disharmony between employees can be a fair reason for dismissing Fred – see **10.4**. However, the law provides that if other employees call or threaten a strike, or other industrial action, then any such pressure placed on you must be disregarded when determining whether Fred has been unfairly dismissed.

Accordingly, therefore, you can sometimes rely on tension in the workplace as a reason for dismissing Fred. However, as soon as things deteriorate and become more formal (due to threatened, or actual, industrial action), you cannot dismiss Fred unless you can show that you would have dismissed without the threatened or actual industrial action.

If you do dismiss Fred because of strikes or industrial action, and the tribunal decides that the dismissal was unfair, you may still be able to show that Fred's conduct contributed to the industrial action by triggering the enmity of his colleagues. This would lead to a reduction in his award – see **13.24**.

Dismissing the employee after less than one year's continuous service   18.15

At present, employees need to have been working for one year before they become entitled to certain employment rights, such as the right to claim unfair dismissal or a redundancy payment. There are, however, two exceptions to the need for Fred to have been working for one year before he can claim:

- where the dismissal is for an automatically unfair reason (except when it arises out of a transfer of undertakings) – see **18.2**;

- where you did not give Fred his statutory minimum notice period (see **12.11** for how to calculate this period) and, if you had given it to him, he would have satisfied the one-year requirement. In practice, this means that if you dismiss Fred without notice after 51 weeks, he is entitled to add-on the one week's statutory minimum notice in order to achieve the necessary year's continuity of employment to claim unfair dismissal.

The 'without prejudice' dismissal 18.16

It is common for employers to call employees into a room and say 'we don't think things are working out – on a "without prejudice" basis, we'll offer you £5,000 if you go'.

In certain circumstances, that can amount to a breach of trust and confidence – and thus entitle the employee to resign and claim constructive dismissal. This will happen if a tribunal thinks you have seriously damaged the ongoing employment relationship by making such a statement. It follows that a tribunal is more likely to think this if there has been no previous complaint about the employee's job performance (or conduct), than if there have been prior complaints and Fred *knows* that the relationship is strained.

And if Fred resigns (and claims constructive dismissal), he is entitled to tell the tribunal about your offer even though you said it was 'without prejudice'. Likewise, if you eventually dismiss Fred after following proper procedures, he is still entitled to tell the tribunal about the 'without prejudice' offer (he would, presumably, be arguing that you had made up your mind to terminate his employment and the procedures were a sham to lay a paper trail). This is because this type of meeting is an exception to the normal 'without prejudice' rule, where litigants cannot tell the tribunal about 'without prejudice' conversations. This is largely a policy exception, reflecting the fact of the unequal bargaining power whilst Fred is still in employment, and the fact that – at that stage – there is no formal dispute which you are trying to resolve.

Statutory Minimum Dismissal Procedures

This Appendix sets out the statutory minimum dismissal procedures which you must comply with, failing which any dismissal will be automatically unfair and an uplift will be applied to any compensation which is payable. The Appendix also summarises the various exceptions, i.e. when the statutory minimum procedures do *not* apply. These laws came into force in October 2004 and have been incorporated into the body of this book.

See also **APPENDIX 2** and **APPENDIX 3**.

The statutory minimum dismissal procedures

The standard procedure

[App 1.1]

Employment Act 2002

'SCHEDULE 2, PART I – DISMISSAL AND DISCIPLINARY PROCEDURES

CHAPTER 1 – STANDARD PROCEDURE

STEP 1: STATEMENT OF GROUNDS FOR ACTION AND INVITATION TO MEETING

1(1)   The employer must set out in writing the employee's alleged conduct or characteristics, or other circumstances, which lead him to contemplate dismissing or taking disciplinary action against the employee.

1(2)   The employer must send the statement or a copy of it to the employee and invite the employee to attend a meeting to discuss the matter.

STEP 2: MEETING

2(1)   The meeting must take place before action is taken, except in the case where the disciplinary action consists of suspension.

2(2)   The meeting must not take place unless–

(a)   the employer has informed the employee what the basis was for including in the statement under paragraph 1(1) the ground or grounds given in it, and

(b)   the employee has had a reasonable opportunity to consider his response to that information.

2(3)   The employee must take all reasonable steps to attend the meeting.

2(4)   After the meeting, the employer must inform the employee of his decision and notify him of the right to appeal against the decision if he is not satisfied with it.

STEP 3: APPEAL

3(1)   If the employee does wish to appeal, he must inform the employer.

3(2)   If the employee informs the employer of his wish to appeal, the employer must invite him to attend a further meeting.

3(3)   The employee must take all reasonable steps to attend the meeting.

3(4)   The appeal meeting need not take place before the dismissal or disciplinary action takes effect.

3(5)   After the appeal meeting, the employer must inform the employee of his final decision.'

In very limited circumstances, where the employee has been guilty of serious gross misconduct, is dismissed immediately, and the tribunal thinks it reasonable for the employer to have dismissed immediately without conducting an investigation, an alternative procedure (known as the 'modified procedure') applies. Although this is listed below for completeness, readers of this book are warned *against* relying on this procedure: it will *always* be safer to comply with the standard procedure – certainly until the courts have had a few years to clarify exactly when the modified procedure is permitted. Using the modified procedure, and a tribunal then deciding you ought to have used the standard procedure, will normally result in an automatically unfair dismissal and an uplift to Fred's award.

The modified procedure

[App 1.2]

Employment Act 2002

'SCHEDULE 2, PART I – DISMISSAL AND DISCIPLINARY PROCE-DURES

CHAPTER 2 – MODIFIED PROCEDURE

STEP 1: STATEMENT OF GROUNDS FOR ACTION

4   The employer must–

    (a)   set out in writing–

        (i)   the employee's alleged misconduct which has led to the dismissal,

        (ii)   what the basis was for thinking at the time of the dismissal that the employee was guilty of the alleged misconduct, and

        (iii)   the employee's right to appeal against dismissal, and

    (b)   send the statement or a copy of it to the employee.

STEP 2: APPEAL

5(1)   If the employee does wish to appeal, he must inform the employer.

5(2)   If the employee informs the employer of his wish to appeal, the employer must invite him to attend a meeting.

5(3)   The employee must take all reasonable steps to attend the meeting.

5(4)   After the appeal meeting, the employer must inform the employee of his final decision.'

General requirements

[App 1.3]

Guidance is given in each of the chapters about what should happen at meetings. However, the following rules are overriding provisions, failure to comply with which normally results in an automatic unfair dismissal and an uplift to Fred's award.

Employment Act 2002

'SCHEDULE 2, PART III – GENERAL REQUIREMENTS

INTRODUCTORY

11   The following requirements apply to each of the procedures set out above (so far as applicable).

TIMETABLE

12   Each step and action under the procedure must be taken without unreasonable delay.

MEETINGS

13(1) Timing and location of meetings must be reasonable.

13(2) Meetings must be conducted in a manner that enables both employer and employee to explain their cases.

13(3) In the case of appeal meetings which are not the first meeting, the employer should, as far as is reasonably practicable, be represented by a more senior manager than attended the first meeting (unless the most senior manager attended that meeting).'

Exceptions

[App 1.4]

When the following exceptions apply, you will not be found to have *automatically* unfairly dismissed Fred if you do not comply with the statutory minimum dismissal procedures. However, a tribunal may think the dismissal is still unfair, even if it is not *automatically* unfair.

Only the important exceptions are listed – this is *not* a comprehensive list (a comprehensive list appears in **APPENDIX 3** at the end of the ACAS Code on Disciplinary and Grievance Procedures). The exceptions which will only arise infrequently are not included; no harm will ever be done by complying with these procedures even if the penalty for failure to comply does not exist.

The exceptions are where:

(1)   the dismissal is for breach of a statutory provision (i.e. the type of dismissal considered in **10.3**);

(2)   you are dismissing all employees in a particular category, and offering to rehire them all on different terms and conditions;

(3)   Fred fails to take reasonable steps to attend the meeting – you are discharged from further steps in the procedure;

(4)   Fred (or his representative) fail to attend two consecutively arranged meetings for a reason that could not have been foreseen at the time the meetings were arranged;

(5)   you have reasonable grounds to believe that following the procedure would result in a significant threat to you, your property, any other person or the property of any other person;

(6) you have been subjected to harassment and have reasonable grounds to believe that following the procedure would result in you being subjected to further harassment;

(7) it is 'not practicable for the party to follow the procedure within a reasonable period' — possibly the exception which will arise most often in practice.

This last exception is, as stated, possibly the most important. Thus if you cannot arrange a meeting with Fred within a reasonable period because he is unwell (which will be common in sickness absence cases) or remanded in custody (in an extreme violence/dishonesty case), the statutory minimum disciplinary procedure will be discharged and you will not be automatically liable for unfair dismissal just because you have not followed every step of the procedure.

A final point to note is that if *Fred* breaches the minimum procedure (for example, by not taking all reasonable steps to attend the meeting) because he has reasonable grounds to believe that following the procedure would result in a threat to person or property or because he has been subject to and fears further harassment *and* a tribunal agrees with him and thinks his reasons for not following the procedures were your fault, you (not he) will be deemed to be in breach of the procedures.

Appendix 2

DTI Guidance

Disciplinary, Dismissal and Grievance Procedures

Guidance for employers

Foreword

[App 2.1]

On 1 October the *Employment Act 2002* (*Dispute Resolution*) *Regulations 2004* came into force. They lay down disciplinary, dismissal and grievance procedures that provide a framework for discussing problems at work. This guide explains the procedures. It is primarily intended for managers in small firms. Separate guidance will be available for employees from http://www.dti.gov.uk/resolvingdisputes.

This document gives general guidance only. It has no legal force and cannot cover every point and situation. If you would like advice on your particular situation, please see below for Acas contact details.

It is important to note that the Regulations aim to set a minimum standard and are not intended to replace existing best practice and the new procedures should complement your existing disciplinary and grievance procedures, not replace them. Your disciplinary and grievance procedures must be set out in writing (see the following section for more details).

If you need more advice, Acas offers a number of services to help you, from good practice advice on setting up procedures to looking for a resolution if your employee applies to a tribunal. Their website is www.acas.org.uk and they have a helpline on 08457 47 47 47.

Chapter 1: Disciplinary and dismissal procedures

[App 2.2]

This chapter sets out the steps you need to take when you are considering dismissal or disciplinary action. Generally speaking, your aim should be to resolve the problem whilst keeping the employee on. That may not be possible, but you must follow the procedures set out below. Failure to do so may result in a tribunal case that goes against you.

Communicating your disciplinary and grievance procedures

[App 2.3]

From 1 October, all employers will be required to issue a written document that sets out their disciplinary rules and the new minimum procedures. This will only affect you if you haven't already made this information available to your staff or if your procedures change as a result of the new procedures.

This information can either be communicated in the employee's contract, his or her written particulars of employment or the letter sent when offering the employee a job. Alternatively, you could set out the details in a statement of change.

Guidance on producing this statement is available from the DTI and Acas[1].

If you do not issue this statement to your staff, and one of them takes an employment tribunal case against you and wins, you will be liable for an additional fine of up to 4 weeks' wages.

Informal warning

[App 2.4]

When someone is not performing satisfactorily or is misbehaving at work the first priority should be to help them to improve. Have an informal discussion of the problem with them. Make sure they understand what they are doing wrong and what they have to do to come up to standard. To remind yourself, make a brief note of the date on which the issue was discussed and what action was agreed.

Formal warning

[App 2.5]

If the issue isn't resolved or the matter is very serious, you should tackle the matter more formally. Invite the employee to a meeting and have a formal discussion with him or her. The employee has the right to be accompanied by a colleague or trade union representative. If you are not satisfied with the employee's explanation you should write the employee a letter setting out the problem, what you expect him or her to do about it, when you expect to see an improvement and what you will do if there is no improvement. Where the employee's poor performance or misconduct is sufficiently serious, for example because it is having a serious harmful effect on the business, it may be appropriate to issue a final written warning.

For example, an employee in a small shop is responsible for unlocking the premises every morning, but arrives unacceptably late. If informal discussions do not resolve the issue, the employer could issue a final written warning, after holding a formal meeting. The final written warning could state that if the employee is late at any time during the next 6 months, he or she would be subject to dismissal procedures.

A final written warning should give details of and the grounds for the complaint. It should warn the employee that failure to improve or modify behaviour may lead to dismissal, and it should refer to the right of appeal. A tribunal is unlikely to find a dismissal to be fair unless you gave a final written warning (except in cases of gross misconduct). If the situation still does not improve, and you feel further action against the employee is necessary you should start the standard procedure.

Standard procedure

[App 2.6]

The standard three-step disciplinary and dismissal procedures apply to

- All dismissals except:

  o 'collective' or constructive dismissals and dismissals where employment cannot continue for reasons beyond anyone's control (see **[APP 2.17]** 'When procedures do not apply')

  o a very small subset of gross misconduct dismissals (see **[APP 2.23]** 'Modified Procedure' and **[APP 2.17]** 'When procedures do not apply').

- All disciplinary action, such as demotion or reduction of pay, except action which is part of a workplace procedure i.e. warnings (oral or written) and suspension on full pay.

Note that the standard procedure applies to the case of an employee who was on a **fixed term contract** of a year or more which is not renewed. It also applies when someone is dismissed on grounds of **age** and has not reached the age of 65 or whatever is the normal retirement age in the company or when someone is dismissed for **health reason**s. Remember that **part-time** employees must be treated in the same way as full–time ones. You should also use the standard procedure when you are making someone **redundant**². Failure to use the standard procedure in such cases may result in you losing a tribunal case.

The three steps are:

i   The written statement.

ii   The hearing.

iii   The appeal meeting.

The written statement

[App 2.7]

You must prepare a statement setting out what the employee has done, or failed to do that may result in disciplinary action or dismissal. In the case of redundancy, retirement on health grounds or the end of a fixed term contract the statement should set out the circumstances which led you to take the decision to end the person's employment. A copy of this statement must be sent to the employee and you must arrange a meeting to discuss the matter. See **[APP 2.26** Letter 1] for the relevant sample letter.

You do not have to put all the details of the employee's conduct in the written statement. But if you don't, the details must be explained to him or her before the meeting, so there is time for him or her to consider a response. The law does not allow you only to present this information at the meeting.

The hearing

[App 2.8]

When arranging the meeting, bear in mind that:

- The meeting should be far enough ahead that the employee has had time to think about the written statement but it should not be delayed for too long. The employee has a duty to take all reasonable steps to attend.

- The employee has a statutory right to be accompanied to the meeting by a workmate or a trade union representative.

- The meeting must be at a reasonable time and in a convenient location. If the employee or person accompanying them is disabled you must take this into account and make reasonable provision to ensure that they can participate fully.

- If you haven't already done so before writing, ensure you have carried out a thorough investigation of all the relevant circumstances of the case and communicate them to the individual before the meeting. After the meeting you should decide what to do and tell the employee what your decision is. At the same time you must offer the employee the opportunity to appeal against that decision if it goes against him or her. Set a time limit for the appeal (the Acas Code recommends five days). See **[APP 2.26** Letter 2**]** for relevant sample letter.

The appeal meeting

[App 2.9]

If the employee wants to appeal he or she must inform you. You should then arrange a meeting to hear the appeal. A sample letter is [at **APP 2.26** Letter 3**]**. The same rules apply to this meeting as to the hearing. If possible a manager more senior than the manager who held the disciplinary hearing should hold the appeal meeting. If the size of your firm makes this impossible you will need to make an extra effort to deal with the matter impartially. Following the appeal meeting you must inform the employee of your decision, making clear that it is final. A sample letter is [at **APP 2.26** Letter 4**]**.

Getting the most out of the meetings

[App 2.10]

The way you run the meeting could have important implications if the matter subsequently goes to an employment tribunal. Start the meeting by introducing all the people present and ensuring that everyone knows the background to and the purpose of the meeting. Remember that you are aiming to resolve the dispute and keep an open mind, listening carefully to what is said. If you can, have a fellow manager at the meeting who can take notes and discuss the meeting with you afterwards. Finish the meeting by summarising what has happened and telling everyone when you will give your decision. Leave yourself some time after the meeting to consider what has been said and follow up any new points that came out of the meeting. If a particularly significant new fact emerges it may be best to adjourn the meeting while you look into it.

Dealing with delays

[App 2.11]

If the employee is genuinely unable to attend any meeting you arrange, for example if he or she is ill, you must offer another reasonable date. If you cannot make the meeting, you must offer an alternative date. If the person the employee has chosen to accompany him cannot make the date of the meeting you offer, the employee must propose another date and time which should be no more than five days later than the original date. If this second meeting is missed, the law considers the procedure to be at an end and you can proceed with the dismissal or disciplinary action without going through any more steps.

Instant dismissal

[App 2.12]

It is almost always unfair to dismiss an employee without first making any investigation of the circumstances. However in very rare cases it has been known for tribunals to rule that an instant dismissal was fair because the circumstances made an investigation unnecessary. For example an employee who engaged in serious misconduct in front of witnesses and there was no likely explanation or mitigating circumstances. In these rare circumstances, the Regulations allow an employer to move directly from the written statement to the appeal without having to hold a hearing. So it is a two-step procedure. You must follow these two steps or the dismissal is automatically unfair.

The written statement

[App 2.13]

You must prepare a written statement, setting out what the employee has done, or failed to do that resulted in their dismissal. It should also mention that the employee has the right of appeal against this decision. A copy of this statement must be sent to the employee.

The appeal meeting

[App 2.14]

If the employee wants to appeal he or she must inform you. You should then arrange a meeting to hear the appeal. A sample letter is [at **APP 2.26** Letter 3]. Following the appeal meeting you must inform the employee of your decision, making clear that it is final. A sample letter is [at **APP 2.26** Letter 4].

It is best to regard the modified procedure as a safeguard rather than a viable option.

Employment Tribunals

[App 2.15]

If the grievance, disciplinary or dismissal procedures are not completed when the case goes to a tribunal the tribunal will decide whether that is the fault of the employee or employer. If it is the fault of the employer the compensation payable will be increased by at least 10% and possibly up to 50%. If it is the employee's fault the compensation will be decreased in the same way. If there is no award, there is no additional penalty.

Be aware that a tribunal can rule that a **dismissal** is unfair or that a grievance is justified even though you have stuck to the letter of the procedures. The tribunal must be satisfied that you acted reasonably in the circumstances (taking into account the size and resources of your organisation).

The law on dismissal

[App 2.16]

If disciplinary action could end in dismissing an employee, employers must ensure the dismissal is fair. Fairness involves 2 key points:

• The reason for the dismissal must be one allowed by the law

- ○ Capability or qualifications of the employee

- ○ Conduct of the employee

- ○ Redundancy

- ○ Contravention of a duty or restriction or

- ○ Some other substantial reason

- The employer must act fairly. This means following the key principles set out below.

PRINCIPLES OF REASONABLE BEHAVIOUR (drawn from the Acas Code of Practice on Disciplinary and Grievance Procedures)

- Procedures should be used to encourage employees to improve, where possible, rather than just as a way of imposing a punishment

- You must inform the employee about the complaint against him or her; the employee should be given an opportunity to state his or her case before decisions are reached

- The employee is entitled to be accompanied at disciplinary meetings

- You should not take disciplinary action until the facts of the case have been established

- You should never dismiss an employee for a first disciplinary offence, unless it is a case of gross misconduct

- You should always give the employee an explanation for any disciplinary action taken and make sure the employee knows what improvement is expected

- You must give the employee an opportunity to appeal

- You should act consistently

Note that an employee cannot take a case of unfair dismissal against you until he or she has been employed by you for a year or more. There are some important exceptions to this rule. Some dismissals are **automatically unfair** whenever they occur. In particular you cannot fairly dismiss a woman for becoming pregnant or a trade union official or health and safety officer for carrying out legitimate duties.[3]

When procedures do not apply

[App 2.17]

There are some circumstances where the law recognises it isn't practical to expect an employer to go through the procedures before dismissing employees or taking disciplinary action. These are:

- Collective issues, where discussion between management and employee representatives is the appropriate way of taking matters forward. For example, when an employer dismisses a whole group of staff and immediately offers them re-employment on different terms.

- When employees are dismissed for taking industrial action (in the case of lawful, officially-organised action, special arrangements apply).

- When it is not possible for employment to continue, for example when a factory burns down.

- When one party behaves in such a violent or unreasonable manner that the other party could not be expected to sit down with them and go through the procedures. You should note that the fact that an employee is behaving unpleasantly and causing you stress and anxiety will not normally be taken as a reason for doing without the procedures. This exemption is to cover cases in which people have real reason to fear violence, harassment or vandalism if the procedures are gone through.

Chapter 2: Grievance procedures

[App 2.18]

A grievance is defined as some action that the employer or a colleague has taken or proposes to take which affects him or her, and which the employee considers has been taken for some reason that is not connected with the way he or she is doing the job. Employees should be encouraged to raise these issues informally. This may solve the problem quickly, and protect good working relations. However, if this informal approach does not work, then the employee must formally raise the grievance. You are required to participate in the following procedure.

Your employee cannot take you to an employment tribunal unless he or she has written to you about the grievance and waited 28 days (although there are some exceptions to this). The 28 day period is to allow you to respond but you should not wait that long if you can help it. If you fail to complete your side of the procedures, any award made in a tribunal case could be increased by 10% and maybe up to 50%. But if the employee starts the procedures but doesn't complete them, his or her award could be reduced by 10% and maybe up to 50%. If there is no award, there is no additional penalty.

Standard procedure

[App 2.19]

The standard three-step grievance procedure applies to almost all grievances (see the following section for exceptions).

Actions which are part of normal workplace procedures such as warnings and paid suspensions can be the subject of grievance procedures as can behaviour by colleagues. Dismissal, however, cannot be the subject of a grievance – you must deal with this as explained in **CHAPTER 1**.

There are a few exceptions to the standard procedure (see **[APP 2.24]** 'When procedures do not apply')

The three steps are:

1   The written statement

2   The meeting

3   The appeal

Written statement

[App 2.20]

The employee must set out his/her grievance in writing and send a copy to the employer.

Meeting

[App 2.21]

The employer must invite the employee to a meeting to discuss the grievance. You should not delay the meeting unreasonably but give yourself time to look into the background to the grievance and check what action has been taken in similar cases.

The meeting should be at a reasonable time and location and the employee has a duty to attend. The employee has a right to be accompanied by a colleague or employee representative. If the employee or the companion is disabled you should take all reasonable steps to ensure that they have no problems participating fully in the meeting. (see 'Getting the most out of the meetings' [at **APP 2.10** above]).

After the meeting you must inform the employee of your decision and offer an appeal meeting if the decision goes against him or her.

Appeal

[App 2.22]

If the employee is still dissatisfied, he or she should tell the employer that he or she wishes to appeal against the decision or lack of one. You must arrange a meeting to discuss the appeal. If possible a manager more senior than the manager who chaired the grievance meeting should chair the appeal meeting. If the size of your firm makes this impossible you will need to make an extra effort to deal with the matter impartially. After the meeting you should tell the employee of your decision, making it clear that it is final.

Modified procedure

[App 2.23]

In general, the standard grievance procedure will apply even after the employee has left your organisation. However there is a shorter procedure that can be used when the aggrieved employee is no longer working for the employer and:

–   Both parties agree in writing that it should apply; **or**

–   It is not reasonably practicable for one or other party to carry out the standard procedure. For example if one of them has left the country for an extended period.

The two steps are:

1   The ex-employee sends a written statement of grievance to his former employer

2   The employer writes back to the ex-employee giving his response to the points raised.

When procedures do not apply

[App 2.24]

The procedures do not need to be completed if the grievance is of a 'collective' nature. The grievance is counted as collective if it is raised by a recognised trade union or a workplace representative on behalf of two or more employees.

The procedures will not apply when one party behaves in such a violent and unreasonable manner that the other party could not be expected to sit down with them and go through the procedures.

Finally there will be circumstances when factors beyond the control of either party mean that it is effectively impossible for the procedure to be gone through, for example if one of the parties concerned leaves the country or becomes seriously ill.

Chapter 3: When procedures overlap

[App 2.25]

Complications can arise when the employee feels that a disciplinary action is unfair or involves unlawful discrimination. **It is very important that you carefully examine the case for any action to make sure that it is firmly based on the conduct or capability of the employee.** If the employee is dismissed for any reason, or subjected to some other action on conduct or capability grounds, and considers that you have acted unlawfully, he or she does not need to raise a separate grievance before being allowed to take you to an employment tribunal. But if the employee believes that disciplinary action, short of dismissal, was not genuinely based on conduct or capability, and/or that it involved unlawful discrimination, he or she would need to start a grievance procedure before being allowed to take you to tribunal.

In practice this should be less complicated than it looks. If you feel one of your employees deserves to be disciplined or dismissed and you are satisfied that your reasons are sound, then you should start the disciplinary proceedings by giving the employee the written statement and arranging the first meeting. If the employee feels that you are being unfair it is up to him or her to raise the matter in writing to you. This written statement can then be discussed at the first hearing or the appeal meeting. If the case then goes to a tribunal, the employee will not have disqualified himself or herself on the technical grounds that he or she failed to start a grievance procedure, and you will not have had to arrange two sets of meetings. The important thing is that the matter will have been properly discussed in the workplace before any further action is taken.

Chapter 4: Sample letters

[App 2.26]

Letter 1: to be sent by the employer, setting out the reasons for the proposed disciplinary action or dismissal and arranging the hearing.

Dear .... Date ....

I am writing to tell you that .... [insert organisation name] is considering dismissing OR taking disciplinary action [insert proposed action] against you.

This action is being considered with regard to the following circumstances:

....

....

You are invited to attend a disciplinary hearing on .... at .... am/pm which is to be held in .... where this will be discussed.

You are entitled, if you wish, to be accompanied by another work colleague or a trade union representative.

Yours sincerely.

Signed .... Manager

Letter 2: to be sent by the employer after the hearing

Dear .... Date ....

On .... you were informed that .... [insert organisation name] was considering dismissing OR taking disciplinary action [insert proposed action] against you.

This was discussed in a meeting on .... Following that meeting, it was decided that: [delete as applicable]

Your conduct/ performance/ etc was still unsatisfactory and that you be dismissed.

Your conduct/ performance/ etc was still unsatisfactory and that the following disciplinary action would be taken against you ....

No further action would be taken against you.

I am therefore writing to you to confirm the decision that you be dismissed

and that your last day of service with the Company will be .... The

reasons for your dismissal are:

....

....

I am therefore writing to you to confirm the decision that disciplinary action will be taken against you. The action will be .... The reasons for this disciplinary action are:

....

....

You have the right of appeal against this decision. Please [write] to ....

within .... days of receiving this disciplinary decision.

Yours sincerely

Signed .... Manager

Letter 3: Notice of appeal hearing

Dear .... Date ....

You have appealed against your dismissal on .... , confirmed to you in writing on .... Your appeal will be heard by .... in .... on .... at ....

You are entitled, if you wish, to be accompanied by another work colleague or a trade union representative.

The decision of this appeal hearing is final and there is no further right of review.

Yours sincerely.

Signed .... Manager

Letter 4: Notice of result of appeal hearing

Dear .... Date ....

You appealed against the decision of the disciplinary hearing that you be dismissed/ subject to disciplinary action [delete as appropriate]. The appeal hearing was held on ....

I am now writing to confirm the decision taken by .... [insert name of the manager] who conducted the appeal hearing, namely that the decision to .... stands/ the decision to .... be revoked (specify if no disciplinary action is being taken or what the new disciplinary action is).

You have now exercised your right of appeal under the Company Disciplinary Procedure and this decision is final.

Yours sincerely

Signed .... Manager

Notes

1   DTI guidance on producing a written statement of employment particulars can be downloaded from http://www.dti.gov.uk/er/individual/statement-pl700.htm or a sample written statement can be obtained from http://www.dti.gov.uk/er/individual/example-pl700a.htm. Acas guidance can be accessed at http://www.acas.org.uk/publications/g01.html.

2   Except when you are making more than twenty people redundant at one establishment in a period of ninety days when a different statutory regime applies.

3   For further information see http://www.dti.gov.uk/er/individual/fair-pl714b.htm#04.

ACAS Code of Practice

Disciplinary and grievance procedures

ACAS Code of Practice, September 2004

[App 3.1]

This Code of Practice provides practical guidance to employers, workers and their representatives on:

• The statutory requirements relating to disciplinary and grievance issues;

• What constitutes reasonable behaviour when dealing with disciplinary and grievance issues;

• Producing and using disciplinary and grievance procedures; and

• A worker's right to bring a companion to grievance and disciplinary hearings.

The statutory dismissal, disciplinary and grievance procedures, as set out in the *Employment Act 2002*, apply only to employees as defined in the 2002 Act and this term is used throughout SECTIONS 1 and 2 of the Code. However, it is good practice to allow all workers access to disciplinary and grievance procedures. The right to be accompanied applies to all workers (which includes employees) and this term is used in SECTION 3 of the Code.

A failure to follow any part of this Code does not, in itself, make a person or organisation liable to proceedings. However, employment tribunals will take the Code into account when considering relevant cases. Similarly, arbitrators appointed by ACAS to determine relevant cases under the ACAS Arbitration Scheme will take the Code into account.

A failure to follow the statutory disciplinary and grievance procedures where they apply may have a number of legal implications which are described in the Code.

The Code (from page 2 to page 29) is issued under *section 199* of the *Trade Union and Labour Relations (Consolidation) Act 1992* and was laid before both Houses of Parliament on [date to be inserted]. The Code comes into effect by order of the Secretary of State on [date to be inserted].

More comprehensive, practical, advice and guidance on disciplinary and grievance procedures is contained in the ACAS Handbook *Discipline and Grievances at Work* which also includes information on the *Disability Discrimination Act 1995* and the *Data Protection Act 1998*. The Handbook can be obtained from the ACAS website at www.acas.org.uk. Further information on the detailed provisions of the statutory disciplinary and grievance procedures can be found on the Department of Trade and Industry's website at www.dti.gov.uk/er.

Appendix 3 — ACAS Code of Practice

Section I

Disciplinary rules and procedures

[App 3.2]

At a glance

Drawing up disciplinary rules and procedures

- Involve management, employees and their representatives where appropriate. (Paragraph 52).

- Make rules clear and brief and explain their purpose (Paragraph 53).

- Explain rules and procedures to employees and make sure they have a copy or ready access to a copy of them. (Paragraph 55).

Operating disciplinary procedures

- Establish facts before taking action (Paragraph 8).

- Deal with cases of minor misconduct or unsatisfactory performance informally (Paragraphs 11–12).

- For more serious cases, follow formal procedures, including informing the employee of the alleged misconduct or unsatisfactory performance (Paragraph 13).

- Invite the employee to a meeting and inform them of the right to be accompanied. (Paragraph 14–16).

- Where performance is unsatisfactory explain to the employee the improvement required, the support that will be given and when and how performance will be reviewed. (Paragraphs 19–20).

- If giving a warning, tell the employee why and how they need to change, the consequences of failing to improve and that they have a right to appeal (Paragraphs 21–22).

- If dismissing an employee, tell them why, when their contract will end and that they can appeal (Paragraph 25).

- Before dismissing or taking disciplinary action other than issuing a warning, always follow the statutory dismissal and disciplinary procedure (Paragraphs 26–32).

- When dealing with absences from work, find out the reasons for the absence before deciding on what action to take (Paragraph 37).

Holding appeals

- If the employee wishes to appeal invite them to a meeting and inform the employee of their right to be accompanied (Paragraphs 44–48).

- Where possible, arrange for the appeal to be dealt with by a more senior manager not involved with the earlier decision (Paragraph 46).

- Inform the employee about the appeal decision and the reasons for it (Paragraph 48).

274

Records

* Keep written records for future reference (Paragraph 49).

Guidance

Why have disciplinary rules and procedures?

[App 3.3]

1 Disciplinary rules and procedures help to promote orderly employment relations as well as fairness and consistency in the treatment of individuals. Disciplinary procedures are also a legal requirement in certain circumstances (see paragraph 6).

2 *Disciplinary rules* tell employees what behaviour employers expect from them. If an employee breaks specific rules about behaviour, this is often called misconduct. Employers use disciplinary procedures and actions to deal with situations where employees allegedly break disciplinary rules. Disciplinary procedures may also be used where employees don't meet their employer's expectations in the way they do their job. These cases, often known as *unsatisfactory performance* (or capability), may require different treatment from misconduct, and disciplinary procedures should allow for this.

3 Guidance on how to draw up disciplinary rules and procedures is contained in paragraphs 52–62.

4 When dealing with disciplinary cases, employers need to be aware both of the law on unfair dismissal and the statutory minimum procedure contained in the *Employment Act 2002* for dismissing or taking disciplinary action against an employee. Employers must also be careful not to discriminate on the grounds of gender, race (including colour, nationality and ethnic or national origins), disability, age, sexual orientation or religion.

The law on unfair dismissal

[App 3.4]

5 The law on unfair dismissal requires employers to act *reasonably* when dealing with disciplinary issues. What is classed as reasonable behaviour will depend on the circumstances of each case, and is ultimately a matter for employment tribunals to decide. However, the core principles employers should work to are set out in the box overleaf. Drawing up and referring to a procedure can help employers deal with disciplinary issues in a fair and consistent manner.

The statutory minimum procedure

[App 3.5]

6 Employers are also required to follow a specific statutory minimum procedure if they are contemplating dismissing an employee or imposing some other disciplinary penalty that isn't suspension on full pay or a warning. Guidance on this statutory procedure is provided in paragraphs 26–32. If an employee is dismissed without the employer following this statutory procedure, and makes a claim to an employment tribunal, providing they have the necessary qualifying service and providing they are not prevented from claiming unfair dismissal by virtue of their age, the dismissal will automatically be ruled unfair. The statutory procedure is a minimum requirement and even where the relevant procedure is followed the dismissal may still be unfair if the employer has not acted reasonably in all the circumstances.

[App 3.6]

7 In small organisations it may not be practicable to adopt all the detailed good practice guidance set out in this Code. Employment tribunals will take account of an employer's size and administrative resources when deciding if it acted reasonably. However, all organisations regardless of size must follow the minimum statutory dismissal and disciplinary procedures.

Core principles of reasonable behaviour

[App 3.7]

- Use procedures primarily to help and encourage employees to improve rather than just as a way of imposing a punishment.

- Inform the employee of the complaint against them, and provide them with an opportunity to state their case before decisions are reached.

- Allow employees to be accompanied at disciplinary meetings.

- Make sure that disciplinary action is not taken until the facts of the case have been established and that the action is reasonable in the circumstances.

- Never dismiss an employee for a first disciplinary offence, unless it is a case of gross misconduct.

- Give the employee a written explanation for any disciplinary action taken and make sure they know what improvement is expected.

- Give the employee an opportunity to appeal.

- Deal with issues as thoroughly and promptly as possible.

- Act consistently

Dealing with disciplinary issues in the workplace

[App 3.8]

8 When a potential disciplinary matter arises, the employer should make necessary investigations to establish the facts promptly before memories of events fade. It is important to keep a written record for later reference. Having established the facts, the employer should decide whether to drop the matter, deal with it informally or arrange for it to be handled formally. Where an investigatory meeting is held solely to establish the facts of a case, it should be made clear to the employee involved that it is not a disciplinary meeting.

9 In certain cases, for example in cases involving gross misconduct, where relationships have broken down or there are risks to an employer's property or responsibilities to other parties, consideration should be given to a brief period of suspension with full pay whilst unhindered investigation is conducted. Such a suspension should only be imposed after careful consideration and should be reviewed to ensure it is not unnecessarily protracted. It should be made clear that the suspension is not considered a disciplinary action.

10 When dealing with disciplinary issues in the workplace employers should bear in mind that they are required under the *Disability Discrimination Act 1995* to make reasonable adjustments to cater for employees who have a disability, for example providing for wheelchair access if necessary.

Informal action

[App 3.9]

11 Cases of minor misconduct or unsatisfactory performance are usually best dealt with informally. A quiet word is often all that is required to improve an employee's conduct or performance. The informal approach may be particularly helpful in small firms, where problems can be dealt with quickly and confidentially. There will, however, be situations where matters are more serious or where an informal approach has been tried but isn't working.

12 If informal action doesn't bring about an improvement, or the misconduct or unsatisfactory performance is considered to be too serious to be classed as minor, employers should provide employees with a clear signal of their dissatisfaction by taking formal action.

Formal action

Inform the employee of the problem

[App 3.10]

13 The first step in any formal process is to let the employee know in writing what it is they are alleged to have done wrong. The letter or note should contain enough information for the individual to be able to understand both what it is they are alleged to have done wrong and the reasons why this is not acceptable. If the employee has difficulty reading, or if English is not their first language, the employer should explain the content of the letter or note to them orally. The letter or note should also invite the individual to a meeting at which the problem can be discussed, and it should inform the individual of their right to be accompanied at the meeting (see **SECTION 3**). The employee should be given copies of any documents that will be produced at the meeting.

Hold a meeting to discuss the problem

[App 3.11]

14 Where possible, the timing and location of the meeting should be agreed with the employee. The length of time between the written notification and the meeting should be long enough to allow the employee to prepare but not so long that memories fade. The employer should hold the meeting in a private location and ensure there will be no interruptions.

15 At the meeting, the employer should explain the complaint against the employee and go through the evidence that has been gathered. The employee should be allowed to set out their case and answer any allegations that have been made. The employee should also be allowed to ask questions, present evidence, call witnesses and be given an opportunity to raise points about any information provided by witnesses.

16 An employee who cannot attend a meeting should inform the employer in advance whenever possible. If the employee fails to attend through circumstances outside their control and unforeseeable at the time the meeting was arranged (e.g. illness) the employer should arrange another meeting. A decision may be taken in the employee's absence if they fail to attend the re-arranged meeting without good reason. If an employee's companion cannot attend on a proposed date, the employee can suggest another date so long as it is reasonable and is not more than five working days after the date originally proposed by the employer. This five day time limit may be extended by mutual agreement.

Decide on outcome and action

[App 3.12]

17 Following the meeting the employer must decide whether disciplinary action is justified or not. Where it is decided that no action is justified the employee should be informed. Where it is

decided that disciplinary action is justified the employer will need to consider what form this should take. Before making any decision the employer should take account of the employee's disciplinary and general record, length of service, actions taken in any previous similar case, the explanations given by the employee and – most important of all – whether the intended disciplinary action is reasonable under the circumstances.

18 Examples of actions the employer might choose to take are set out in paragraphs 19–25. It is normally good practice to give employees at least one chance to improve their conduct or performance before they are issued with a final written warning. However, if an employee's misconduct or unsatisfactory performance – or its continuance – is sufficiently serious, for example because it is having, or is likely to have, a serious harmful effect on the organisation, it may be appropriate to move directly to a final written warning. In cases of gross misconduct, the employer may decide to dismiss even though the employee has not previously received a warning for misconduct. (Further guidance on dealing with gross misconduct is set out at paragraphs 36–37.)

First formal action – unsatisfactory performance

[App 3.13]

19 Following the meeting, an employee who is found to be performing unsatisfactorily should be given a written note setting out:

* the performance problem;

* the improvement that is required;

* the timescale for achieving this improvement;

* a review date; and

* any support the employer will provide to assist the employee.

20 The employee should be informed that the note represents the first stage of a formal procedure and that failure to improve could lead to a final written warning and, ultimately, dismissal. A copy of the note should be kept and used as the basis for monitoring and reviewing performance over a specified period (e.g. six months).

First formal action – misconduct

[App 3.14]

21 Where, following a disciplinary meeting, an employee is found guilty of misconduct, the usual first step would be to give them a written warning setting out the nature of the misconduct and the change in behaviour required.

22 The employee should be informed that the warning is part of the formal disciplinary process and what the consequences will be of a failure to change behaviour. The consequences could be a final written warning and ultimately, dismissal. The employee should also be informed that they may appeal against the decision. A record of the warning should be kept, but it should be disregarded for disciplinary purposes after a specified period (e.g. six months).

23 Guidance on dealing with cases of gross misconduct is provided in paragraphs 35–36.

Final written warning

[App 3.15]

24 Where there is a failure to improve or change behaviour in the timescale set at the first formal stage, or where the offence is sufficiently serious, the employee should normally be issued with a final written warning – but only after they have been given a chance to present their case at a meeting. The final written warning should give details of, and grounds for, the complaint. It

should warn the employee that failure to improve or modify behaviour may lead to dismissal or to some other penalty, and refer to the right of appeal. The final written warning should normally be disregarded for disciplinary purposes after a specified period (for example 12 months).

Dismissal or other penalty

[App 3.16]

25 If the employee's conduct or performance still fails to improve, the final stage in the disciplinary process might be dismissal or (if the employee's contract allows it or it is mutually agreed) some other penalty such as demotion, disciplinary transfer, or loss of seniority/pay. A decision to dismiss should only be taken by a manager who has the authority to do so. The employee should be informed as soon as possible of the reasons for the dismissal, the date on which the employment contract will terminate, the appropriate period of notice and their right of appeal.

26 It is important for employers to bear in mind that before they dismiss an employee or impose a sanction such as demotion, loss of seniority or loss of pay, they must as a minimum have followed the statutory dismissal and disciplinary procedures. The standard statutory procedure to be used in almost all cases requires the employer to:

Step 1

Write to the employee notifying them of the allegations against them and the basis of the allegations and invite them to a meeting to discuss the matter;

Step 2

Hold a meeting to discuss the allegations – at which the employee has the right to be accompanied – and notify the employee of the decision;

Step 3

If the employee wishes to appeal, hold an appeal meeting at which the employee has the right to be accompanied – and inform the employee of the final decision.

---

27 More detail on the statutory standard procedure is set out at Annex A. There is a modified two step procedure for use in special circumstances involving gross misconduct and details of this are set out at Annex B. Guidance on the modified procedure is contained in paragraph 36. There are a number of situations in which it is not necessary for employers to use the statutory procedures or where they will have been deemed to be completed and these are described in Annex E.

28 If the employer fails to follow this statutory procedure (where it applies), and an employee who is qualified to do so makes a claim for unfair dismissal, the employment tribunal will automatically find the dismissal unfair. The tribunal will normally increase the compensation awarded by 10 per cent, or, where it feels it is just and equitable to do so, up to 50 per cent. Equally, if the employment tribunal finds that an employee has been dismissed unfairly but has failed to follow the procedure (for instance they have failed to attend the disciplinary meeting without good cause), compensation will be reduced by, normally, 10 per cent, or, if the tribunal considers it just and equitable to do so, up to 50 per cent.

29 If the tribunal considers there are exceptional circumstances, compensation may be adjusted (up or down) by less than 10 per cent or not at all.

30 Employers and employees will normally be expected to go through the statutory dismissal and disciplinary procedure unless they have reasonable grounds to believe that by doing so they might be exposed to a significant threat, such as violent, abusive or intimidating behaviour, or they will be harassed. There will always be a certain amount of stress and anxiety for both parties when dealing with any disciplinary case, but this exemption will only apply where the employer or

employee reasonably believes that they would come to some serious physical or mental harm; their property or some third party is threatened or the other party has harassed them and this may continue.

31 Equally, the statutory procedure does not need to be followed if circumstances beyond the control of either party prevent one or more steps being followed within a reasonable period. This will sometimes be the case where there is a long-term illness or a long period of absence abroad but, in the case of employers, wherever possible they should consider appointing another manager to deal with the procedure.

32 Where an employee fails to attend a meeting held as part of the statutory discipline procedure without good reason the statutory procedure comes to an end. In those circumstances the employee's compensation may be reduced if they bring a successful complaint before an employment tribunal. If the employee does have a good reason for non-attendance, the employer must re-arrange the meeting. If the employee does not attend the second meeting for good reason the employer need not arrange a third meeting but there will be no adjustment of compensation.

What if a grievance is raised during a disciplinary case?

[App 3.17]

33 In the course of a disciplinary process, an employee might raise a grievance that is related to the case. If this happens, the employer should consider suspending the disciplinary procedure for a short period while the grievance is dealt with. Depending on the nature of the grievance, the employer may need to consider bringing in another manager to deal with the disciplinary process. In small organisations this may not be possible, and the existing manager should deal with the case as impartially as possible.

34 Where the action taken or contemplated by the employer is dismissal the statutory grievance procedure does not apply. Where the action taken or contemplated is paid suspension or a warning the statutory grievance procedure and not the dismissal and disciplinary procedure applies to any grievance. However, where the employer takes, or is contemplating other action short of dismissal and asserts that the reason for the action is conduct or capability related, the statutory grievance procedure does not apply unless the grievance is that the action amounts, or would amount, to unlawful discrimination, or that the true reason for the action is not the reason given by the employer. In those cases the employee must have raised a written grievance in accordance with the statutory grievance procedure before presenting any complaint to an employment tribunal about the issue raised by the grievance. However, if the written grievance is raised before any disciplinary appeal meeting, the rest of the grievance procedure does not have to be followed, although the employer may use the appeal meeting to discuss the grievance.

Dealing with gross misconduct

[App 3.18]

35 If an employer considers an employee guilty of gross misconduct, and thus potentially liable for summary dismissal, it is still important to establish the facts before taking any action. A short period of suspension with full pay may be helpful or necessary, although it should only be imposed after careful consideration and should be kept under review. It should be made clear to the employee that the suspension is not a disciplinary action and does not involve any prejudgement.

36 It is a core principle of reasonable behaviour that employers should give employees the opportunity of putting their case at a disciplinary meeting before deciding whether to take action. This principle applies as much to cases of gross misconduct as it does to ordinary cases of misconduct or unsatisfactory performance. There may however be some very limited cases where despite the fact that an employer has dismissed an employee immediately without a meeting an employment tribunal will, very exceptionally, find the dismissal to be fair To allow for these cases

there is a statutory modified procedure under which the employer is required to write to the employee after the dismissal setting out the reasons for the dismissal and to hold an appeal meeting, if the employee wants one. The statutory procedure that must be followed by employers in such cases is set out in Annex B. If an employer fails to follow this procedure and the case goes to tribunal, the dismissal will be found to be automatically unfair.

Dealing with absence from work

[App 3.19]

37 When dealing with absence from work, it is important to determine the reasons why the employee has not been at work. If there is no acceptable reason, the matter should be treated as a conduct issue and dealt with as a disciplinary matter.

38 If the absence is due to genuine (including medically certified) illness, the issue becomes one of capability, and the employer should take a sympathetic and considerate approach. When thinking about how to handle these cases, it is helpful to consider:

- how soon the employee's health and attendance will improve;

- whether alternative work is available;

- the effect of the absence on the organisation;

- how similar situations have been handled in the past; and

- whether the illness is a result of disability in which case the provisions of the *Disability Discrimination Act 1995* will apply.

39 The impact of long-term absences will nearly always be greater on small organisations, and they may be entitled to act at an earlier stage than large organisations.

40 In cases of extended sick leave both statutory and contractual issues will need to be addressed and specialist advice may be necessary.

Dealing with special situations

If the full procedure is not immediately available

[App 3.20]

41 Special arrangements might be required for handling disciplinary matters among nightshift employees, employees in isolated locations or depots, or others who may be difficult to reach. Nevertheless the appropriate statutory procedure must be followed where it applies.

Trade union representatives

[App 3.21]

42 Disciplinary action against a trade union representative can lead to a serious dispute if it is seen as an attack on the union's functions. Normal standards apply but, if disciplinary action is considered, the case should be discussed, after obtaining the employee's agreement, with a senior trade union representative or permanent union official.

Criminal charges or convictions not related to employment

[App 3.22]

43 If an employee is charged with, or convicted of, a criminal offence not related to work, this is not in itself reason for disciplinary action. The employer should establish the facts of the case and consider whether the matter is serious enough to warrant starting the disciplinary procedure. The main consideration should be whether the offence, or alleged offence, is one that makes the employee unsuitable for their type of work. Similarly, an employee should not be dismissed solely because they are absent from work as a result of being remanded in custody.

Appeals

[App 3.23]

44 Employees who have had disciplinary action taken against them should be given the opportunity to appeal. It is useful to set a time limit for asking for an appeal – five working days is usually enough.

45 An employee may choose to appeal for example because:

- they think a finding or penalty is unfair;

- new evidence comes to light; or

- they think the disciplinary procedure wasn't used correctly.

It should be noted that the appeal stage is part of the statutory procedure and if the employee pursues an employment tribunal claim the tribunal may reduce any award of compensation if the employee did not exercise the right of appeal.

46 As far as is reasonably practicable a more senior manager not involved with the case should hear the appeal. In small organisations, even if a more senior manager is not available, another manager should hear the appeal, if possible. If that is not an option, the person overseeing the case should act as impartially as possible. Records and notes of the original disciplinary meeting should be made available to the person hearing the appeal.

47 The employers should contact the employee with appeal arrangements as soon as possible, and inform them of their statutory right to be accompanied at the appeal meeting.

48 The manager must inform the employee about the appeal decision, and the reasons for it, as soon as possible. They should also confirm the decision in writing. If the decision is the final stage of the organisation's appeals procedure, the manager should make this clear to the employee.

Keeping records

[App 3.24]

49 It is important, and in the interests of both employers and employees, to keep written records during the disciplinary process. Records should include:

- the complaint against the employee;

- the employee's defence;

- findings made and actions taken;

- the reason for actions taken;

- whether an appeal was lodged;

- the outcome of the appeal;

- any grievances raised during the disciplinary procedure; and

- subsequent developments.

50 Records should be treated as confidential and be kept no longer than necessary in accordance with the *Data Protection Act 1998*. This Act gives individuals the right to request and have access to certain personal data.

51 Copies of meeting records should be given to the employee including copies of any formal minutes that may have been taken. In certain circumstances (for example to protect a witness) the employer might withhold some information.

Drawing up disciplinary rules and procedures

[App 3.25]

52 Management is responsible for maintaining and setting standards of performance in an organisation and for ensuring that disciplinary rules and procedures are in place. Employers are legally required to have disciplinary procedures. It is good practice to involve employees (and, where appropriate, their representatives) when making or changing rules and procedures, so that everyone affected by them understands them.

Rules

[App 3.26]

53 When making rules, the aim should be to specify those that are necessary for ensuring a safe and efficient workplace and for maintaining good employment relations.

54 It is unlikely that any set of rules will cover all possible disciplinary issues, but rules normally cover:

- bad behaviour, such as fighting or drunkenness;

- unsatisfactory work performance;

- harassment or victimisation;

- misuse of company facilities (for example e-mail and internet);

- poor timekeeping;

- unauthorised absences; and

- repeated or serious failure to follow instructions.

55 Rules should be specific, clear and recorded in writing. They also need to be readily available to employees, for instance on a noticeboard or, in larger organisations, in a staff handbook or on the Intranet. Management should do all they can to ensure that every employee knows and understands the rules, including those employees whose first language is not English or who have trouble reading. This is often best done as part of an induction process.

56 Employers should inform employees of the likely consequences of breaking disciplinary rules. In particular, they should list examples of acts of gross misconduct that may warrant summary dismissal.

57 Acts which constitute gross misconduct are those resulting in a serious breach of contractual terms and are best decided by organisations in the light of their own particular circumstances. However, examples of gross misconduct might include:

• theft or fraud;

• physical violence or bullying;

• deliberate and serious damage to property;

• serious misuse of an organisation's property or name;

• deliberately accessing internet sites containing pornographic, offensive or obscene material;

• serious insubordination;

• unlawful discrimination or harassment;

• bringing the organisation into serious disrepute;

• serious incapability at work brought on by alcohol or illegal drugs;

• causing loss, damage or injury through serious negligence;

• a serious breach of health and safety rules; and

• a serious breach of confidence.

Procedures

[App 3.27]

58 Disciplinary procedures should not be seen primarily as a means of imposing sanctions but rather as a way of encouraging improvement amongst employees whose conduct or performance is unsatisfactory. Some organisations may prefer to have separate procedures for dealing with issues of conduct and capability. Large organisations may also have separate procedures to deal with other issues such as harassment and bullying.

59 When drawing up and applying procedures employers should always bear in mind the requirements of natural justice. This means that employees should be given the opportunity of a meeting with someone who has not been involved in the matter. They should be informed of the allegations against them, together with the supporting evidence, in advance of the meeting. Employees should be given the opportunity to challenge the allegations before decisions are reached and should be provided with a right of appeal.

60 Good disciplinary procedures should:

• be put in writing;

• say to whom they apply;

• be non-discriminatory;

• allow for matters to be dealt without undue delay;

• allow for information to be kept confidential;

• tell employees what disciplinary action might be taken;

• say what levels of management have the authority to take disciplinary action;

• require employees to be informed of the complaints against them and supporting evidence, before a meeting;

• give employees a chance to have their say before management reaches a decision;

- provide employees with the right to be accompanied;

- provide that no employee is dismissed for a first breach of discipline, except in cases of gross misconduct;

- require management to investigate fully before any disciplinary action is taken;

- ensure that employees are given an explanation for any sanction; and

- allow employees to appeal against a decision.

61 It is important to ensure that everyone in an organisation understands the disciplinary procedures including the statutory requirements. In small firms this is best done by making sure all employees have access to a copy of the procedures, for instance on a noticeboard, and by taking a few moments to run through the procedures with the employee. In large organisations formal training for those who use and operate the procedures may be appropriate.

Further action

[App 3.28]

62 It is sensible to keep rules and procedures under review to make sure they are always relevant and effective. New or additional rules should only be introduced after reasonable notice has been given to all employees and any employee representatives have been consulted.

Section 2

Grievance procedures

[App 3.29]

At a glance

Drawing up grievance procedures

- Involve management, employees and their representatives where appropriate. (Paragraph 90).

- Explain procedures to employees and make sure they have a copy or ready access to a copy of them. (Paragraph 94).

Operating grievance procedures

- Many grievances can be settled informally with line managers (Paragraph 67).

- Employees should raise formal grievances with management (Paragraph 73).

- Invite the employee to a meeting and inform them about the right to be accompanied (Paragraph 77).

- Give the employee an opportunity to have their say at the meeting (Paragraph 78).

- Write with a response within a reasonable time and inform the employee of their right to appeal (Paragraph 81).

Appeals

- If possible, a more senior manager should handle the appeal (Paragraph 82).

- Tell the employee they have the right to be accompanied (Paragraph 82).

- The senior manager should respond to the grievance in writing after the appeal and tell the employee if it is the final stage in the grievance procedure (Paragraph 83).

Records

- Written records should be kept for future reference (Paragraph 87).

Guidance

Why have grievance procedures?

[App 3.30]

63 *Grievances* are concerns, problems or complaints that employees raise with their employers.

64 *Grievance procedures* are used by employers to deal with employees' grievances.

65 Grievance procedures allow employers to deal with grievances fairly, consistently and speedily. Employers must have procedures available to employees so that their grievances can be properly considered.

66 Guidance on drawing up grievance procedures is set out in paragraphs 90–95.

Dealing with grievances in the workplace

[App 3.31]

67 Employees should aim to resolve most grievances informally with their line manager. This has advantages for all workplaces, particularly where there might be a close personal relationship between a manager and an employee. It also allows for problems to be resolved quickly.

68 If a grievance cannot be settled informally, the employee should raise it formally with management. There is a statutory grievance procedure that employees must invoke if they wish subsequently to use the grievance as the basis of certain applications to an employment tribunal.

69 Under the standard statutory procedure, employees must:

Step 1

Inform the employer of their grievance in writing.

Step 2

Be invited by the employer to a meeting to discuss the grievance where the right to be accompanied will apply and be notified in writing of the decision. The employee must take all reasonable steps to attend this meeting.

> **Step 3**
>
> Be given the right to an appeal meeting if they feel the grievance has not been satisfactorily resolved and be notified of the final decision.

More detail on the standard statutory procedure is set out in Annex C.

70 There are certain occasions when it is not necessary to follow the statutory procedure for example, if the employee is raising a concern in compliance with the *Public Interest Disclosure Act* or a grievance is raised on behalf of at least two employees by an appropriate representative such as an official of an independent trade union. A full list of exemptions is set out in Annex E.

71 It is important that employers and employees follow the statutory grievance procedure where it applies. The employee should (subject to the exemptions described in Annex E) at least have raised the grievance in writing and waited 28 days before presenting any tribunal claim relating to the matter. A premature claim will be automatically rejected by the tribunal although (subject to special time limit rules) it may be presented again once the written grievance has been raised. Furthermore if a grievance comes before an employment tribunal and either party has failed to follow the procedure then the tribunal will normally adjust any award by 10 per cent or, where it feels it just and equitable to do so, by up to 50 per cent, depending on which party has failed to follow the procedure. In exceptional cases compensation can be adjusted by less than 10 per cent or not at all.

72 Wherever possible a grievance should be dealt with before an employee leaves employment. A statutory grievance procedure ('the modified grievance procedure' described in Annex D), however, applies where an employee has already left employment, the standard procedure has not been commenced or completed before the employee left employment and both parties agree in writing that it should be used instead of the standard statutory procedure. Under the modified procedure the employee should write to the employer setting out the grievance as soon as possible after leaving employment and the employer must write back setting out its response.

Raising a grievance

[App 3.32]

73 Employees should normally raise a grievance with their line manager unless someone else is specified in the organisation's procedure. If the complaint is against the person with whom the grievance would normally be raised the employee can approach that person's manager or another manager in the organisation. In small businesses where this isn't possible, the line manager should hear the grievance and deal with it as impartially as possible.

74 Managers should deal with all grievances raised, whether or not the grievance is presented in writing. However, employees need to be aware that if the statutory procedure applies, they will not subsequently be able to take the case to an employment tribunal unless they have first raised a grievance in writing and waited a further 28 days before presenting the tribunal claim.

75 Setting out a grievance in writing is not easy – especially for those employees whose first language is not English or who have difficulty expressing themselves on paper. In these circumstances the employee should be encouraged to seek help for example from a work colleague, a trade union or other employee representative. Under the *Disability Discrimination Act 1995* employers are required to make reasonable adjustments which may include assisting employees to formulate a written grievance if they are unable to do so themselves because of a disability.

76 In circumstances where a grievance may apply to more than one person and where a trade union is recognised it may be appropriate for the problem to be resolved through collective agreements between the trade union(s) and the employer.

Grievance meetings

[App 3.33]

77 On receiving a formal grievance, a manager should invite the employee to a meeting as soon as possible and inform them that they have the right to be accompanied. It is good practice to agree a time and place for the meeting with the employee. Small organisations might not have private meeting rooms, but it is important that the meeting is not interrupted and that the employee feels their grievance is being treated confidentially. If an employee's companion cannot attend on a proposed date, the employee can suggest another date so long as it is reasonable and is not more than five working days after the date originally proposed by the employer. This five day time limit may be extended by mutual agreement.

78 The employee should be allowed to explain their complaint and say how they think it should be settled. If the employer reaches a point in the meeting where they are not sure how to deal with the grievance or feel that further investigation is necessary the meeting should be adjourned to get advice or make further investigation. This might be particularly useful in small organisations that lack experience of dealing with formal grievances. The employer should give the grievance careful consideration before responding.

79 Employers and employees will normally be expected to go through the statutory grievance procedures unless they have reasonable grounds to believe that by doing so they might be exposed to a significant threat, such as violent, abusive or intimidating behaviour, or they will be harassed. There will always be a certain amount of stress and anxiety for both parties when dealing with grievance cases, but this exemption will only apply where the employer or employee reasonably believes that they would come to some serious physical or mental harm; their property or some third party is threatened or the other party has harassed them and this may continue.

80 Equally, the statutory procedure does not need to be followed if circumstances beyond the control of either party prevent one or more steps being followed within a reasonable period. This will sometimes be the case where there is a long-term illness or a long period of absence abroad but wherever possible the employer should consider appointing another manager to deal with the procedure.

81 The employer should respond in writing to the employee's grievance within a reasonable time and should let the employee know that they can appeal against the employer's decision if they are not satisfied with it. What is considered reasonable will vary from organisation to organisation, but five working days is normally long enough. If it is not possible to respond within five working days the employee should be given an explanation for the delay and told when a response can be expected.

Appeals

[App 3.34]

82 If an employee informs the employer that they are unhappy with the decision after a grievance meeting, the employer should arrange an appeal. It should be noted that the appeal stage is part of the statutory procedure and if the employee pursues a n employment tribunal claim the tribunal may reduce any award of compensation if the employee did not exercise the right of appeal. As far as is reasonably practicable the appeal should be with a more senior manager than the one who dealt with the original grievance. In small organisations, even if there is no more senior manager available, another manager should, if possible, hear the appeal. If that is not an option, the person overseeing the case should act as impartially as possible. At the same time as inviting the employee to attend the appeal, the employer should remind them of their right to be accompanied at the appeal meeting.

83 As with the first meeting, the employer should write to the employee with a decision on their grievance as soon as possible. They should also tell the employee if the appeal meeting is the final stage of the grievance procedure.

84 In large organisations it is good practice to allow a further appeal to a higher level of management, such as a director. However, in smaller firms the first appeal will usually mark the end of the grievance procedure.

Special considerations

[App 3.35]

85 Complaints about discrimination, bullying and harassment in the workplace are sensitive issues, and large organisations often have separate grievance procedures for dealing with these. It is important that these procedures meet the statutory minimum requirements.

86 Organisations may also wish to consider whether they need a whistleblowing procedure in the light of the *Public Interest Disclosure Act 1998*. This Act provides protection to employees who raise concerns about certain kinds of wrongdoing in accordance with its procedures.

Keeping records

[App 3.36]

87 It is important, and in the interests of both employer and employee, to keep written records during the grievance process. Records should include:

- the nature of the grievance raised;

- a copy of the written grievance;

- the employer's response;

- action taken;

- reasons for action taken;

- whether there was an appeal and, if so, the outcome; and

- subsequent developments.

88 Records should be treated as confidential and kept in accordance with the *Data Protection Act 1998*, which gives individuals the right to request and have access to certain personal data.

89 Copies of meeting records should be given to the employee including any formal minutes that may have been taken. In certain circumstances (for example to protect a witness) the employer might withhold some information.

Drawing up grievance procedures

[App 3.37]

90 When employers draw up grievance procedures, it pays to involve everybody they will affect, including managers, employees and, where appropriate, their representatives.

91 Grievance procedures should make it easy for employees to raise issues with management and should:

- be simple and put in writing;

- enable an employee's line manager to deal informally with a grievance, if possible;

- keep proceedings confidential; and

- allow the employee to have a companion at meetings.

92 Issues that may cause grievances include:

- terms and conditions of employment;

- health and safety;

- work relations;

- bullying and harassment;

- new working practices;

- working environment;

- organisational change; and

- equal opportunities.

93 Where separate procedures exist for dealing with grievances on particular issues (for example, harassment and bullying) these should be used instead of the normal grievance procedure.

94 It's important to ensure that everyone in the organisation understands the grievance procedures including the statutory requirements and that, if necessary, supervisors, managers and employee representatives are trained in their use. Employees must be given a copy of the procedures or have ready access to them, for instance on a noticeboard. Large organisations can include them with disciplinary procedures as part of an induction process.

95 Take the time to explain the detail of grievance procedures to employees. This is particularly useful for people who don't speak English very well or who have difficulty with reading.

Section 3

A worker's right to be accompanied

[App 3.38]

At a glance

The right to be accompanied

- All workers have the right to be accompanied at a disciplinary or grievance hearing (Paragraph 96).

- Workers must make a reasonable request to the employer if they want to be accompanied (Paragraph 96).

- Disciplinary hearings, for these purposes, include meetings where either disciplinary actions or some other actions might be taken against the worker. Appeal hearings are also covered (Paragraphs 97–99).

- Grievance hearings are defined as meetings where an employer deals with a worker's complaint about a duty owed to them by the employer (Paragraphs 100–102).

The companion

- The companion can be a fellow worker or a union official (Paragraph 104).

- Nobody has to accept an invitation to act as a companion (Paragraph 107).

- Fellow workers who are acting as companions can take paid time off to prepare for and go to a hearing (Paragraph 109).

Applying the right

- Agree a suitable date with the worker and the companion (Paragraph 110).

- The worker should tell the employer who the chosen companion is (Paragraph 112).

- The companion can have a say at the hearing but can't answer questions for the worker (Paragraph 113–114).

- Don't disadvantage workers who have applied the right, or their companions (Paragraph 116).

Guidance

What is the right to be accompanied?

[App 3.39]

96 Workers have a statutory right to be accompanied by a fellow worker or trade union official where they are required or invited by their employer to attend certain disciplinary or grievance hearings. They must make a reasonable request to their employer to be accompanied. Further guidance on what is a reasonable request and who can accompany a worker appears at paragraphs 103–109.

What is a disciplinary hearing?

[App 3.40]

97 For the purposes of this right, disciplinary hearings are defined as meetings that could result in:

- a formal warning being issued to a worker (i.e. a warning that will be placed on the worker's record);

- the taking of some other disciplinary action (such as suspension without pay, demotion or dismissal) or other action; or

- the confirmation of a warning or some other disciplinary action (such as an appeal hearing).

98 The right to be accompanied will also apply to any disciplinary meetings held as part of the statutory dismissal and disciplinary procedures. This includes any meetings held after an employee has left employment.

99 Informal discussions or counselling sessions do not attract the right to be accompanied unless they could result in formal warnings or other actions. Meetings to investigate an issue are not disciplinary hearings. If it becomes clear during the course of such a meeting that disciplinary action is called for, the meeting should be ended and a formal hearing arranged at which the worker will have the right to be accompanied.

What is a grievance hearing?

[App 3.41]

100 For the purposes of this right, a grievance hearing is a meeting at which an employer deals with a complaint about a duty owed by them to a worker, whether the duty arises from statute or common law (for example contractual commitments).

101 For instance, an individual's request for a pay rise is unlikely to fall within the definition, unless a right to an increase is specifically provided for in the contract or the request raises an issue about equal pay. Equally, most employers will be under no legal duty to provide their workers with car parking facilities, and a grievance about such facilities would carry no right to be accompanied at a hearing by a companion. However, if a worker were disabled and needed a car to get to and from work, they probably would be entitled to a companion at a grievance hearing, as an issue might arise as to whether the employer was meeting its obligations under the *Disability Discrimination Act 1995*.

102 The right to be accompanied will also apply to any meetings held as part of the statutory grievance procedures. This includes any meetings after the employee has left employment.

What is a reasonable request?

[App 3.42]

103 Whether a request for a companion is reasonable will depend on the circumstances of the individual case and, ultimately, it is a matter for the courts and tribunals to decide. However, when workers are choosing a companion, they should bear in mind that it would not be reasonable to insist on being accompanied by a colleague whose presence would prejudice the hearing or who might have a conflict of interest. Nor would it be reasonable for a worker to ask to be accompanied by a colleague from a geographically remote location when someone suitably qualified was available on site. The request to be accompanied does not have to be in writing.

The companion

[App 3.43]

104 The companion may be:

- a fellow worker (ie another of the employer's workers);

- an official employed by a trade union, or a lay trade union official, as long as they have been reasonably certified in writing by their union as having experience of, or having received training in, acting as a worker's companion at disciplinary or grievance hearings. Certification may take the form of a card or letter.

105 Some workers may, however, have additional contractual rights to be accompanied by persons other than those listed above (for instance a partner, spouse or legal representative). If workers are disabled, employers should consider whether it might be reasonable to allow them to be accompanied because of their disability.

106 Workers may ask an official from any trade union to accompany them at a disciplinary or grievance hearing, regardless of whether the union is recognised or not. However, where a union is recognised in a workplace, it is good practice for workers to ask an official from that union to accompany them.

107 Fellow workers or trade union officials do not have to accept a request to accompany a worker, and they should not be pressurised to do so.

108 Trade unions should ensure that their officials are trained in the role of acting as a worker's companion. Even when a trade union official has experience of acting in the role, there may still be a need for periodic refresher training.

109 A worker who has agreed to accompany a colleague employed by the same employer is entitled to take a reasonable amount of paid time off to fulfil that responsibility. This should cover the hearing and it is also good practice to allow time for the companion to familiarise themselves with the case and confer with the worker before and after the hearing. A lay trade union official is permitted to take a reasonable amount of paid time off to accompany a worker at a hearing, as long as the worker is employed by the same employer. In cases where a lay official agrees to accompany a worker employed by another organisation, time off is a matter for agreement by the parties concerned.

Applying the right

[App 3.44]

110 Where possible, the employer should allow a companion to have a say in the date and time of a hearing. If the companion can't attend on a proposed date, the worker can suggest an alternative time and date so long as it is reasonable and it is not be more than five working days after the original date.

111 In the same way that employers should cater for a worker's disability at a disciplinary or grievance hearing, they should also cater for a companion's disability, for example providing for wheelchair access if necessary.

112 Before the hearing takes place, the worker should tell the employer who they have chosen as a companion. In certain circumstances (for instance when the companion is an official of a non-recognised trade union) it can be helpful for the companion and employer to make contact before the hearing.

113 The companion should be allowed to address the hearing in order to:

- put the worker's case

- sum up the worker's case

- respond on the worker's behalf to any view expressed at the hearing.

114 The companion can also confer with the worker during the hearing. It is good practice to allow the companion to participate as fully as possible in the hearing, including asking witnesses questions. The companion has no right to answer questions on the worker's behalf, or to address the hearing if the worker does not wish it, or to prevent the employer from explaining their case.

115 Workers whose employers fail to comply with a reasonable request to be accompanied may present a complaint to an employment tribunal. Workers may also complain to a tribunal if employers fail to re-arrange a hearing to a reasonable date proposed by the worker when a companion cannot attend on the date originally proposed. The tribunal may order compensation of up to two weeks' pay. This could be increased if, in addition, the tribunal finds that the worker has been unfairly dismissed.

116 Employers should be careful not to disadvantage workers for using their right to be accompanied or for being companions, as this is against the law and could lead to a claim to an employment tribunal.

Section 4

Annexes

Annex A

Standard statutory dismissal and disciplinary procedure

[App 3.45]

(**This is a summary of the statutory procedure which is set out in full in** *Schedule 2* **to the** *Employment Act 2002.*)

This procedure applies to disciplinary action short of dismissal (excluding oral and written warnings and suspension on full pay) based on either conduct or capability. It also applies to dismissals (except for constructive dismissals) including dismissals on the basis of conduct, capability, expiry of a fixed term contract, redundancy and retirement. However, it does not apply in certain kinds of excepted cases that are described in Annex E.

Step 1

Statement of grounds for action and invitation to meeting

- The employer must set out in writing the employee's alleged conduct or characteristics, or other circumstances, which lead them to contemplate dismissing or taking disciplinary action against the employee.

- The employer must send the statement or a copy of it to the employee and invite the employee to attend a meeting to discuss the matter.

Step 2

The meeting

- The meeting must take place before action is taken, except in the case where the disciplinary action consists of suspension.

- The meeting must not take place unless:

    (i) the employer has informed the employee what the basis was for including in the statement under Step 1 the ground or grounds given in it; and

    (ii) the employee has had a reasonable opportunity to consider their response to that information.

- The employee must take all reasonable steps to attend the meeting.

- After the meeting, the employer must inform the employee of their decision and notify them of the right to appeal against the decision if they are not satisfied with it.

- Employees have the right to be accompanied at the meeting (see SECTION 3).

Step 3

Appeal

- If the employee wishes to appeal, they must inform the employer.

- If the employee informs the employer of their wish to appeal, the employer must invite them to attend a further meeting.

- The employee must take all reasonable steps to attend the meeting.

- The appeal meeting need not take place before the dismissal or disciplinary action takes effect.

- Where reasonably practicable, the appeal should be dealt with by a more senior manager than attended the first meeting (unless the most senior manager attended that meeting).

- After the appeal meeting, the employer must inform the employee of their final decision.

- Employees have the right to be accompanied at the appeal meeting (see SECTION 3).

Annex B

Modified statutory dismissal and disciplinary procedure

[App 3.46]

(**This is a summary of the statutory procedure which is set out in full in** *Schedule 2* **to the** *Employment Act 2002.*)

Step 1

Statement of grounds for action

- The employer must set out in writing:

  (i)   the employee's alleged misconduct which has led to the dismissal;

  (ii)   the reasons for thinking at the time of the dismissal that the employee was guilty of the alleged misconduct; and

  (iii)   the employee's right of appeal against dismissal.

- The employer must send the statement or a copy of it to the employee.

Step 2

Appeal

- If the employee does wish to appeal, they must inform the employer.

- If the employee informs the employer of their wish to appeal, the employer must invite them to attend a meeting.

- The employee must take all reasonable steps to attend the meeting.

- After the appeal meeting, the employer must inform the employee of their final decision.

- Where reasonably practicable the appeal should be dealt with by a more senior manager not involved in the earlier decision to dismiss.

- Employees have the right to be accompanied at the appeal meeting (see SECTION 3).

Annex C

Standard statutory grievance procedure

[App 3.47]

(This is a summary of the statutory procedure which is set out in full in *Schedule 2* to the *Employment Act 2002.*)

Step 1

Statement of grievance

- The employee must set out the grievance in writing and send the statement or a copy of it to the employer.

Step 2

Meeting

- The employer must invite the employee to attend a meeting to discuss the grievance.
- The meeting must not take place unless:
  - the employee has informed the employer what the basis for the grievance was when they made the statement under Step 1; and
  - the employer has had a reasonable opportunity to consider their response to that information.
- The employee must take all reasonable steps to attend the meeting.
- After the meeting, the employer must inform the employee of their decision as to their response to the grievance and notify them of the right of appeal against the decision if they are not satisfied with it.
- Employees have the right to be accompanied at the meeting (see SECTION 3) (25)

Step 3

Appeal

- If the employee does wish to appeal, they must inform the employer.
- If the employee informs the employer of their wish to appeal, the employer must invite them to attend a further meeting.
- The employee must take all reasonable steps to attend the meeting.
- After the appeal meeting, the employer must inform the employee of their final decision.
- Where reasonably practicable, the appeal should be dealt with by a more senior manager than attended the first meeting (unless the most senior manager attended that meeting).
- Employees have the right to be accompanied at the appeal meeting (see SECTION 3).

Annex D

Modified statutory grievance procedure

[App 3.48]

(This is a summary of the statutory procedure which is set out in full in *Schedule 2* to the *Employment Act 2002*.)

Step 1

Statement of grievance

- The employee must set out in writing:
    - ○ the grievance; and
    - ○ the basis for it.
- The employee must send the statement or a copy of it to the employer.

Step 2

Response

- The employer must set out their response in writing and send the statement or a copy of it to the employee.

Annex E

Statutory Procedures: Exemptions and Deemed Compliance

[App 3.49]

The *Employment Act 2002* (*Dispute Resolution*) *Regulations 2004* contain detailed provisions about the application of the Statutory Dispute Resolution Procedures. This Annex summarises the particular provisions of the 2004 Regulations which describe:

(a)   certain situations in which the statutory procedures will not apply at all; and

(b)   other situations in which a party who has not completed the applicable procedure will nevertheless be treated as though they had done so.

Where a statutory procedure applies *and* one of the conditions for extending time limits contained in the 2004 Regulations has been met, then the normal time limit for presenting an employment tribunal claim will be extended by three months. The guidance notes accompanying tribunal application forms describe those conditions. However, in cases where the procedures do not apply at all, there can be *no* such extension.

(a)   *Situations in which the Statutory Procedures do not apply at all*

The Disciplinary and Dismissal Procedures do not apply where:

- Factors beyond the control of either party make it impracticable to carry out or complete the procedure for the foreseeable future; or

- The employee is dismissed in circumstances covered by the modified dismissal procedure and presents a tribunal complaint before the employer has taken step 1; or

- All of the employees of the same description or category are dismissed and offered re-engagement either before or upon termination of their contract; or

- The dismissal is one of a group of redundancies covered by the duty of collective consultation of worker representatives under the *Trade Union and Labour Relations (Consolidation) Act 1992*; or

- The employee is dismissed while taking part in unofficial industrial action, or other industrial action which is not 'protected action' under the 1992 Act, unless the employment tribunal has jurisdiction to hear a claim of unfair dismissal; or

- The employee is unfairly dismissed for taking part in industrial action which is 'protected action' under the 1992 Act; or

- The employer's business suddenly and unexpectedly ceases to function and it becomes impractical to employee any employees; or

- The employee cannot continue in the particular position without contravening a statutory requirement; or

- The employee is one to whom a dismissal procedure agreement designated under *section 110* of the *Employment Relations Act 1996* applies.

The Grievance Procedures do not apply where:

- The employee is no longer employed, and it is no longer practicable for the employee to take step 1 of the procedure; or

- The employee wishes to complain about an actual or threatened dismissal; or

- The employee raises a concern as a 'protected disclosure' in compliance with the public interest disclosure provisions of the 1996 Act;

- The employee wishes to complain about (actual or threatened) action short of dismissal to which the standard disciplinary procedure applies, unless the grievance is that this involves unlawful discrimination (including under the Equal Pay Act) or is not genuinely on grounds of capability or conduct.

In addition, neither party need comply with an applicable statutory procedure where to do so would be contrary to the interests of national security.

(b) Situations in which the Statutory Procedures have not been completed but are treated as having been complied with

The Disciplinary and Dismissal Procedures are treated as having been complied with where all stages of the procedure have been completed, other than the right of appeal, and:

- The employee then applies to the employment tribunal for interim relief; or

- A collective agreement provides for a right of appeal, which the employee exercises.

The Grievance Procedures are treated as having been complied with where:

- The employee is complaining that action short of dismissal to which the standard disciplinary procedure applies is not genuinely on grounds of conduct or capability, or involves unlawful discrimination, and the employee has raised that complaint as a written grievance before any appeal hearing under a statutory procedure or, if none is being followed, before presenting a tribunal complaint; or

- The employment has ended and the employee has raised a written grievance, but it has become not reasonably practical to have a meeting or an appeal. However, the employer must still give the employee a written answer to the grievance; or

- An official of a recognised independent union or other appropriate representative has raised the grievance on behalf of two or more named employees. Employees sharing the grievance may choose one of their number to act as a representative; or

- The employee pursues the grievance using a procedure available under an industry-level collective agreement.

(c) Other Special Circumstances in which the Statutory Procedures need not be begun or completed

In addition, neither the employer nor employee need begin a procedure (which will then be treated as not applying), or comply with a particular requirement of it (but will still be deemed to have complied) if the reason for not beginning or not complying is:

- The reasonable belief that doing so would result in a significant threat to themselves, any other person, or their or any other persons' property;

- Because they have been subjected to harassment and reasonably believe that doing so would result in further harassment; or

- Because it is not practicable to do so within a reasonable period.

Sample Written Statement of Terms and Conditions of Employment

Note: this is a very basic written statement of terms and conditions of employment. It contains the minimum amount of information that an employer is obliged to provide within one month of an employee joining. Unless your business is small, it is by far preferable to have a properly drafted contract of employment and appropriate employment policies in place.

Employer: _____

Employee: _____

This is the written statement of the terms and conditions of your Employment as required by the *Employment Rights Act 1996*.

1. Dates of Employment

Your employment with us began on _____. You had not previously been employed by us or an associated company, and so your continuity of employment also started on _____.

2. Job Title

You are employed as an administrative assistant to the managing director,_____. Your duties include general administration, filing, dealing with customers' enquiries and general secretarial duties. You may, however, be required to undertake any reasonable tasks that are necessary in the interests of the business.

3. Place of Work

Your normal place of work is _____, although you may be required to travel around Great Britain on an occasional basis. We reserve the right to change your normal place of work to any location within 50 miles of _____but will give you at least 28 days' notice before doing this.

Our offices are a non-smoking environment.

4. Hours of Work

Your normal working hours are 8.00am to 5.00pm Monday to Friday, although we may require you to work overtime on occasion. Any overtime will be paid at time-and-a-half. You are entitled to a one-hour break for lunch and a 10-minute coffee break each morning and afternoon.

5. Remuneration

As at _____, your remuneration is _____pa, payable monthly in arrears.

You are entitled to 20 days' paid holiday per year plus authorised bank holidays, which accrues on a *pro rata* basis. The holiday year runs from 1 January to 31 December. Up to five days' holiday may be carried over into the next holiday year. All holiday entitlements shall be taken entirely at our discretion, although we will not unreasonably refuse your requests for holiday.

Your remuneration does not include any pension contributions. A stakeholder pension is available: if you wish to join the scheme, details are available from _____.

6. Termination of Employment

We reserve the right to terminate your employment immediately in cases of gross misconduct. In all other cases, periods of notice required are as follows:

- If we dismiss you: you are entitled to one week's notice during your first two years of employment. After this, we will give you one week's notice for every complete year that you have worked, up to a maximum of 12 weeks.

- If you resign: you must give us one weeks' notice during your first two years of employment. After this, you must give us one month's notice.

7. Sickness

In the event of sickness we will pay you full sick-pay for six weeks, after which you will be placed on statutory sick-pay. 'Qualifying days' for the purpose of statutory sick-pay are those days on which you normally work under this contract.

In order to qualify for sick-pay, you must inform us of the reason for your absence not later than midday on the first day of your absence and must complete a self-certification form if you return to work within seven days.

If you are sick for longer than seven days, you must provide a doctor's medical certificate by the eighth day of sick-leave, and must produce further certificates as necessary upon the expiry of each of the previous certificates.

We reserve the right to require you to undergo a medical examination in the event that you have been absent through sickness for over four weeks.

8. Confidentiality

Any information about the company, including any information about our customers and suppliers, of which you become aware due to your employment must be treated as confidential. It must not be disclosed to any third person, or used for your own advantage, either during your employment or after termination of your employment.

9. Disciplinary Procedure

We regard high standards of conduct as crucial. This disciplinary procedure sets out the procedure which we will follow, and the possible disciplinary sanctions that may be applied, if you fall short of the standard expected of you. Since we are a small business, the disciplinary procedure will usually be carried out by _____.

- In any case of misconduct, we will undertake a full investigation into the circumstances surrounding the misconduct before undertaking any disciplinary action. This will include a meeting with you (at which you may have a representative present) during which the allegations are discussed and you are given a full opportunity to put your case.

- In cases of minor misconduct: you will either be given an oral warning or a written warning, depending on the seriousness of the misconduct. A record of the warning will be kept for two years, after which time it will be discarded.

- In cases of gross (or very serious) misconduct, you will either be dismissed or, if there are extenuating circumstances, you will be given a written warning.

- In the case of repetition of minor misconduct (whether of the same or a different nature) you may be dismissed.

- The following are examples of minor misconduct which would warrant an oral or a written warning: poor job performance, absence from work, smoking, poor timekeeping, failure to comply with an instruction, mild intoxication due to alcohol, swearing, rudeness to colleagues. This list is not exhaustive.

- The following are examples of gross misconduct which would warrant dismissal: intoxication at work in front of customers, illegal use of drugs, theft, actual or threatened violence, malicious damage to property, personal use of confidential information, falsification of records, negligence resulting in serious loss or injury, harassment of employees, customers or any other third parties on grounds of sex, race, age, sexual orientation or disability. This list is not exhaustive.

- In the event of an allegation of gross misconduct, you may be suspended on full pay whilst the allegation is being investigated and the disciplinary action considered. Any period of suspension without pay will not normally exceed four weeks.

302

- You are entitled to appeal against any disciplinary decision with which you do not agree. An appeal should be sent in writing to John Alexander within seven days of the decision, stating your grounds for the appeal.

- At any stage of the disciplinary process, you may be accompanied by a workplace colleague or a trade union representative.

10. Grievances

In the event of any grievance arising out of your employment, you should firstly discuss the matter informally with _____. If the matter cannot be resolved you should address your grievance in writing to _____, who will respond in writing and take such action as is appropriate within 14 days (or such longer period as is reasonable). You may be accompanied, at any stage, by a workplace colleague or a trade union representative.

11. Dismissal Procedures

In the event we have to contemplate dismissal for a conduct reason, we will follow the disciplinary process above.

If contemplating dismissal for any other reason (for example absence, poor performance or redundancy) we will follow the following procedure:

- we will write to you, setting out the reasons why we are considering dismissal, and invite you to a meeting;

- you are entitled to be accompanied by a trade union representative or a workplace colleague;

- at the meeting, we will discuss all relevant matters with you. These may include the possibility of obtaining medical evidence, setting clear guidelines and targets for you, selection methods for redundancy or possible alternative employment;

- after the meeting, we will notify you of our decision. If you are dismissed, you will be offered a right of appeal.

I acknowledge receipt of this written statement of Particulars of Employment and confirm that this constitutes my understanding of my contract of employment.

Signed _____ Dated_____
[Employee]

Signed _____ Dated_____
[Employer]

Appendix 5

Sample Compromise Agreement

This compromise agreement is made between _____ ('the employer') and _____ ('the employee').

WHEREAS:

(1) the employee has brought a claim against the employer under the *Employment Rights Act 1996*, the *Sex Discrimination Act 1975* and for wrongful dismissal (application number _____); and

(2) the parties have agreed a compromise of his claims

IT IS AGREED THAT:

(1) subject to paragraph 2, this agreement is in full and final settlement of any and all contractual and/or statutory claims that the employee could bring against the employer arising out of his contract of employment (or contract for services), or the termination thereof, in an employment tribunal or a civil court, including any claims (or possible claims) that he might have under the *Employment Rights Act 1996*, the *Equal Pay Act 1970*, the *Race Relations Act 1976*, the *Disability Discrimination Act 1995*, the *Sex Discrimination Act 1975*, the *Equal Pay Act 1970*, the *Trade Union and Labour Relations (Consolidation) Act 1992* and the *Working Time Regulations 1998 (SI 1998 No 1833)*.

(2) this agreement does not compromise any claims the employee has for personal injuries arising out of her employment (or contract for services).

(3) the employer shall pay the sum of £10,000 to the employee in instalments by the following dates:

- £3,000 by 23 January 2005

- £3,500 by 16 February 2005

- £3,500 by 16 March 2005

(4) the employer shall provide, upon request, a reference for the employee in the following terms:

'Alf worked for this company as an administrative assistant between January 1997 and August 2004. He was a hard and diligent worker during his period of employment and his work was always of the highest standard. He was dismissed because of a misunderstanding between himself and another member of staff.'

(5)   the parties agree to keep this settlement, and the fact of settlement, confidential (except that it may be disclosed to the parties' spouses, and their legal and financial advisors).

(6)   the employee has received independent legal advice from Neville Smith of Messrs Smith, Bloggs and Jones ('the independent legal adviser')

(7)   the independent legal adviser hereby declares and warrants that the relevant conditions relating to compromise agreements have been satisfied pursuant to *section 203* of the *Employment Rights Act 1996* and/or *sections 9* and *10* of the *Employment Rights* (*Dispute Resolution*) *Act 1996* – in particular, that the employee has been advised of the effect of this agreement upon his statutory and contractual rights, and that the independent legal adviser is a qualified solicitor holding a current practising certificate and that he/his firm has an insurance policy in force concerning the risk of a claim by the employee in respect of any loss arising in consequence of his advice.

Signed: _____Date
[Employee]

Signed: _____Date
[Employer]

Signed: _____Date
Messrs Smith, Bloggs and Jones (independent legal adviser)

Useful Telephone Numbers

Central Office of the Employment Tribunals	01284 762171
Employment Tribunal Helpline (free telephone helpline)	0845 795 9775
ACAS Head Office	020 7396 5100

Employment tribunals

Aberdeen	01224 593 137
Ashford	01233 621 346
Bedford	01234 351 306
Birmingham	0121 236 6051
Bristol	0117 929 8261
Bury St. Edmunds	01284 762 171
Cardiff	029 2067 8100
Dundee	01382 221 578
Exeter	01392 279 665
Leeds	0113 245 9741
Leicester	0116 255 0099
Liverpool	0151 236 9397
London (North) (*Watford*)	01923 281 750
London (Central) (*Woburn Place*)	020 7273 8575
London (East) (*Stratford*)	020 8221 0921
London (South) (*Croydon*)	020 8667 9131
Manchester	0161 833 0581
Newcastle	0191 260 6900
Nottingham	0115 947 5701
Reading	0118 959 4917

Sheffield	0114 276 0348
Shrewsbury	01743 358 341
Southampton	023 8071 6400

Appendix 7

Useful Websites

The links below were correct as at September 2004.

For those who seek regular updating by email, the Employment Law (UK) mailing list (produced by the author of this book!), can be joined at www.danielbarnett.co.uk. This sends out breaking news on employment law matters once or twice a week.

Age Discrimination

Shorthand title	Notes	Web-address (*url*)
Employers Forum on Age	EFA home page	http://www.efa.org.uk/
Articles on age discrimination	Articles written by Daniel Barnett	http://www.danielbarnett.co.uk/article-index.html

Data Protection

Shorthand title	Notes	Web-address (*url*)
Information Commissioner	Responsible for Data Protection & Freedom of Information	http://www.dataprotection.gov.uk/

Disability

Shorthand title	Notes	Web-address (*url*)
Rising Dawn	(Formerly Disability Advice and Welfare Network)	http://www.patient.co.uk/showdoc/26739844
Disability	General assistance and advice, managed by the Disability Unit in the Department for Work and Pensions	http://www.disability.gov.uk

| Disability Rights Commission | Profile of the DRC | http://www.disability.gov.uk/drc/ |

Discrimination (General)

Shorthand title	Notes	Web-address (*url*)
Advisory, Conciliation & Arbitration Service (ACAS)	ACAS home page	http://www.acas.org.uk/
Equal Opportunities Commission	EOC home page	http://www.eoc.org.uk/

Dispute Resolution

Shorthand title	Notes	Web-address (*url*)
ADR Group	Dispute Resolution specialists – the home page	http://www.adrgroup.co.uk/
Arbitration, ADR & Mediation site by Delia Venables	Alternative Dispute Resolution (ADR) including Adjudication, Arbitration and Mediation	http://www.venables.co.uk/adr.htm
ODR site by Delia Venables	Online Dispute Resolution (ODR)	http://www.venables.co.uk/odr.htm
Dispute Resolution	Expert Evidence, Arbitration and Mediation	http://www.endispute.co.uk/

Employee Relations and Policies

Shorthand title	Notes	Web-address (*url*)
Hamiltons Solicitors	Criminal litigation, regulation of the Internet, data protection	http://www.hamiltons-solicitors.co.uk

Employment Lawyers

Shorthand title	Notes	Web-address (*url*)
Bar Directory	On-line access to the directory	http://2.sweetandmaxwell.co.uk/bardirectory/website/
Barristers on the Web – site maintained by Delia Venables	Chambers and Barristers on the Web in England and Wales	http://www.venables.co.uk/bar.htm
Clifford Chance	Clifford Chance home page	http://www.cliffordchance.com/
Daniel Barnett's Employment Law Mailing List	Daniel Barnett's home page	http://www.danielbarnett.co.uk/
Employment Lawyers' Association	ELA home page	http://www.elaweb.org.uk/
Fox Williams	Fox Williams home page	http://www.foxwilliams.com
Law Society	Law Society home page	http://www.lawsociety.org.uk/homelaw
Lawrite Legal	Employment law, health and safety law and HR solutions for business	http://www.lawrite.co.uk/index.htm

Employment Related Organisations

Shorthand title	Notes	Web-address (*url*)
Citizen's Advice Bureau	CAB home page	http://www.citizensadvice.org
Chartered Institute of Personnel and Development	CIPD home page	http://www.cipd.co.uk/default.cipd
Jobcentre Plus	Part of the Department for Work and Pensions	http://www.jobcentreplus.gov.uk/cms.asp?Page=/Home
Incomes Data Services	IDS home page	http://www.incomesdata.co.uk/
Warwick Institute for Employment Research	WIER home page	http://www2.warwick.ac.uk/fac/soc/ier/

Institute of Employment Rights	A think tank for the Labour movement	http://www.ier.org.uk/
Institute of Directors	IOD home page	http://www.iod.com/is-bin/ INTERSHOP.enfinity/eCS/ Store/en/-/GBP/IOD-Start
Institute of Management Services	Institute of Management Services home page	http:// www.ims-productivity.com
Low Pay Commission	LPC home page	http://www.lowpay.gov.uk/
Occupational Pensions Regulatory Authority	OPRA home page	http://www.opra.co.uk/
Public Concern at Work (Whistleblowing)	Public Concern at Work home page	http://www.pcaw.co.uk/
British Employment Law	Emplaw home page	http://www.emplaw.co.uk/

Europe

Shorthand title	Notes	Web-address (*url*)
Amsterdam Treaty	The Amsterdam Treaty home page	http://europa.eu.int/abc/ obj/amst/en/index.htm
Bulletin of the European Union	An Account of the activities of the European Commission and the other Community Institutions	http://europa.eu.int/abc/ doc/off/bull/en/ welcome.htm
EUR-Lex European Union Law	EUR-Lex home page	http://europa.eu.int/ eur-lex/en/
European Commission	The European Commission Representation in the United Kingdom	http://www.cec.org.uk/
European Industrial Relations Observatory On-line	EIRO home page	http:// www.eiro.eurofound.ie/
European Links – site maintained by Delia Venables	Portal to European Resources (non-UK)	http://www.venables.co.uk/ europe.htm

European Parliament	Europarl home page	http://www.europarl.eu.int/default.htm
European Union	EU home page	http://www.europa.eu.int/
European Union Employers' Network	The Federation of European Employers home page	http://www.fedee.com/index.shtml
UK Government Euro Site	Euro information	http://www.euro.gov.uk/home.asp?f=1

Government and Parliament

Shorthand title	Notes	Web-address (*url*)
Department of Trade and Industry	DTI home page	http://www.dti.gov.uk/
DTI Employment Relations	Department of Trade and Industry – Employment Relations Directorate home page	http://www.dti.gov.uk/er/index.htm
Foreign & Commonwealth Office	FCO home page	http://www.fco.gov.uk/ servlet/Front?pagename =OpenMarket/Xcelerate/ ShowPage&c=Page&cid =1007029390554
HM Treasury	HM Treasury home page	http://www.hm-treasury.gov.uk/
Hansard: House of Commons Debates	The five most recent editions of Hansard that are available for browsing	http://www.parliament. the-stationery-office. co.uk/pa/cm/ cmhansrd.htm
Hansard: House of Lords Debates	House of Lords debates available for browsing	http://www.parliament. the-stationery-office. co.uk/pa/ld/ ldhansrd.htm
House of Commons	House of Commons home page	http://www.parliament.uk/about_commons/about_commons.cfm
House of Lords	House of Lords home page	http://www.parliament.uk/about_lords/about_lords.cfm
Stationery Office	TSO home page	http://www.tso.co.uk/

Harassment

Shorthand title	Notes	Web-address (*url*)
Success Unlimited	Large Internet resource on bullying	http://www.successunlimited.co.uk/
Harassment Law	Practical information and relevant web links on harassment	http://www.harassment-law.co.uk/

Health and Safety

Shorthand title	Notes	Web-address (*url*)
Health & Safety Executive	HSE home page	http://www.hse.gov.uk/index.htm
HSE Books	Bookfinder catalogue	http://www.hsebooks.com/Books

Human Rights

Shorthand title	Notes	Web-address (*url*)
European Court of Human Rights	ECHR home page	http://www.echr.coe.int/
Women's Human Rights Sources	Women's Human Rights Resources Database	http://www.law-lib.utoronto.ca/Diana/

Law Reports and Judgments

Shorthand title	Notes	Web-address (*url*)
European Court Reports	Curia home page	http://www.curia.eu.int/
House of Lords Judgments	Judgments delivered since 14 November 1996	http://www.parliament.the-stationery-office.co.uk/pa/ld199697/ldjudgmt/ldjudgmt.htm

Industrial Relations Law Reports	IRS home page	http://www.irsonline.co.uk/
Law Reports for England and Wales	ICLR home page	http://www.lawreports.co.uk/

Legislation

Shorthand title	Notes	Web–address (*url*)
HMSO	Her Majesty's Stationery Office	http://www.hmso.gov.uk/
HMSO Guidance Notes: Publishing and Copyright	Guidance Notes	http://www.hmso.gov.uk/ copyright/guidance/ guidance_notes.htm
Statutory Instruments	UK SIs	http://www.legislation.hmso.gov.uk/ stat.htm

Racial Discrimination

Shorthand title	Notes	Web–address (*url*)
Commission for Racial Equality	CRE home page	http://www.cre.gov.uk/

Sex Discrimination

Shorthand title	Notes	Web–address (*url*)
Equal Opportunities Commission	EOC home page	http://www.eoc.org.uk/
Sexuality, Gender & the Law	Sex laws worldwide	http://www.lib.uchicago.edu/ ~llou/sexlaw.html

Tribunals and Courts

Shorthand title	Notes	Web-address (*url*)
Employment Appeal Tribunal	EAT home page	http:// www.employmentappeals. gov.uk/
European Court of Human Rights	ECHR home page	http://www.echr.coe.int/
European Court of Justice	Court of Justice and Court of First Instance	http://europa.eu.int/cj/en/ index.htm
High Court: QBD	A Guide to the working practices of the Queen's Bench Division within the Royal Courts of Justice	http:// www.courtservice.gov.uk/ using_courts/guides_notices/ notices/queens/ qb_sec_1.htm
House of Lords	House of Lords home page	http://www.parliament.uk/ about_lords/about_lords.cfm
Tribunals Review	Review of Tribunals – Sir Andrew Leggatt's report	http:// www.tribunals-review.org.uk/

Index

C

G

H

I

T

U

W